"Bearing Each Other's Burdens"

A History of St. John's Community Centre, Pumwani

By James Richardson & Pat Richardson

A painting given to us by Elimo Njau, a Tanzanian recognised as one of East Africa's foremost artists and famous for his murals in St. James and all Martyrs Memorial Cathedral, an Anglican church built as a memorial to the Christians who died in the Mau Mau conflict.

The painting, depicting the woman bearing her burdens, is inscribed:

"DIGNITY, HUMANITY AND INTEGRITY

Elimo Njau for Pat & Jim

22/2/2001".

It was a present from his workshop and gallery to the authors when they visited him there shortly after a fire at the Paa ya Paa Centre, Ridgeways, Nairobi.

Published by Dolman Scott Ltd 2019

Copyright © 2019 James Richardson & Pat Richardson

The author asserts the moral right under the Copyright, Designs and Patents Act 1988 to be identified as the author of this work. All rights reserved. No part of this publication may be reproduced, stored in a retrieval system, or transmitted, in any form or by any means without the prior written consent of the author, nor be otherwise circulated in any form of binding or cover, other than that in which it is published and without a similar condition being imposed on the subsequent purchaser.

Although the authors have made every effort to ensure that the information in this book was correct at the time of going to press, they do not assume and hereby disclaim any liability to any party for any loss or damage caused by errors or omissions, howsoever arising. In the event of any disappointment or distress caused through description, or inclusion in or omission from the book, the authors apologise. This would have been entirely unintentional.

ISBN: 978-1-911412-98-4

Printed for Dolman Scott
www.dolmanscott.co.uk

About the authors

Pat Richardson, nee Rose, known in Pumwani as "Patrose", sailed to Kenya in January 1959 on the '*Rhodesia Castle*', with three other missionary recruits. She worked in Pumwani for four years as a social case worker and warden of St. John's Community Centre. During that time, she met her husband James (Jim) Richardson. They were married in December 1962 at St. John's Church, Pumwani, and lived in Kenya with their four children until 1980.

James worked in Nairobi as an Advocate. Alongside his professional career, he was the Chairman of the Finance & General Purposes Committee of the Community Centre for 15 years and was a Lay Reader at St. John's Church for nearly 20 years.

Since leaving Kenya, they have remained in contact with Centre staff and maintain an interest in its progress.

The Authors' wedding at St John's Church, Pumwani, with the reception in St. John's Community Centre – Dec 1962

By the same author

'PRAYERS FOR TODAY'
- James Richardson & William N. Richards
- Published 1977 by:
  Uzima Press Ltd, Imani House, PO Box 48127, Nairobi, Kenya

Acknowledgements

We are indebted to the many people who have helped us, providing information and giving us guidance in the writing of this book.

The Church Mission Society in England and the Church Missionary Society of New South Wales Australia have provided from their archives, reports and photographs which have enabled us to write the history of mission activity in Pumwani preceding the establishment of St. John's Community Centre.

We received valued information from Marjorie Oludhe Macgoye, the well-known Kenyan author, Joyce Burns, a daughter of Archdeacon Burns, Margaret Pattinson, Michael Nunn, Ken Ashton and others, who have written to or spoken with us.

We would not have been able to deal with the Centre's activities after we left Kenya in 1980, without records and information provided by the Centre itself. We are particularly grateful to our long-standing friend, Eunice Kamau, who gave us an account of her time as Director and, more recently, to Sally Gatei, the Centre Project Manager, who amidst her busy life patiently responds to all our queries and requests.

Friends like John & Shirley Ridout and Lynn Wilkinson have read the contents and given us their views and we are grateful to them and everybody else who have encouraged us over many years to bring this project to a conclusion, not least our long-suffering children Heather, Sarah, Emma & Simon who have made no small contribution in terms of constantly recurring advice, IT expertise, formatting of the book and liaison with the publisher.

Contents

About the authors i
By the same author ii
Acknowledgements iii
Table of Photographs xiii
Abbreviations xvi
Prologue xvii

PART I - "IN THE BEGINNING…" 1

Chapter 1 – How it Began for Us 3
   Bristol 1955 3
   The journey up-country 4
   Arrival 6

Chapter 2 – Adjusting to the Status Quo… 10
   Foxbury 10
   Wake-up call 11
   The earlier history of CMS in Pumwani 13
   "Bwana Burns" 13
   Sister Maude Pethybridge 16
   "Burns Memorial Hall" 18
   Charles & Helen Tett 21
   St. John's Community Centre: its beginning 22
   The Mau Mau Rebellion 24

Chapter 3 – The People of Pumwani 28
   Living Conditions in Pumwani 30
   Prostitution and Beer-brewing – a local economy 32

Chapter 4 – Housing & Development 35
   The original development and housing 35
   Religious & Social Facilities 36

Chapter 5 – The Activities of the Community Centre in its Early Years 41
   Informal school 41
   Adult Education 44
   Special Group for Teenage Girls 44

    More Formality!... 45
    Distribution of milk and food 47

Chapter 6 – Early Development & Growth 49
    Small Beginnings.. 49
    Transport... 52
    The return visit of John Taylor 53
    Jim's involvement... 54
    The Christian Industrial Training Centre (CITC) 56
    Emerging financial empowerment.. 58
    Emergence of the Centre's Governance... 59

Chapter 7 – Overseas Church Support.. 61
    The Anglican Church... 61
    Mutual Responsibility and Interdependence 61
    The Diocese of Rochester 62
    Competing Claims 63
    A Community Church.. 64
    To be or not to be!.. 65
    Financial Empowerment from Other Churches –
    "Bread for the World".. 70

PART II - "POWER TO THE PEOPLE…" 73
Chapter 8 – The Concept of Community Empowerment 75
    British Council of Churches 75
    Policy Committee & its Report.. 76
    How to achieve a change 77
    Staff involvement at all levels 79
    Policy & Governance... 79
    A Second Policy Statement.. 80
    The thrust of the new Policy Statement 80
    User Involvement... 81
    The contents of the Second Policy Statement..................................... 81
    The Paradigm Shift.. 83
    What is Community Empowerment or Development?........................ 85
    The Community Development Worker.. 86
    Working in Special Populations... 87
    "Bearing each other's burdens" 88

Chapter 9 – Empowerment Through Education 89
    The Girls' Training Scheme... 90

Women's Classes 91
First-aid Education.. 91
Margaret Pooley.. 95
Non-Formal Education 95
Adult Education 96
Commercial Classes.. 96
Changing Patterns in the demand for education 98

Chapter 10 – Empowerment Through Employment........................... 100
Early attempts to break the cycle 100
The Break-through 101
Mary Politeyan.. 102

Chapter 11 – What's Brewing in The Beer Hall?............................... 106
At the cross-roads 106
The way forward 109
Dorothy Udall 112
Management of the Business 113

Chapter 12 – Social Casework: Its Use & Relevance 115
"What are you going to do?" 115
Visiting in the location.. 115
Language... 115
Relationship changes within the family 116
Relationships between young persons of the opposite sex 118
Fear of the law 118
Stella Purchase - a prophet?.. 120
Training social caseworkers.. 121
Outreach by Community Centre staff to other agencies........................... 125
The Kenya-Israel School of Social Work 126
All Saints' Cathedral... 127
Joint Refugee Service of Kenya 127

PART III - "MORE POWER TO THE CENTRE" 129

Chapter 13 – Selecting & Empowering the New Leader................... 131
Uhuru & Expectations of the Labour Market 131
"Africanisation"... 132
The Private Sector... 132
Training in the Professions 132
St. John's Community Centre 133
"Africanisation" of the Warden's post 134

Overseas training for the Warden & his family 134
Temporary replacement warden 135
Training for the Warden's wife 135

Chapter 14 – Creating an Endowment 137
Sponsorship Schemes 137
Core-funding 138
Eastleigh flats 138
Wood Avenue 139
Maridadi Fabrics Profits 139
Percentage Levy on Earmarked Funds 140

Chapter 15 – The Role of the Volunteer 141
The American Contingent 141
Growth 143
Full-time Volunteers 144
Immi Tivola 145
Richard Hess 148

Chapter 16 – Voluntary Financial & Business Expertise 150
Clive Ashton 151
The Dilemma 151
CMS to the rescue 152
A hot potato 153
Ken Pattinson 155

Chapter 17 – Developing a New Industry 157
Governance 157
The Sewing Project 158
Methods and Systems 161
CORAT 162

Chapter 18 – Accommodating Maridadi Fabrics 165
Options for additional space 165
Elsbeth's Report 166
God's Guidance? – an unexpected solution! 167
Negotiations, Plans & Squatters 168
Finance 170

PART IV - "A DECADE OF DISASTER" 173

Chapter 19 – The Gathering Storm 175
Ken Pattinson's Final Report 175
Cash flow 177

    Centre Building Development 177
    The Nursery School 178
    The Last Straw 179
    Financial Control and Management.. 181

Chapter 20 – Struggling to Survive.. 183
    Information Sources... 183
    Marjorie Oludhe Macgoye (nee King) 183
    Information source provided by Marjorie.. 185
    Caretaker Committee 186
    Re-organisation of the Centre's governance.. 188
    Management or Merger?... 190
    New Committees 191

Chapter 21 – Back to Square One 195
    More change 195
    A new Board of Management 195
    'Children Incorporated' of USA 198
    Matumaini House & Centre Buildings 199
    The Executive Committee 199

PART V - "THE PARADIGM SHIFT"... 203

Chapter 22 - Renaissance 205
    New Leadership 205
    The Induction.. 205
    A poisoned chalice!   A rich inheritance!... 206
    The Financial Challenge 209
    Mounting opposition... 210
    A time for rationalisation: Territory - Staff – Governance 211
    St. John's High School.. 212

Chapter 23 – Strategic Planning... 215
    The Baseline Survey Report & New Programmes 215
    A New Strategy 216
    Upgrading of staff and activities... 216
    Financial Correction & Re-arrangement 217
    Deeper needs... 218
    Water supply 219
    The environmental conditions 220
    The Tudor Trust 221

Table of Contents

Chapter 24 – The Paradigm Shift 226
Answers to prayer 226
A new positive inter-faith relationship 227
Time to move on 228
The "Paradigm Shift" 228
Continuing Opposition 229
The "mind-set" created by poverty 230
The psychological effect of "Livelihood Training" given
    to the Youth Groups 232
Sammy Kymana 233
The Spiritual Dimension 236
Eunice: A personal appreciation 236
Peter Njuguna 238

PART VI - "THE BIGGER PICTURE" 239

Chapter 25 – HIV/AIDS Orphans & Vulnerable Children 241
Pumwani 242
Partnerships & the Larger Scenario 242
Small Community Projects 243
Apprenticeships 245
Revolving Funds 246
Sensitisation of the Community 248
Child Protection 250
Health and Hygiene 251
Psycho-social support 252
Continuing effectiveness 254

Chapter 26 - HIV/AIDS "Springs of Life" 255
Stigma 255
The Centre's Response 256
Behaviour Change – Abstinence 259
Faithfulness in Marriage 260
HIV Counselling & Testing 260
Conclusions 261
"Hope" 262
"Aphia Plus" 264
"Dreams" 265
"Nilinde" 267
Child and Maternal Health – something different –
    something new 268

Chapter 27 – Empowerment of Women 270
Political Inequality – a historical perspective 270
Inequality in the workplace 270
Sexual mistreatment 271
Pumwani 272
Gender Budgeting of Devolved Funds 273
The need for political education in Pumwani 274
Women & Youth - the need of literacy 274
Area committees 276
Monitoring & Audit 276
Widening horizons 277
The Future 280

Chapter 28 – Non-Formal Education (NFE) 281
Parking Boys 281
The history of the Centre's informal school 283
The Current Programme 283
Classification of the Non-Formal Education (NFE) Programme 285
"Choices" 286
Assessment 288
Performance 288
Update 290
Future Challenges 292

Chapter 29 - "Blessed Are the Peacemakers" 295
Election fears 295
Church involvement and initiatives 295
Nairobi North outreach 296
Monitors & Peace Committees 297
Training 297
The Situation Room 297
Conclusions 298

PART VII - "CONCLUSION" 301

Chapter 30 – Outcomes in Pumwani 303
International & National Challenges 303
Sectoral Areas of Activity 304
Economic Empowerment 304
Education & Training 305
Youth Empowerment 308
Uprising 310

"Chipukizi Youth Group" 313
Mustakabal Women Group 313
Group Training...315
Pumwani Youth Group...316
Sponsorship..317
Health - HIV/AIDS – Child Mortality..320
Governance & Human Rights...322

Chapter 31 – The Future Role of the Centre..324
The Centre workforce 324
Strategic Management 325
Participatory involvement & Institutional Achievement 325
Empowerment of local groups...327
Young People & Crime..328
The Performing Arts 332
The International Arena 334
Church Community Mobilization Transformational
  Development (CCMTD)..335
What of the future?..337

Epilogue 339

Index..340

Table of Photographs

Ch.	Page	Caption
-	i	The Authors' wedding at St John's Church, Pumwani, with the reception in St. John's Community Centre – Dec 1962
1	7	St. John's Church, Pumwani
1	7	A family living in staff housing on the church compound
1	9	The view from Pat's window in 1959
1	9	Volleyball in the Centre's field
2	12	Another view from Pat's window
2	14	Bwana Burns and his wife Sibella
2	19	Miss Pethybridge - much loved - "the one who prays for us"
2	20	The opening of the Centre: Archbishop Beecher (2nd from right) in attendance
2	20	Archbishop Leonard Beecher and his wife Gladys
2	26	Students at Kigari Teacher Training College enacting an oathing ceremony
3	29	Two Pumwani residents finding peace in the Community Centre grounds
3	31	The view today from St. John's Community Centre
4	39	The new Pumwani – 'California' – behind the existing location
5	42	Some of the 120 children in the Primary School classes 1958
5	43	Georgina talking with Dishon
5	43	Georgina (right) with Martha (centre)
5	45	"The group cooked drop-scones"
5	46	"The girls all received a uniform"
5	48	Mark Shiundu stirring the posho
6	50	Alexander, deputy warden, settles new residents into the old people's home
6	51	Hadijah, a regular visitor to the casework office
6	53	The Rev'd Dishon Mwangola, Vicar of St. John's Church
6	57	An early cohort of CITC trainees
7	65	The Rev'd Anne Barnett speaking with Ephantus Mugo, the new Centre Director
7	68	Matumaini Old People's Home downstairs, with the Girls' hostel upstairs (photo taken July 2019 – 46 years after it was opened)

Table of Photographs

Ch.	Page	Caption
7	69	St. John's ACK Church Pumwani "spanking new church building"
7	71	The Rev'd Dishon Mwangola, the vicar, with Charles Rubia, Mayor of Nairobi, opening the first Old Peoples' Home
9	89	An older girls' class in 1960 with Naomi their teacher (4th from left)
9	92	Women's classes learning English – "It was all very low key. A simple beginning..."
9	93	Martha Wambui, - "one of its most valued teachers" - with her husband James
9	93	Martha & James' wedding party
10	103	Basket weaving
11	108	Wambui, watching the churchgoers
11	110	Water damaged photo of early screen-printing by hand in the Beerhall
12	121	Emma – now an enthusiastic member of the Mothers Union
12	124	Emma provided advice to mothers with malnourished children
13	131	Crowd celebrating outside Legco (the Legislative Council)
17	160	Developing a sewing section
18	172	The new Maridadi Fabrics factory (recent photo)
19	182	St. John's Church Nursery School (above + below)
22	213	Mrs. Eunice Kamau -"She looked forward to meeting the considerable challenge which the job offered."
23	221	Lamu Road - a current street scene without rubbish
23	223	Pat showing Roger Northcott of Tudor Trust around Pumwani - 1998
23	224	Stinking foul water from the lavatory in a pub
23	224	Lavatory block 34 - Wanaume lipa 10 (Men Pay 10) – "taking small payments for their services"
23	225	Lavatory block 32 with its proud custodian
24	235	Sammy Kymana – "a real inspiration to other young people"
26	264	Barolina – "Grateful to the Family Matters Programme"
26	266	Dream girls graduating from vocational courses celebrate as they throw their mortarboards in the air
27	272	Children from the Centre protesting
27	275	Women learning literacy in the early days

Table of Photographs

Ch.	Page	Caption
27	278	Pumwani Youth Club 1961 Netball Team
27	278	A visit to City Park exploring the bigger world
27	279	Enjoying the facilities of City Park
28	282	NFE Schoolchildren washing hands after a lesson on hygiene
28	285	Gordon, himself a former pupil here, now a skilled carpenter inspiring non formal school pupils with his work
28	292	Ezekiel Kamau mentoring pupils at St. John's High School during a coffee break
28	294	Thousands of children have over the years benefited from the NFE programme
28	294	"…the children ate a healthy lunch three times a week"
30	307	Facilities like homework clubs were introduced
30	310	Eunice Kamau (far right) with community leaders who had organised the care of the lavatories and stand pipes
30	311	Winstone Nanjeso - Chairman of Uprising (centre of photo wearing white shirt)
30	312	Uprising has gone from a small kiosk to a multi-storey building for housing
30	314	Leaders interview Chipukizi Youth Group
30	314	Mustakabal Women Group – "enhanced relationships"
30	317	Pumwani Youth Group Car Wash
30	319	Peter Mweke in motivational discussions with street children
31	324	Peter Njuguna – Director of St. John's Community Centre
31	327	Mealtimes at the centre in the past
31	330	Sally Gatei – Projects Manager
31	331	Community cleaning Munyema Street, the "notorious route outside the Centre gates"
31	332	Youth Group in Dancing and Performing Arts
31	336	CCMTD workshop of clergy from implementing parishes and a team from the Centre with the Diocesan Director of Mission mapping the way forward
31	337	"What of the future?"
31	338	Staff, community members and the local government area chief at a stakeholders forum

Abbreviations

"3Cs"	Christian Community Centres
ACK	Anglican Church of Kenya
BCMS	Bible Churchmen's Missionary Society
CCK	Christian Council of Kenya
CCMTD	Church Community Mobilization Transformational Development
CHH	Child Head of Household
CITC	Christian Industrial Training Centre
CMS	Church Missionary Society, later renamed Church Mission Society
CORAT	Christian Organizations Research and Advisory Trust
CPK	Church of the Province of Kenya
Danida	Danish International Development Agency
ECLOF	Ecumenical Church Loan Fund
HOPE	Health Outcomes through Prevention Education
JRSK	Joint Refugee Service of Kenya
KNH	Kindernothilfe - meaning Children's Emergency Help
MRI	Mutual Responsibility and Interdependence
NCCK	National Council of the Churches of Kenya (previously known as Christian Council of Kenya – CCK)
NCA	Norwegian Church Aid
NFE	Non-Formal Education
OVC	Orphans & Vulnerable Children
PEPFAR	President's Emergency Plan For AIDS Relief
PYGRON	Pumwani Youth Groups Network
SAMS	South American Missionary Society
UNHCR	United Nations High Commissioner for Refugees
UNICEF	United Nations International Children's Emergency Fund
USPG	United Society for the Propagation of the Gospel
USAID	United States Agency for International Development

Prologue

The French doors leading out of our Dorset home into the conservatory have four glass panels in them. The glass was brought back by us from Nairobi aboard a British Airways jumbo-jet and cosseted amongst the smart uniforms of the crew, who kindly provided space in their locker, despite the rather grubby cardboard into which it had been packed and tied up with old rope. Thanks to their TLC it arrived back safely in England as did the stowaway gecko, who had successfully infiltrated the packaging, only to find himself in Britain during the middle of winter. He remained in a margarine tub on a desk at the office, which was always warm, until Pat's secretary thought he should go off to a local aquarium which collected him within half an hour and welcomed him with open arms.

Safe landings too for the glass! Why, however, the concern? It consisted of some windows from St. John's Church Pumwani, the first Anglican church building in Nairobi which had stood originally on the site of the Parliament Buildings and was dismantled and re-erected in Pumwani to make way for the first Legislative Council when it was formed. The old church building, constructed for the most part of corrugated iron sheets but unmistakably a traditional church of Victorian vintage, had stained glass windows and a friend had rescued and retained them for us at the time of demolition, when the new St. John's Pumwani was built.

The glass is delicate, pale green in colour, beautifully set in diamond-shaped lead. At the foot the glaziers have preserved a thin, horizontal, mauve strip, which, as luck had it, perfectly matches the dining room wallpaper. Notwithstanding its delicate hue, the glass is opaque, ensuring that no glare from the African sun would have interrupted the churchgoers' view of the activities within the church and the worship taking place. It also excluded entirely any sight of the mud and wattle buildings, the deplorable conditions and the daily life of the people of Pumwani which was going on outside. The congregation was cocooned from the poverty, misery and suffering which surrounded it and was not involved.

Prologue

It was to redress this situation that St. John's Community Centre was established in 1956. There was a need to understand the meaning of Christian compassion and to offer it to the under-privileged population of Pumwani giving practical expression to the Biblical exhortation "Bear each other's burdens". In the pages which follow, we hope you will see how, over a period of sixty years, these words have motivated and inspired the leaders, staff and volunteers of St. John's Community Centre, Pumwani.

Pat & Jim Richardson
Poole, England
June 2019

Part I - "In the Beginning…"

Chapter 1 – How it Began for Us

Bristol 1955

It all began for Pat one afternoon in the late Autumn of 1955, when there was a knock at the door of her room. She was working at the time on a research project in Bristol, where families, who had lived in the old slum area of Barton Hill, were being resettled in other parts of the city, following the demolition of their homes and familiar surroundings. Pat was working in a team, who interviewed the families before they moved and afterwards at regular intervals in their new homes. The project was conducted from the University Settlement in Barton Hill, where there was a wealth of knowledge about the life of the community over many years and a positive relationship between the Settlement residents and other members of the community.

When Pat answered the door, it was to see John Taylor, the late Bishop of Winchester and a missionary at that time working with the Church Missionary Society (CMS). He had come to Bristol to speak at Fishponds Teacher Training College and had called to invite her to consider a position with the Society, working in St. John's Community Centre Pumwani, the oldest African location in the City of Nairobi in Kenya.

In 1951 Pat had gone up to Birmingham University to read for a degree in Social Studies. Throughout the early fifties the English newspapers were full of headlines about the horrific activities of the Mau Mau in Kenya. We shall explore more of this but, in the meantime, suffice it to say that the causes of this uprising were of great interest to a budding sociologist!

Following the visit of John Taylor to Barton Hill, and Pat's offer to CMS and acceptance as a mission partner, the Mission thought that Pat should obtain further experience in other fields of social work. She spent some months in Church Army-run institutions and then completed a post-graduate course in generic social casework before moving to Kenya. It was not until January 1959, that she set sail on the *"Rhodesia Castle"*, to take up her post in Nairobi.

Part I - "In the Beginning..."

The journey up-country

Pat and three other missionary recruits arrived in Mombasa, a large port on the East coast of Kenya, three weeks later. Barbara, a teacher, was bound for Juba in the Southern Sudan; Jane, an occupational therapist, for a leprosy settlement in Uganda; Pat Lisk, another teacher, for a girls' school in Nyanza, North-Western Kenya and Pat Rose for the Community Centre in Pumwani.

Having said good-bye to Barbara, the three who were remaining in East Africa climbed aboard the long train hissing in Mombasa Railway Station and set off travelling through the night on the narrow-gauge railway line, which would take them the 300 miles to Nairobi. They were both apprehensive and excited, wondering what they would find at the end of this train journey, but so happy that the past few years of preparation had brought them to this new country and an exciting future.

Shortly after the train left Mombasa an African, wearing a red fez and long white kanzu with a broad red cummerbund around his waist, came along the corridor banging a gong to signify that the first sitting for dinner was ready to be served. Whilst the three young white women enjoyed an amazing colonial-type dinner, including curry, complete with white damask table-cloths and napkins, another steward prepared their beds back in their carriage.

Very few Africans ate in the dining room and the majority travelled in over-crowded carriages, sitting on hard benches or the floor. At this point in Kenya's history there was very little social mixing between the African, Asian and European communities, who each lived in their separate areas. The three missionary recruits knew that this railway passed through the Tsavo National Park where Indians who had built the railway at the end of the nineteenth century had struggled and managed to complete the work despite the terrifying attacks of the "man-eaters of Tsavo". It was, however, too dark to see any lions or animals through the windows of their carriage. The only excitement was caused by the vendors of oranges, bananas and maize-cobs, who thronged the platform when the train stopped at Voi and tried to draw the attention of the passengers to their wares. The next morning the three returned to the dining room and enjoyed their last luxurious meal for a long time. As they approached Nairobi in the early sunlight they saw giraffe and antelope scattered on the plains between tiny African huts and patches of maize and banana trees. A first impression of a quiet, beautiful country!

They arrived in Nairobi in brilliant sunshine at about 8am but the air was fresh and cool, in contrast to the humid heat of Mombasa. During the journey they had climbed about 5500 feet from sea-level and passed through the dry, scrubby Akamba countryside. The train stopped to disgorge a large group of passengers, among whom were European settlers heading eventually for the "white highlands" where they grew coffee and tea, farmed vast areas of wheat and grazed their sheep and cattle. Crowds of Africans, interspersed with groups of Asians, were returning to the city where they worked or hoped to find ways of earning much-needed cash.

After all the excitement of the last three weeks and facing so much uncertainty in the future, it was re-assuring to be met on the station platform by a group of CMS missionaries.

Pat was greeted warmly by Helen and Charles Tett, her senior missionaries in Pumwani, who drove her there from Nairobi station. It was a short journey of about two miles through crowded streets, which looked nothing like the very beautiful city centre portrayed in the inviting brochure put out by the municipality and entitled "City in the Sun".

Opposite the station stood Church House, the first of the new generation of taller buildings bringing in the age of the sky-scrapers to Nairobi. As they left this behind them, they passed the headquarters of the Kenya Planters Co-operative Union and Mincing Lane Market, where Pat would later buy fruit and vegetables. The car made slow progress as the streets were packed with poorly-dressed, often bare-footed Africans, some walking and others pushing wooden barrows. Opposite the market was an ornate mosque, which Pat was told had been built with money sent from Pakistan.

Arrival

As they drove into the Pumwani location they passed the large government maternity hospital, which served the whole of Nairobi. They entered the CMS compound where the old Anglican church of St. John's was standing, clad in corrugated iron, but unmistakably a church just as the Victorians would have designed it. It was surrounded by small stone-built houses, which were the homes of the employees of the Anglican church and its institutions, such as the Nairobi Bookshop in Church House. The vicar, the Rev'd Dishon Mwangola, with his wife and three grown-up children, lived in one of these buildings, which the Archbishop of Kenya later compared to a "dog kennel". This home was to become very familiar to Pat as she visited Ethelreda, the vicar's wife, each morning for some months gaining practice in speaking Kiswahili.

Ethelreda was a very large Mtaita lady, who came with her family from the coast and, therefore, spoke very good grammatical Swahili, influenced by the Arabs who had settled near to Taita country. Ethelreda taught Pat colloquial Swahili and shared her Christian faith. She also freely criticised Europeans and CMS missionaries for such heinous sins as wearing short skirts.

The area occupied by the church and the church employees was fenced off, separating it from the new Community Centre, the 'Burns Memorial Hall', where Pat would be working. A large open space around the Centre was used for volleyball, football and "socializing". Many young males who enjoyed meeting there, were in fact buying and smoking "bhang", a kind of cannabis, which resulted in blood-shot eyes, extreme lethargy and not infrequently aggression and fighting.

Chapter 1 – How it Began for Us

St. John's Church, Pumwani

A family living in staff housing on the church compound

Finally, at long last, they arrived at CMS Pumwani. As they got out of Charles' car, the smell of Pumwani hit them. Charles led the way up a wooden staircase and on to the long wooden landing, which provided access to the missionaries' flats. He took Pat's cases along to the farthest door, showed Pat inside and left her to recover. Pat was standing in an L shaped room built of rough stone blocks, which were covered in cream emulsion paint and red dust. A dining table and chairs stood in one end of the room and a sofa along the opposite wall. In the other corner of the rectangle was the toilet and a small kitchen. Adjacent to this rectangle was a bathroom and two bedrooms, in one of which Charles had placed Pat's luggage.

She would be sharing the flat with Georgina Serpell, a missionary from Australia CMS. Georgina welcomed Pat into the flat, which she had equipped, and introduced her to Mary Shadrack, a young, unmarried Kikuyu mother, whom she had taught to do simple domestic chores. Pat benefited from Georgina's hospitality and her generosity in introducing her to members of the Church, the Centre staff and some of the Pumwani residents. This induction was completed before Georgina had to return home because of her mother's ill-health. She returned to Kenya later but went to work with CMS in Nakuru and did not come back to Pumwani.

Having seen around the flat, Pat stood at the window and looked out at Pumwani or 'Majengo' as it was known to its residents. The houses were small, rectangular, made from mud and wattle and roofed by pieces of corrugated iron or recycled tins, which had been beaten flat.

It had taken over four years of extra training and experience for her to reach this place and, for the next four years, this would be her home where she would remain.

Chapter 1 – How it Began for Us

The view from Pat's window in 1959

Volleyball in the Centre's field

Chapter 2 – Adjusting to the Status Quo…

Those four years spent in preparation for her work in Africa included over a year of "missionary training" at "Foxbury", a centre near Chislehurst in Kent, where the Church Mission Society (CMS) prepared women missionaries, or mission partners as they are now called, for the cultural differences which they would find upon arrival abroad. We have observed over the years how valuable this could be and the problems faced by missionaries of other societies who did not provide orientation.

Foxbury

Foxbury had not been an easy period while Pat was prepared, one might even say moulded, by CMS for her new vocation. When she had offered to CMS it was a lifetime commitment. Most of her colleagues would remain in the mission for the rest of their working lives. Although missionaries usually went to destinations where they had felt called to serve, there was no guarantee that they would spend the rest of their working lives in that country or region. Situations might change for a variety of reasons, not least politically and one had, therefore, to be prepared to go wherever in the world CMS wanted one to be. A degree of versatility and flexibility was required. Hence the need for missionary training as it was called.

The staff at Foxbury had first-hand experience of the mission field and knew that many problems, which arose on mission stations, were due to the eccentricities and unloving behaviour of a small number of people living and working together in close communion. They tried to help those missionaries in training who were obviously going to find themselves in such difficult situations. They needed to be strong characters, who would hold fast to their conviction but at the same time understand their need to be adaptable and sensitive to others' needs. During their time at Foxbury, the trainees were divided up into small groups where their inter-personal behaviour was studied by the staff and senior students. In many ways this was helpful but to some of the students it caused serious stress. Because of her professional training, Pat was often critical of the dynamics which were created, making her a target for well-meaning criticism and advice.

Some single missionaries later married and usually it would be to another missionary. Missionaries, for the most part, lived in remote situations and the likelihood of their meeting other people with a similar vocation, who shared the same values and objectives, was equally remote. Whether single or married, missionaries and their children would stay essentially within the CMS family and the mission would undertake the responsibility for their well-being and that of their children.

This was not, however, a life for the faint-hearted and physical, sometimes hazardous, conditions might be encountered. Nor would it suit those anxious to preserve their creature comforts. Allowances were adequate and the necessities of life were provided for but they were designed to provide simple, comfortable living and did not in the least spill over into the luxurious category. So, one could plan to take a reasonable local holiday for rest and recreation but it would be nothing fancy. Periodically, of course, one was required to return to the United Kingdom for holiday and deputation, the latter designed to inform CMS members at home of the work which they were supporting.

Wake-up call

Waking up to her first morning in Pumwani, Pat could understand why that difficult period of training had been required of her. Consciously, or unconsciously, she found herself in an environment like she had never experienced before. She had been welcomed by colleagues, whom she would have around her; similarly-minded people but all of them strong personalities, certainly not, as we have noted, faint-hearted.

Here, out of her window, she witnessed, in the extreme, how the other half lived. Here was life in the raw. It started soon after daybreak, with people on the move. They were opening up their shops or "dukas" from which they would hope to sell the day-to-day requirements of their neighbours. There were no supermarkets here. They simply opened up a shutter which had protected their wares during the night and they were open for business.

Another view from Pat's window

The other ingredient of movement in Pumwani, like most of the African locations, was the ubiquitous barrow, pushed by hand and transporting the goods required. In the countryside we would see these barrows pulled by hungry, emaciated donkeys, who looked as though they might drop and were very largely ill-treated, more used to the stick than the carrot. They were, however, not so much in evidence in the metropolis, busy with all kinds of motorised traffic.

All this started up at about 6 a.m., perhaps earlier, as another day dawned in Pumwani. Pat probably had little idea what that day would hold for her but she was excited. This was what it had all been about. Here was the culmination of years of academic education at school and at university:

years of practical post-graduate research under the watchful and skilful direction of Hilda Jennings at the Bristol settlement; months helping with the laundry in the Church Army approved school, with all the trauma of those deprived, unhappy girls, who needed love not harsh, sadistic treatment at the hands of those who controlled them; weeks spent at the "Mothers", where unmarried mothers gave birth to their illegitimate children and looked after them under the watchful gaze of abler women; and finally, a year working with, and learning from, the medical social workers at the Queen Elizabeth Hospital and Dr. Stirret a psychiatrist in Birmingham. All this leading up to this very first morning, when Pat would look out on a whole new vista of life and work, into which she was expecting to become immersed. Immersed to the point at which she would become a part of it and into which she might hope to bring some meaning.

We shall explain in later chapters how difficult it was for the local Church to understand Pat's work as a social caseworker and indeed the need to grapple with social conditions and social needs. This was something with which the Church was unfamiliar: earlier missionaries had come primarily as evangelists, establishing at the same time schools and hospitals to deal with the basic needs of the people. A community centre and its wider remit would prove to be a bridge too far for the local church congregation. She would be bringing a new concept and new ideas: to do that she would have to understand what her predecessors had accomplished and how she would build on that.

The earlier history of CMS in Pumwani

"Bwana Burns"

The first missionary to Nairobi had been Archdeacon George Burns, after whom the Community Centre building, the Burns Memorial Hall, had been named. "Bwana Burns", as he was known amongst the residents of Pumwani, had been sent by the Church Missionary Association, New South Wales, Australia in 1896 and, like the very early missionaries, had started his missionary career at the coast. He married Sibella Bazett, who had come to Kenya from England in 1892, with her two sisters, as a single lady missionary. They had had two children, both of whom they had buried in Frere Town. The Burns were not the first missionary family to have experienced such a tragedy. Burns himself contracted black water fever, a deadly disease, and although he survived, he was not allowed to continue his work at the coast or in the Shimba Hills.

Bwana Burns and his wife Sibella

After leave in England, he was sent to East Africa on the 12th May 1906 to open a new mission station in Nairobi. He had two more children and when Joyce, his daughter, was only three months old, they travelled there by train as far as the railway had been constructed. Thereafter, they completed the journey to Nairobi on foot.

Once there, George Burns started work in the back of an Indian duka (shop) with a colleague Canon Elijah Gacanja. Burns was the first CMS missionary to work in Nairobi and, with Elijah's help, was as such the founder of the Anglican Church in what would become the capital city. St. John's Church in Pumwani was originally erected in Jackson Road in the centre of the city and when it came time to exchange this central site, to make way for the new Parliament or Legislative Council as it was known in colonial days, it was George who arranged for it to be taken down and re-erected on its present site in Pumwani. Constructed of corrugated iron it was nevertheless unmistakably a Victorian church building in cultural shape and appearance. The thriving Christian population now worshipping at All Saints' Cathedral and numerous Churches across the City and its surrounding suburbs can trace their roots back to Archdeacon George Burns OBE. Burns himself was to become one of the Members of the Legislative Council (Legco as it came to be known) and was chosen to be the Representative of African Interests.

The situation Burns found on his arrival in Nairobi is described in the CMS Proceedings of 1907:

> "Nearly half of the native Christians in British East Africa are found in Nairobi; they have not been baptised at that station for the Society only began work there in 1906, but they have flocked thither from other places, chiefly from the Coast, in search of employment. It is said the women among them are a hindrance rather than a help, for drink has a sad hold on some of their number and they show no desire to attend any of the services, while there are nearly always to be found in the prison some lads who have been in touch with missionaries".

The social life which Pat found in Pumwani just over fifty years later was not so very different, although a group of elderly women describing themselves as members of "Dini ya Burnsi" (Burns religion) attended St. John's Church services and women's meetings held in the Community Centre. Some were retired prostitutes and beer brewers and one or two others had come to the city with their European employers, for whom they had worked as ayahs (nannies) or house-servants.

Burns on his arrival in Nairobi had found there the Rev'd W.M. Faloon, a chaplain who had been appointed earlier by the Colonial and Continental Church Society to minister to the European community. Faloon had also conducted Kiswahili services for approximately 100 African Christians. Burns relieved him of the Kiswahili services. He also opened a school which began with four pupils and by the end of the year had about thirty in regular attendance, most of them being young men serving in hotels and such places. One adult was baptised. Burns was ordained in 1910 and remained serving the Church in Nairobi until his retirement in 1932.

Sister Maude Pethybridge

In 1918, the last year of the Great War, Sister Maude Pethybridge was sent out to British East Africa. Her first post was as Nursing Sister in the C.M.S. Mzizima Hospital at Frere Town, a short distance from Mombasa. It was a busy hospital with over 1,000 in-patients during the first year of her arrival. Like the other missionaries, she was saddened by the cruel suffering caused by the paganism there but that was lightened by the realisation that they had many special opportunities of reaching the hearts of the people through kindness and sympathy.

She was reported as carrying on there "valiant service against the odds", following which she was relocated to Embu, but after five years' service in Kenya she was forced to return to Australia for a complete rest, followed by a special course of training there at the Women's Hospital.

Thus equipped, and having fully recovered, she returned to Africa in 1924. She was much loved by African Christians in Butere, Nyanza, where she worked as an evangelist and established church services in

Luyhia and Luo. Joined by a Miss Moller and Miss Lee Appleby, they wrote in 1935 speaking of their busy life, full of bustling activity, in kindergarten, dispensary, and other similar work and rejoicing that, in their part of Kenya, there was a fine response on the part of the people, young and old, to missionary endeavour.

In the early 1940s, Sister Pethybridge (who had become affectionately known as "Pethy") developed asthma and was moved to Nairobi where, with the help of Mrs. Pittway and Miss Mary Plummer from England, she encountered a very different environment and attitude to her work amongst the town women of Nairobi. These women were living out of their natural environment and, as a result, found "pitfalls at every turn." Pethy organised three groups of Christian women, meeting weekly in three places in the African suburbs, many of whom, in their turn, became keen workers among their own fellow-country women. As a result, the number of non-Christians coming for instruction increased.

During the years 1943 to 1945, the same development of African Church responsibility was to be seen in "the great Church of St. Stephen", with its hundreds of worshippers, which was then wholly under African pastoral supervision. The city work extended from Nairobi for seventy miles to the east and north-east, where there were large estates owned by Europeans and mission work developed amongst huge numbers of labourers from all around, as far away as Kavirondo, coming under the care of the African Padre in Nairobi.

Pethy coveted prayer in her difficult, heart-breaking work among the women in Nairobi and these out-districts. Her work was as varied as it was exacting. She wrote of spiritual and practical teaching for the Christian women, of sewing classes and classes for instruction, of sick visiting and work amongst the women of the Nairobi Jail. As we would have expected, she made efforts to reclaim prostitutes, of which there were then over 1,000 in the city, and to guard others in the ever-present moral danger which surrounded them. She was visiting in the homes and also in the different hospitals: "European", "African", "Mental" and "Infectious Diseases". And, as if all this was not enough, there is mention of European soldiers coming in for meals, because we are talking about the closing years of World War II. The work in the city, on the surrounding farms, and in the great districts which border the Nairobi confines, all came under direct African supervision, with Canon Shadrack Mliwa, three evangelists, and Pethy in full-time work. The peculiar problems of the work in great African cities – cosmopolitanism, detribalisation, class-consciousness, broken homes, immorality and many more, called for most earnest prayer. The burden was beyond description and requesting prayer also for herself, she wrote: "I need much prayer for health and wisdom, and really to be indwelt and governed by God. There are difficulties, and I often cry to God in the night. Pray for me." Prayer was at the heart of Pethy's long missionary career and in Butere the people called her "Bibi Bahoia" – "the one who prays for us".

Moving on from the immediate post-war period to 1953, she found herself living and working in an area of Mau Mau activity and Australian CMS asked Kenya whether Pethy should be recalled in view of her 35 years of service and the danger in Pumwani. Concerns continued to be expressed by Australia on the same account over the next few years without any action being thought to be necessary. Finally, in February 1957 Pethy retired, well after retirement age, completing 39 years of service and very hard work, officially recorded as "characterised by her unswerving loyalty to her Lord and her great love of the African people."

"Burns Memorial Hall"

In recognition of the contribution made by Burns to the work of the church in Nairobi, the new Community Centre building was named the "Burns Memorial Hall" and opened by his successor, Miss Pethybridge, in June 1956. It comprised a hall, canteen, clubrooms, an office and a nearby store. The opening ceremony and dedication service were conducted by the Bishop of Mombasa, the Rt Rev'd Leonard Beecher. The building was one of seven such centres built in Nairobi at the same time and each of the church organisations responsible for these was helped by substantial contributions from the Government and Nairobi City Council.

Chapter 2 – Adjusting to the Status Quo...

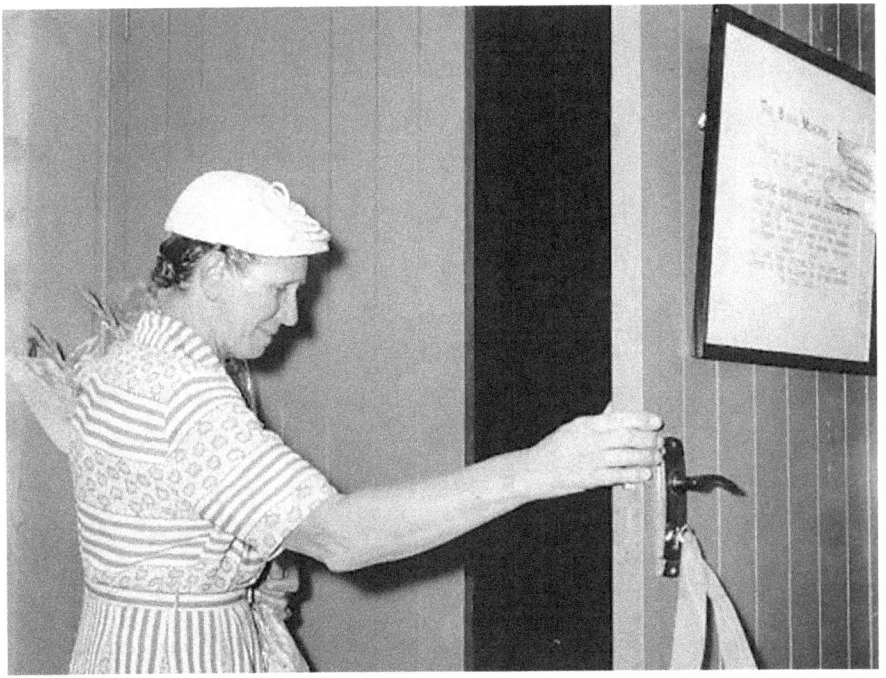

Miss Pethybridge - much loved - "the one who prays for us"

At the same time as the new building was erected, extensions were made to the existing CMS building in Pumwani, which had been in existence before 1920, when Pumwani was set out. The ground floor was being used as Dr. Aggrey Primary School and the floor above for the accommodation of women missionaries. Indeed, many generations of missionaries had lived there, including Edith Wiseman and Mary Rickman. A new flat on each end of the first floor was now constructed to increase the missionary accommodation and it was one of those which Pat occupied.

CMS had identified the Rev'd Charles and Mrs. Helen Tett as new CMS missionaries, who would come to Pumwani and take charge of the new Community Centre. They arrived in 1957 together with Jean Hake (nee Besgrove) who was a moral welfare worker from England. She was to work with women and girls alongside Gladys Beecher, the wife of the Archbishop of East Africa; Gladys, who had been born in Kenya, was a member of the well-known Leakey family and spoke fluent Kikuyu.

Part I - "In the Beginning..."

The opening of the Centre: Archbishop Beecher (2nd from right) in attendance

Archbishop Leonard Beecher and his wife Gladys

Gladys and Jean organised many helpful discussion groups among African women and girls, social workers and church members on aspects of Christian Home & Family Life. There was a particular emphasis on the problem of female genital mutilation, something which is illegal in England and for which the law is now being enforced.

Charles & Helen Tett

Charles and Helen had both been Sudan United Mission (SUM) missionaries in Nigeria employed in medical and educational work. They were married at Jos in Nigeria and then returned to England, where Charles was ordained before coming out to Kenya with their children, Robin aged nine years and Pauline aged two. Although they had no directly appropriate training or experience for their new job, they agreed to try it for six months and stayed fourteen years.

When they arrived, the Vicar of St. John's Church was the Rev'd David Mzungu, who led well-attended services in Kiswahili. Charles initiated an English-speaking service soon after his arrival. Miss Pethybridge had organised a church women's meeting and Helen was soon involved in this on Wednesday afternoons in the Community Centre. Georgina Serpell ran the Sunday School in which there were 300 pupils and just one other teacher! She was also responsible for the Youth Church, which met on Sunday afternoons in the Centre.

Charles and Helen were not well off but money and possessions did not worry them and they were generous in the way they shared their lives and belongings. Early on after her arrival, Pat was taken by them to spend her holiday with them at the coast. They invited her to do some of the driving but due to her inexperience of African murrum roads, she turned the car over on the very loose and dusty surface. It created considerable disruption of the holiday and involved a lot of travel for Charles, obtaining spare parts, but the matter was never mentioned and no resentment was created by the accident.

Charles' total involvement in his work and ministry was demonstrated on one occasion at their meal table. He had taken apart an old car with boys he was training at the trade school, and because of shortage of space the engine was to be seen hiding beneath their dining table.

St. John's Community Centre: its beginning

As the Tetts did not arrive in Kenya until September 1956 an Mkamba catechist named Daniel Waswa was appointed as Assistant Sub-Warden and a Management Committee was constituted, composed mostly of elders from St. John's Church, with the pastor David Mzungu as chairman. This committee met on the 7th August, 19th September, 20th November and the 19th December 1956. At these meetings it was decided to grant temporary membership of the Centre until the 31st December and issue membership cards on payment of twenty cents.

Sub-committees agreed to arrange football, a library, classes in advanced English, a choir and regular film shows by the Christian Council of Kenya (CCK) film unit. Miss Mary Eyre, a member both of the Cathedral congregation and of the Revival Brethren, together also with Mrs. Daniel Waswa, started a sewing class on Thursday afternoons and soon there were thirty-six members. The free film shows attracted packed houses on alternate Thursdays and a concert party made up of fourteen young Muslim men, who were known as the Coast Youth Dramatic Society, gave several concerts on the other Thursdays.

Unfortunately, the Management Committee decided that the sketches performed by the young Muslim boys aged between 11 and 21, were not helpful to the other Centre members and they were, therefore, discontinued. This was typical of the attitude of the Church elders.

The East African Literature Bureau agreed to loan 100 books to the Centre. The Centre bought two copies of Baraza and the East African Standard each Friday for reading in the library. Local people came to the Centre to listen to the wireless, play indoor games, buy refreshments from the canteen and listen to lectures from visiting speakers. There is still in existence a list of the boys selected to play football for the Kangundo Youth Football Club, CMS Pumwani, who were lined up against Misyani team, presumably a Kamba club, on the 7th October 1956.

The Centre attracted famous visitors during its early years. On the 21st October 1956 Princess Margaret drove through Pumwani and later Field Marshall Sir Claude Auchinlech visited the Centre. He was a cousin of Mary Eyre and was particularly interested in the Centre's youth work, having been President of the London Federation of Boys Clubs for seven years. Following their return from England, a tea party was held in the Centre for Bishop and Mrs. Obadiah Kariuki, whose daughter Eugenia later joined the staff of the Church Army Community Centre in Doonholm Road. The Pumwani residents were excited by the visits of these dignitaries and a sense of pride in their community became noticeable.

Several years following Pat's arrival, Helen Tett told her that the local church had been apprehensive about the nature of the work which she and Charles might be intending to do and the Revival Brethren had been particularly suspicious. She said that after some months they discovered that Daniel, who had been the acting Warden, had been dishonest and he was sacked. His dismissal did not improve inter-racial attitudes, which underlay problems between the local church and the missionaries for many years to come.

Helen found a way into fellowship with women church members by following in the steps of Pethy, who was loved and trusted by them. Pethy's mantle fell upon Helen. She also served the church by giving hospitality to school parties in the Centre at a charge of Shs.3/50 per person per day. Likewise, she arranged accommodation for pastors who came to Nairobi for meetings of Synod and catered for wedding receptions at a charge of Shs.1/- per head. The refreshments consisted of buns spread with red jam and cups of milky tea.

Helen was a woman of diverse abilities and incredible energy. Her nursing gifts and compassionate nature were fully used as she visited the sick and often the terminally ill in Pumwani. In the late fifties Helen arranged a jumble sale in the Centre to raise money for the purchase of typewriters for it. This was one of many extraordinary events, which would have quickly deteriorated into chaos but for the able-bodied friends of the Centre, recruited to maintain a semblance of order and control.

When Pat arrived in January 1959 there were 150 children attending an informal school at the Centre. This had been arranged by Barbara McDougal of CCK and she did similar work in the other Christian Community Centres. Working among these children was Miss Martha Wambui, an untrained teacher, who did an amazing job and who introduced first Helen, and then Pat, to the women and girls of Pumwani. She was also a support to Georgina in her Sunday School and youth work.

Soon after his arrival Charles Tett began to concentrate on a boys' club, which eventually became the Christian Industrial Training Centre (CITC) and at the end of 1958 this club moved into the ground floor formerly occupied by Dr. Aggrey School, which was then accommodated in one of the newly-erected primary school buildings in Racecourse Road. Charles' work amongst boys was never really integrated into the other activities of St. John's Community Centre, although it had had its roots there. Charles' interest and energy were almost exclusively devoted to this work amongst boys, which quickly developed its own separate entity and national reputation. As a result, the future activities of the Centre became largely orientated towards women, girls and young children. This situation persisted for many decades, until a High School was built some twenty years later. Eventually the cycle turned full circle and some sixty years on the Centre is now fully committed to vocational training for boys as well as girls.

Whilst Charles mechanical skills attracted boys and young men to the Centre, he was not devoid of many other skills. Trained in First Aid, he responded one evening to a call from Pat, who had with her a woman going into labour. Turning on the lights of his car, he successfully delivered the baby in the open air.

The Mau Mau Rebellion

The other aspect of the status quo, with which Pat had to familiarise herself, was the political spectrum.

We have spoken of the interest shown by Pat in the uprising amongst the Kikuyu. Her first impressions in England had been of European settlers and a missionary being murdered in their homes. Further first-hand knowledge revealed the more extensive suffering of Kikuyu Africans who had refused to take the Mau Mau oath. On the 26th March 1953 during the notorious massacre of the villagers of Lari, Chief Luka, who had been appointed by the colonial government, together with more than a hundred loyalists were slaughtered for that very reason. They were regarded as traitors by the nationalists. Indeed, during the whole uprising no fewer than 1800 Kikuyu and fellow Africans from other tribes were murdered, one such being the verger of St. John's Church, Pumwani. Pumwani had apparently been a significant centre for Mau Mau activity, although the authors' knowledge of this is almost non-existent.

Kenya was still a colony and the British Government declared a state of emergency in 1952, sending British troops to help in putting down the rebellion. As a result, hundreds of members of the Mau Mau and nationalist suspects were killed, beaten and tortured as they opposed the government forces. At the root of the conflict lay the feelings of the Kikuyu as they saw expatriates taking possession of large tracts of their land. After the Second World War many Europeans went to Kenya seeking a new way of life and the British Government encouraged them to develop land which did not appear to be achieving its full potential. The Government had compensated the Kikuyu after their protests but the amount paid was regarded as insufficient by the Africans. To the Kikuyu the monetary value of the land was not the primary consideration. Geographical features such as rocks and trees had peculiar associations with ancestors and spirits, which local people were determined to keep.

During World War II many Kenyans had visited new places and experienced new conditions. They had been taught new skills and responsibilities. On their return to Kenya they were unable to obtain employment in responsible positions and were treated paternalistically by the European settlers. The coming of Western culture was causing old tribal customs and standards to crumble: the young, and especially the educated, Kenyans were confused. Many Kikuyu were drifting to the towns. They were pulled between the old and the new ways. Some became frustrated and bitter, especially as they experienced racial discrimination and they were unable to obtain the employment, which would provide them with a decent living.

Students at Kigari Teacher Training College enacting an oathing ceremony

Aware then of what had been done previously in Pumwani by CMS, perceptive of the stance taken by the parish church on social conditions and at the same time conscious of the "wind of change" then sweeping across Africa, Pat had particularly to acquaint herself with the special people, whom she had come to serve and whose needs and burdens she had come to bear.

Living in Pumwani she became aware of the situation. After a few weeks, a car journey out of town to visit Limuru and later a visit to the CMS mission station at Weithaga revealed a different side of the problem. The Kikuyu were living in very small houses, which were grouped tightly together as they had been ordered to do by the colonial regime for security purposes. The villagers' freedom had been tightly restricted by curfew regulations, traditional family accommodation was no longer possible and sudden searches and cross-questioning as soldiers searched for Mau Mau activists were frequent. Unhappiness and resentment resulted in grave discontent.

Two months after Pat arrived in Pumwani, the missionaries in Kenya received a visit from Canon Cecil Bewes, the Africa Secretary of CMS, who lived and worked in London. He had encouraged Pat to pursue her interest in Kenya and she was thrilled to meet him again in this very country. Canon Bewes and his wife and children had lived for more than twenty years in Kenya. He knew the country well and spoke fluent Kikuyu. As Africa Secretary, Canon Bewes received frequent letters and reports from CMS missionaries and during his visits to Kenya and their visits to the U.K. he had many opportunities for private conversations with his Kikuyu friends. He was, therefore, well aware of the growing tensions between blacks and whites, Christians and Mau Mau followers in Kenya. In England he reported this situation and was therefore selected to be a member of the Hola Commission which investigated and reported on the events in Hola in March 1959. It was for this he made a visit to Pumwani.

The Hola massacre of twelve Mau Mau detainees took place on the 3rd March 1959 when one African soldier was ordered by the colonial government to use force to ensure that the political detainees performed a physical task which they had refused to undertake. Eleven men were killed and many more maimed or injured by the blows administered by soldiers with sticks. Africans and many white settlers alike were horrified by this event and the colonial administration feared repercussions. The Hola Report marked a point in the history of Kenya when the colonial regime was seen as inappropriate and nationalism consequently surged forward.

Chapter 3 – The People of Pumwani

During her brief stay in Mombasa Pat had seen similar areas where she understood "Swahilis" lived. These were the descendants of Arab traders, who had formed families with African women and developed the language known as Kiswahili. Both at the coast and in Nairobi the areas where they lived were called "Majengo" or "the buildings" and most of the people who lived in Pumwani were Muslim. For them the mosque in Pumwani was very important both spiritually and socially. It had been rebuilt in 1930. Others who came to the area often adopted Muslim dress, either a long white kanzu and embroidered round hat for the men or an all-enveloping black bui bui for the women. Many adopted a Muslim name. Some of the Kikuyu who did not want to be involved in the conflict between Christian loyalists and Mau Mau nationalists found the Muslim umbrella an easy way out.

The population of Pumwani was not a homogenous group and it was very difficult to find any overall social or political grouping in the location. On her arrival in 1959, Charles Tett, Pat's senior CMS missionary remarked to her that he believed that it was home to about 10,000 people but others suggested 20,000 or even 30,000. There was no up-to-date demographic data as to their ages, sex, occupation, education or living conditions.

Central Government had nominated a chief and sub-chief whom Pat gradually came to know but they did not seem to be universally acknowledged in practice as leaders to be consulted. One day the local European District Officer, David Lowther, came to Pat's flat to greet her armed with a bunch of flowers: a nice touch appreciated by a young missionary and a gesture which one might imagine to be in the style or tradition of the British Colonial Administration. However, David, although respected as part of the "Kizungu" administration, did not usually seem to be part of the thinking or lives of the Pumwani residents.

It was easy to meet these residents because many of them were sitting outside their houses or standing about in the narrow roads as one walked around the area. Some congregated in the field behind the Centre in their search for an oasis of peace. There was no hustle or bustle.

Two Pumwani residents finding peace in the Community Centre grounds

Some men stood behind vegetable stalls in the streets and hanging over the stalls were bunches of banana leaves, which indicated that here it was possible to buy miraa, the illegal drug which came in by lorry from Somalia or Ethiopia. Other men and boys enjoyed smoking "bhang" or "cannabis", sitting on an empty grassy patch outside the Community Centre. Some of these boys took part in Centre activities and were friendly towards the Centre workers. Others were aggressive and expressed their dislike for Wazungu (Europeans).

In the evenings, the shops would still be open, welcoming their customers with the warm glow of their oil lamps hanging over the open hatch, their shopfront through which they did their trade. Trading also occurred outside the houses, where older women sat beside small heaps of tomatoes, onions and sweetcorn, which they sold for ten cents a heap. Playing in the mud and ditches of filthy water were small children, whose mothers or grandmothers gossiped and lit charcoal-burning braziers or jikos to cook tea or the family meal. One was often invited to a mug of tea or "chai" which was made by boiling milk, water, large helpings of sugar and tealeaves together in one large saucepan, sometimes with a touch of ginger added.

Even for those who found in Pumwani a unique visual attraction, the aroma greeting newly arriving visitors was unwelcoming. The stench produced by open drains and rotting vegetation was unbelievably strong, enough to make anybody heave who had a weak stomach and a sensitive nose.

Living Conditions in Pumwani

Pat spent her early weeks visiting in Pumwani, learning at first-hand about the conditions in which the inhabitants lived. For example, a mother and her large family of children lived and slept in one dark, overcrowded room eight or ten feet square; some sleeping on the bed and others beneath it on the mud floor. The charcoal brazier, on which the food was cooked, was sometimes in the passage, which ran down the centre of the mud and wattle houses and from which up to ten rooms led off. In other homes the brazier was in the room with the family and the cats and dogs which roamed around. Many of the children received horrific burns from souffrirs, stews or tea. Other children were bitten by rats in the night, which could run easily from room to room because there were no ceilings.

It was not easy to wash up used utensils or wash clothes or bodies because water was such a precious commodity. In Pumwani there were only eight standpipes where water supplied by the City Council came through the taps in a slow drizzle. The pipework had been laid some forty years earlier and water leaked from the pipes connecting the main City Council supply and the standpipes. These smaller connecting pipes had become furred up with the passage of time. There were always queues of women and children waiting to fill their five-gallon debbies. The small children loved playing in the mud. Unfortunately, some of the liquid was escaping from the communal lavatory and shower blocks, most of which were built adjoining a standpipe. The row of male lavatories was back-to-back with the lavatories for women, which consisted of long ditches without any privacy and which had once flushed but no longer did so. At night plastic bags full of human excrement were hurled from some of the

The view today from St. John's Community Centre

houses; "flying bombs" they were called. There was no running water for washing in the ablution blocks and no drains to carry away waste water from these or the houses.

Prostitution and Beer-brewing – a local economy

Regular and organised case-work by social workers, who were being professionally trained at the Community Centre in the 1960's, soon demonstrated that many of the social problems of Pumwani stemmed from the nature of the economy in that community. It was notorious as the red-light district of Nairobi. It was the place where men of all races came for relaxation and pleasure.

Most African men, of necessity, were separated from their families. Their work demanded it. The old stables, for example, built for the Carrier Corps (a British Regiment) had been converted into small rooms for the occupation of African men working in the City. Tiny, usually fairly squalid, rooms were grouped together with communal latrine blocks but no space was provided for the men's wives or families. Employers were not required to provide family accommodation for married men because it was not the custom to do so and employees did not expect or demand it. Furthermore, the social system did not permit it. Women traditionally worked their land back in the rural areas. They worked hard, growing crops and tending livestock with which they fed their children, selling any surplus for which they obtained cash, a most important commodity. Without cash they could not pay for school fees. Without cash they could not buy school uniforms. Without cash they could not pay for medical treatment nor could they provide their sons with the dowries required for potential daughters-in-law.

Traditionally, therefore, women did not follow their husbands into Nairobi or the other cities, where their men went in search of employment. They continued to maintain their traditional homes and homesteads, even after their husbands found work from which they derived an income in the city. Indeed, the "shamba" or homestead which the women kept and cultivated in their own home area has remained, and probably will for the future remain, the treasured asset of every family, however successful they may become and however much wealth they might acquire. "Home" is their tribal area. They resort there more often than not on public holidays and indeed for their annual holidays. They try to get there in time for clearing and planting their crops before the rains. They expect to finally retire there when their working days in the towns are done. Bodies are taken back to the rural areas for burial after death. Traditionally sacrifices had been made at special places in these home areas and the spirits of ancestors were believed to be there. Whilst these beliefs may have belonged to the past and were laughed at by new generations, a certain amount of superstition remained. Men therefore seeking work in the town in these early days sought a bed space and not a family home.

In the twenty-first century, travel is easier and with the introduction and legalisation of the "matatu" or taxi - a cheap, often dangerous and nail-biting mode of transport - it is within the financial capability of most people to get to and fro to their home areas at not too great a cost. It was not so in the middle of the last century. Men often returned home only for their annual leave, rarely seeing their wives in the meantime.

So the sex industry of Pumwani was a necessity. It was that much more pleasurable, when accompanied by local beer, which was brewed in the Nairobi City Council beer hall and which many Pumwani women were licensed to buy and re-sell – though they usually did so after it had been "doctored" to make it more powerful and popular. Men working in Nairobi visited Pumwani for an evening of leisure and entertainment: it was a social occasion. Indeed, lasting relationships were formed and visits would be made to elderly women, who were no longer able to ply their trade, by men who wanted simply to have a chat or to obtain advice.

Unhappily, the sex industry of Pumwani was also a necessity for the women who lived there. Unlike the men working in the City, many had grown up in Pumwani. They had no land back in the rural areas. Their mothers had come up, many of them from the Coast following the construction of the railway from Mombasa to Nairobi, and the strong Swahili-speaking Muslim influence predominant in Pumwani had originated with them. Others had travelled with European employers to work as domestic servants and had moved to Pumwani when these jobs had come to an end.

Girls and women who came into the City from the rural areas seeking work and a better future, often ended up with neither in Pumwani. As a result, many children never knew their fathers and the incidence of sexually transmitted diseases was high. So in 1950 Nairobi City Council had opened a special VD clinic and dispensary in Pumwani.

So, for lack of other employment, prostitution had become a way of life in Pumwani – a vicious circle. Once a girl had entered upon it, it became almost impossible to break free. Indeed, it was a cycle in the communal life of Pumwani which was perpetuated in the next generation – and the generation following that - a cycle which appeared to be endless.

The only way to break the cycle would be to offer women in the community some alternative and remunerative form of employment. In the meantime, the girls and young women did what all their female friends and relations did and they did so from a very young age. To begin with, while the girls were young and desirable, this life could be financially rewarding. The best payers were the English "johnnies" who came from the RAF camp at Eastleigh, the neighbouring location to Pumwani. Sometimes wealthy Africans brought glamour to the lives of these girls. More usually, however, the clients were the working-men living in Nairobi without their wives. Regular customers were often long-distance lorry drivers, who spent a night in Nairobi breaking their long journeys. Sadly, the inevitable birth of children brought increased responsibility to mothers, who were often young and added to the pressure to find money for food and accommodation for their growing families.

Chapter 4 – Housing & Development

The housing and living conditions which Pat found when she arrived and which were described in the last chapter, have persisted very largely although they have been kept under review by the Nairobi City Council. It has been the intention for at least sixty years to redevelop the area and some work has been done on this but the problems attendant on redevelopment are huge and diverse.

The original development and housing

Pumwani, indeed Nairobi itself, had its beginnings with the arrival of the new railway line from Mombasa to Uganda, which attracted people to the area.

Some employers such as the Railways, who owned the housing estate at Muthurwa, the Central Government, Local Government and the Ministry of Works provided housing for their employees. Other Africans were not so fortunate and for them, in 1919, the Municipal Council acquired an area of about 40 acres and set it aside for their housing. This area, which was known as Pumwani, was divided into stands and plots. Roads were constructed and eight water standpipes and twelve blocks of lavatories and ablutions were set out. It was an early site and service scheme. Individuals were invited to rent a stand and on this construct a house of daub and wattle, which had to conform to certain regulations with regard to size. These house-owners were the elite, many of them being prostitutes who established Pumwani as Nairobi's red-light district. The original scheme was planned for 4,150 people.

As more women and girls arrived from the country-side or other areas of Nairobi, they were encouraged to live in mud shanties, which they built for themselves and these temporary shelters were called "Majengo" (the buildings), a name which was later applied to Pumwani as a whole.

Part I - "In the Beginning..."

Religious & Social Facilities

When the plans were made for the development of this area, a plot was allocated for a Protestant Church and, in the course of time, Canon Burns supervised the move of a corrugated iron building, which became known as the "tin church", from Jackson Road, where Parliament Buildings now stand in the Centre of Nairobi, to Pumwani, where it was called "St. John's".

Of more interest to the Muslim population was a Social Hall, erected as a War Memorial for Africans, who had died in the first world-war. At the time of Pat's arrival this Municipal Hall was a popular venue for watching films but nothing was ever shown which was educational, or which even seemed attractive to the Centre workers. After the Community Centre was opened in 1957, films were sometimes shown there but the most popular events in Pumwani were political meetings addressed by African nationalists and other politicians.

In 1931 the population of Pumwani was 7,173 and by 1939 it had grown to over 8,000. Although Pumwani had begun as a planned settlement, many of the rooms were added to the houses without permission. After the second world-war the Municipal Council again began to discuss the demolition and reconstruction of Pumwani and because of this anticipated development, money was not spent on maintenance or improvements. In the early days of the Community Centre, the anticipated reconstruction of Pumwani was frequently referred to, but the availability of finance was the critical issue which delayed any action.

In 1960 Nairobi City Council had explained to the village committee a scheme for redevelopment, which they then amended in 1961. Nationalists were convinced that following the declaration of "Uhuru" or "Freedom" in December 1963 something would then be done and in that year a scheme for improving the roads and sewers was prepared. Another report recommending a new scheme was prepared in 1964. This scheme incorporated plans for tenant purchase and council letting but it advised against self-built housing. The estimated cost was comparatively

Chapter 4 – Housing & Development

low, K£750,000[1], and this plan was discussed with the landlords who approved it.

However, in 1965 yet another new plan was prepared, for which the costing was K£2,000,000 and it became obvious that many existing Pumwani tenants would not be able to afford the new rents. In September the City Council prepared a social survey of Pumwani and this was led by the Rev'd Swailem Sidhom, who involved amongst other people, students from St Paul's Theological College, Limuru. Mr. Sidhom estimated that the average monthly Pumwani rent at that time was Shs.32/50 but the City Council proceeded with a scheme in which room rents would turn out to be no less than Shs.120/- per month due to a large rise in building costs.

The Community Centre became very concerned about the social implications of this redevelopment. Its effect upon the Pumwani residents and the life of the community would be immense. Important as it was that living conditions should be improved, the outcome for the people who were living there would be devastating.

We were going to England for leave in 1966 and Jim purchased a small Super 8 cine-camera, putting together a home-made film with music and commentary to demonstrate to our Churches and links there, the fears we had for the people of Pumwani, who would find it impossible to purchase or rent property in the only area they had called home. We recall photographing through lettering stuck on the back window of our car, portraying the title of the film against a moving backdrop of Pumwani houses as we drove along. We can still visualise a session sprawled out on the living room floor, timing selected pieces of music to synchronise with certain scenes. Finally, a session at the Forces Broadcasting Station

---

[1] Currency: The unit of currency during the years 1959-1963 was the East African Shilling, which was tied to sterling on the basis of E.A. Shs.20 =£1.Following Independence in 1963, the Kenya Shilling became the unit of currency, which is no longer at parity with sterling. In the early 1970s - even in 1980 – the rate of exchange was approximately K.Sh 17 = £1. The Kenya pound has sometimes been used for expressing larger amounts, and the notation K£1 = Sh.20 is sometimes followed in the text. 100 Cents = one Kenya shilling.

in Eastleigh, Nairobi organised by a friend, where a "mix" was achieved of film, music and commentary.

You can imagine our disappointment when we arrived back in England and hired from a photographic shop a new projector, which proved to be defective and scored a green line through the entire film. Sadly, we did not have a copy but we showed it as it was, at Pat's previous Church of St. Matthew's in Harwell and at my previous Church of St. Stephen's, Chatham. We then sent it to CMS but cannot think it was ever shown again. At least a few Christian friends were prayerfully aware of the problems likely to be experienced by the people of Pumwani if the bulldozers were to move in.

Following the showing of this film at Chatham, Pat was invited to address a Rochester Diocesan meeting which provided MRI[2] funds for Pumwani.

In 1966 the City Council's plans were once more revised and the estimated building costs of Phase 1 was K£600,000. This bill eventually reached K£1,154,000. So, Central Government made money available and in March 1967 the work started to provide rooms for tenant-purchase and for letting. The new Pumwani, known as "California", was erected on vacant land adjacent to the existing location and this was fortunate because the following February rents for the new flats were fixed at Shs.260 and Shs.280 per month. The people in Pumwani were not pleased and were disturbed by the fear of homelessness.

During the latter half of 1967 the Centre realised that action should be taken on its part on two counts. The general fear of homelessness on the part of the community needed to be addressed and more specifically the imminence of the proposed demolition of the building occupied by eight destitute old people housed by the Parish and the Centre in the house made available by the City Council required some plans for re-housing them.

Ephantus Mugo, the then Warden of the Community Centre, supported by the Board attended a number of community meetings called by the chief in

---

[2] Mutual Responsibility and Interdependence (MRI) – see chapter 7.

Chapter 4 – Housing & Development

The new Pumwani – 'California' – behind the existing location

1968 and 1969 but they were not successful in coming to any conclusion. Perhaps in consequence, the City Council asked the Centre to join in a survey of old people, their needs and condition, as a basis upon which the Council might base its future decisions. The Centre in fact carried out its own survey at the beginning of 1968, enlisting the support of two interviewers from Ofafa and Bahati Community Centres to work with three members of its own staff and working full time they interviewed 120 old people within the space of two weeks. Pat was asked to become involved in this and the Board congratulated her upon her report, which demonstrated the enormous support these old people received from their neighbours, friends or relatives upon whom they depended. It pointed out that any disruption to the existing community by redevelopment, would place a much greater burden upon government and voluntary social services.

At a public meeting in August 1968 Mr. Mugo suggested that plans for the demolition of Pumwani should be dropped and be re-thought. The demolition planned to start in October 1968 was postponed and it was not till 1970 that demolition of the old Pumwani began. Just one of those houses demolished in March of that year rendered 40 people homeless. The scheme would destroy a way of life which had many good attributes, without replacing them.

Chapter 5 – The Activities of the Community Centre in its Early Years

The Centre opened whilst the State of Emergency was still in existence and there was considerable suspicion on the part of local residents about the activities and purpose of those working there. The African staff were all Christians and therefore known to be unsympathetic to Mau Mau. The motives of the expatriates for living and working among the people of Pumwani, were the subject of speculation and misunderstanding. When, soon after their arrival, Helen and Charles Tett walked through the muddy streets of Pumwani, they were met with silent stares and sullen expressions, especially on the faces of the Kikuyu. Only after much hard work, building relationships and talking openly were these barriers broken down.

Interestingly, a CMS Year Book commenting on the atmosphere surrounding the Tetts, observed that Pauline, their three-year-old daughter was "a great asset and the doors of many homes have been opened because of her." It also made the comment: "There is a price to pay for this friendship, however – lack of privacy, continual demands for help and advice. This is the only way, in this situation, to hope to have opportunities for communicating the Gospel of Christ."

Informal school

Large numbers of children were, however, interested to find out what the Centre could offer them. Some of these children were orphans or had only one parent, who could not afford to pay their school fees or buy the school uniforms which were a requirement before a child could be admitted to a government school. Others could not find a school place because the schools were too few for the demands of the population. These children spent their days roaming the streets and were attracted by the games and activities organised at the Centre.

In February 1957, it was decided to run daily classes for these children and this was achieved, as we have mentioned, with the help of Barbara McDougal the Christian Council of Kenya (CCK) worker, who was employed to supervise these classes in the Community Centres. Georgina Serpell, aided by Martha Wambui, took responsibility for them at Pumwani. By the end of 1957 there were about 160 such children known to Georgina, of whom 120 attended regularly at the Primary School Classes.

City Council Education Department was happy for this informal education to continue and it was used, where possible, as a first-aid project to enable unschooled children to catch up and enter normal schools in classes of their own age groups.

At a public rally in 1963, President Kenyatta announced the abolition of fees for Primary education, however this promise was only partially fulfilled in 1974 and only for the first 4 years of schooling. So, the Centre still provides education for children unable to access the national education system, even at the present day.

Some of the 120 children in the Primary School classes 1958

Chapter 5 – The Activities of the Community Centre in its Early Years

Georgina talking with Dishon

Georgina (right) with Martha (centre)

Adult Education

Helen Tett and Georgina Serpell started classes for women in homecraft and adult literacy and in 1958 the number attending daily had grown to 44. In the evenings subjects as diverse as photography and shorthand were taught to anybody who was interested whilst the standards ranged from literacy for the uneducated to Makerere University extra-mural studies. An average of 70 to 80 attended such classes each evening, many of them Muslim but also including Revival Brethren and other Christians.

Special Group for Teenage Girls

In February 1959, Pat arrived as the first social caseworker at the Centre. During her work the needs of the teenage girls in the area became more apparent. As a result, an informal group of these girls, who were mostly living as juvenile prostitutes, some of whom were mothers, many of whom were illiterate and almost all of whom showed signs of anti-social behaviour, began to meet informally with Pat each afternoon. To begin with they chatted, told their life histories and discussed their problems and possible solutions. They themselves suggested that they would like to learn to read and write and do useful arithmetic.

Others began to sew and knit and the group did some simple cooking. Sometimes they went on outings such as walking to the City gardens at Pangani, which was a new experience for most.

One afternoon the group cooked drop-scones on charcoal "jikos" and went home triumphantly bearing the products. Unfortunately, two of the girls took the scones to the Mosque, where they were gladly received and eaten by the elders. Later Pat received a visit from a very senior Muslim official, who came to complain that these men had been contaminated by food cooked with the infidels' utensils. Another mistake was more keenly felt by Pat. It appeared that three or four of these girls had nowhere to sleep and after Georgina, with whom Pat had shared a flat, had returned to Australia, there was an empty bedroom. It seemed appropriate, therefore, that while accommodation for the girls was being sorted out, they should sleep in the spare room. The following day Pat went out for a short time leaving the girls alone in her flat. When she returned the girls and some of Pat's best clothes and her jewellery had gone. Thanks to the group's dynamics it was all returned to Pat but those three members of the group never appeared in the Centre again.

"The group cooked drop-scones"

More Formality!

In December 1961 Margaret Pooley, a CMS headmistress, who had been ordered to leave their country by the Sudanese Government, arrived in Pumwani. As she took over all of the girls' classes she injected the discipline which she felt was lacking. When Pat explained that the Muslim girls had an unpleasant habit during Ramadhan of leaving the classroom at frequent intervals to spit, Margaret made it clear that in her school in the Sudan the Muslim girls swallowed their saliva and in Pumwani they would do the same. Margaret transformed all the informal girls' classes, working out new syllabi and introducing a new atmosphere of order and discipline.

The girls all received uniform which gave them a sense of belonging and following the famine in 1961 they were provided with a midday meal, which increased their sense of being cared for. Gradually qualified teachers were employed for the girls' classes.

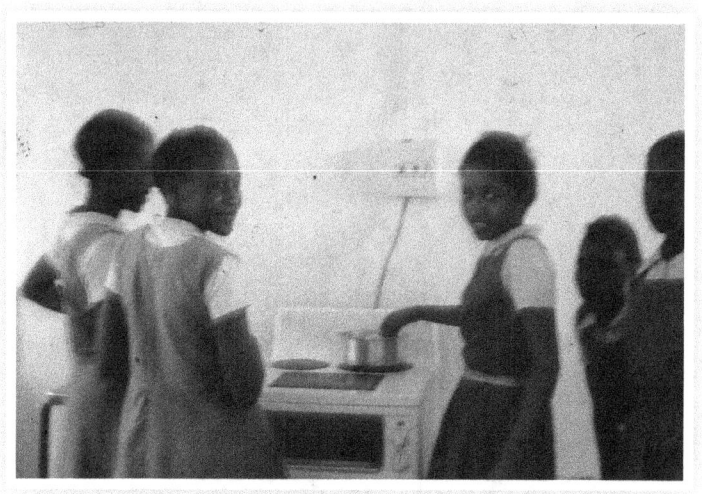

"The girls all received a uniform"

Some of Pat's older teenage group moved into these classes. Most of the others remained associated with the Centre, joining in games and social events. They remained, however, a distinct group; they never identified themselves with the more formal classes. When Pat was married in December 1962 some of them spent hours the day before the wedding preparing gallons of fruit cup, which Pat thought would be suitable for the Christian brethren, who were teetotal and came in large numbers to the reception. In view of the temperature prevailing in Nairobi during December, a preservative was required to inhibit the fermentation process and the addition of brandy enhanced the wedding libation. It might not have been Moet & Chandon but it was well received by the guests, whatever their background and their usual tipple. Some of the same girls came to the wedding in their Muslim black bui-buis to sing in the special choir, which had been trained by Hazel Houston, the wife of the Minister of Nairobi Baptist Church.

Distribution of milk and food

It was arranged for the Nairobi City Council to deliver milk to the Centre daily so that this could be distributed to children who had special needs, such as malnutrition and tuberculosis.

Living on the CMS compound was a young Mluhia man, named Mark Shiundu. He was a committed Christian, educated to Standard IV and had good Swahili and English[3]. Totally trustworthy, together with Alexander Shewera the deputy warden, he provided a link with the Revival Brethren and worked at the Centre for twenty years. Mark supervised the milk distribution, laughing and joking with the children and he quickly spotted any strange children who might have insinuated themselves into the queue.

It was also Mark's job to cook and distribute a meal at lunch time to the members of the girls' classes and others who were thought to be in special need. This continued until Anne Barnett, a later caseworker, concluded that this distribution of cooked food encouraged family breakdown. Instead, she gave food to mothers to cook at home with the result that the children went home to eat with their families.

---

[3] Primary education was completed at the end of Standard VIII.

Part I - "In the Beginning..."

Mark Shiundu stirring the posho

Chapter 6 – Early Development & Growth

Small Beginnings

Like those whom it came to serve and the area in which it served, the Centre itself was in considerable need of empowerment and resources at the time when Pat arrived. There were three African members of staff, only one of whom, Alexander Shewera, had much education. He was a qualified and experienced teacher, who had retired from being headmaster of the local protestant primary school named Dr. Aggrey. Mark Shiundu, who acted as caretaker and odd job man, and also looked after the garden, had only completed half of his primary education. Martha Wambui, who also had four years of primary education, was a dedicated worker amongst women and girls. All were committed members of the Revival Brethren.

The premises were woefully inadequate, insufficient in size and in need of a coat of paint. There was no Centre transport. Most worrying of all there was no core-financing.

As there was no Centre transport, neither Pat nor staff nor clients had easy access to the centre of the City. To the best of her recollection there was no public transport although matatus were available along the Racecourse Road, a quarter of a mile away.

Equipment was very basic and included newspapers, a poorly stocked library, blackboard and chalks, sewing materials mainly provided by British volunteers from the Cathedral and the Baptist Church, netballs, footballs and canteen equipment. It resembled what today might be called a 'drop-in centre'. Pat later acquired a casework office with a desk, two chairs and a cupboard which could be locked where she kept her files. Behind her chair she placed a picture of Holman Hunt's "The Light of the World."

From the beginning it had been recognised that a youth wing would have been desirable, where young people could meet in a healthier

Part I - "In the Beginning... "

atmosphere than that offered by the bars of the district. They needed a quiet room, in which they could read and do their homework. Lack of funds precluded this.

The Centre had been opened in June 1956 by Miss Pethybridge, shortly before she retired in 1957. Building costs had been received from Central government and Nairobi City Council and expatriate staff was provided by CMS. To begin with, the Centre was supervised by Miss Mary Eyre, a volunteer from All Saints' Cathedral, and she was joined by four African volunteers, two of whom came four nights a week. Later some African staff were appointed. When Helen and Charles Tett and their family arrived in October 1956 Charles became the Warden. It would not be unfair to say that CMS had done little financially to prime the pump for this project. They provided the salary and housing for the Tetts and this was more or less where their help stopped.

There were five Church Community Centres in the African locations in Nairobi. Their work was co-ordinated by a special committee – the **C**hristian **C**ommunity **C**entres ("3Cs") Co-ordinating Committee - set

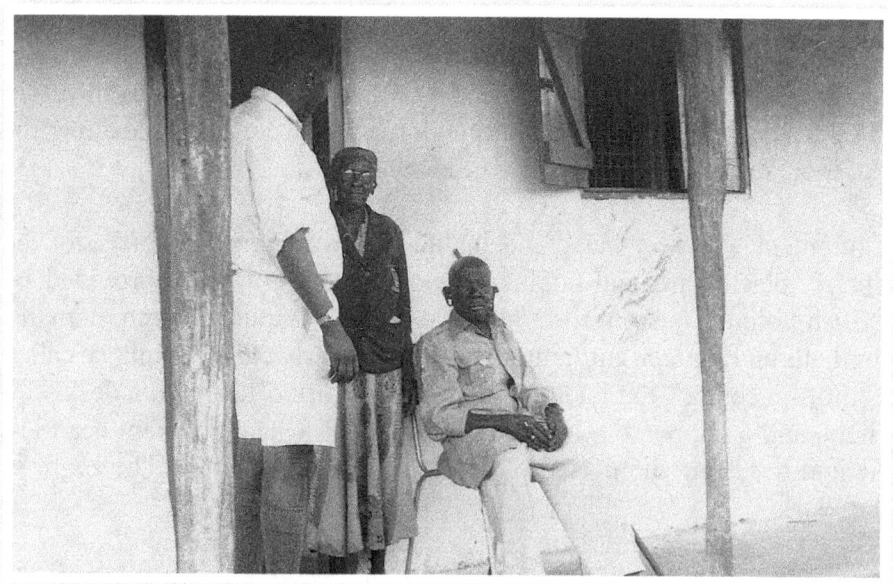

Alexander, deputy warden, settles new residents into the old people's home

Chapter 6 – Early Development & Growth

Hadijah, a regular visitor to the casework office

up by the Christian Council of Kenya (CCK), but each centre developed its own pattern. Financially, the CMS Community Centre was very similar to the other Community Centres. It was in fact the smallest of the CCK Centres and had the least facilities. They were, however, all working on a shoestring. Later the Southern Baptists from America set up a centre in Shauri Moyo, in the location next to Pumwani. As one might have expected, they did not experience any shortage of funds. The Revival Brethren in Pumwani disapproved of the Southern Baptist missionaries because they wore necklaces and make-up. On the other hand, the Baptist missionaries felt it was necessary to re-baptise any Anglican young people, who were attracted to their facilities as they had been heretically baptised as infants. The Southern Baptists did not join the "3Cs" Co-ordinating Committee and so there was little co-operation between them and the other centres, although there were good informal relationships between the staff of all the centres.

For any activity of the Centre, certainly any new activity, Pat had to find the funding. In the course of her casework activities she discovered individuals in desperate need of financial support, such as the cost of medical treatment. So she would tote around her European friends and acquaintances to solicit donations – something at which she became quite adept. When visiting Jim, who became a lay reader at St. John's in 1960, in the YMCA at Hospital Hill and meeting his friends there, it would not be unknown to see them getting out their cheque books in an attempt to finance the importunity of a client or meet a current crisis at the Centre.

Transport

A year or so after her arrival Pat managed to purchase at auction a Lloyd van, with an engine capacity of 600cc, a rare, little-known, German vehicle because only twelve of them had been imported into the country. She paid £125 for it with a loan from CMS. It proved to be a bargain because it had only five hundred miles on the clock and was trouble-free. It was an enclosed van, with a rear door, and an entire girls' netball team could be seen climbing regularly into the back of it: it became the forerunner par excellence of the matatu. Unfortunately, there was no budget for the running costs, even when it was being used on Centre business and activities. So, the recurrent expenditure and the loan repayments had to come out of the Shs.400/- (£20) monthly allowance, which Pat received as a single missionary.

The van became the subject of many disagreements as it was thought to belong to the church and Pat had to resist attempts to commandeer it although she was happy to drive the Pastor, the Rev'd Dishon Mwangola around his far-flung parish. When Pat resigned as Warden, everybody was amazed that the van disappeared with her. We knew that if she had given it to the Centre when she left, the staff and the church would all have suspected her of deceiving them.

The Rev'd Dishon Mwangola, Vicar of St. John's Church

The return visit of John Taylor

Then quite suddenly a change took place in 1962. John Taylor, then CMS Africa Secretary, the same person who had visited Pat at her flat in Bristol in 1955, knocked the door once more, this time at her flat in

Pumwani. He was appalled to find that she had no core-funding for the project. Following his visit, major advances were made in the Centre's empowerment both in terms of its governance and in the understanding of its financial situation.

A decision was taken to form a Management Committee and the reason for its formation became clear from the very first minute of that Committee setting out its Terms of Reference:

> "The Acting Chairman (Jesse Hillman a senior missionary in the CMS Kenya Mission) told the members that the Committee had been set up to advise on the Management of the Centre, to draw up a Constitution for the Community Centre and to decide on the best way of keeping the accounts. The Committee was under the Standing Committee of the CMS Kenya Mission, who would be responsible for the Centre only whilst it remained under CMS. *The Standing Committee had received a report concerning the financial position of the Centre and had decided to form a Management Committee as a result.*" (Authors' italics for emphasis)

John Taylor's visit to the flat for a second time had again been timely and critical. The meeting which followed was a landmark for the Centre. Decisions were taken in principle for the construction of new buildings and consideration was given to the kind of person to replace the Warden who was to be married at the end of the year and would be leaving her post. But more of that later.

Jim's involvement

It was also a landmark for Jim, because he was invited to be one of the founder members of the new Management Committee. It became his first official involvement with the Community Centre. He had previously helped Pat in the Contact Club, a social group which Pat had gathered together, composed of educated young African and Asian men and women. They were all English-speaking, most of whom had School Certificate and included young nurses from Pumwani Maternity Hospital.

Jim had felt called to come to Africa, after reading Keith Cole's book, "Kenya hanging in the Middle Way". He met up with Cyril Hooper, the Youth Secretary of CMS. Cyril had come from a Kenya missionary family and he encouraged Jim in his vocation, suggesting he might apply to become a District Officer with the Colonial Administration. Upon reflection, the Colonial Office might not have regarded his Christian vocation the ideal motivation for that kind of appointment. Had he been successful, his service would very likely have been curtailed soon afterwards, when Kenya was granted political independence.

At last Jim found an advertisement for a qualified solicitor with a firm of Advocates in Nairobi and it was not long before he was travelling out on the Comet, armed with letters of introduction from CMS addressed to key members of the Mission and the Church in Nairobi. He soon met up with Stanley Giltrap, the person in charge of the CMS Kenya Mission: Stanley was a caring person and spent time to welcome Jim into the family of CMS, collecting him each week for their Bible study which met in his home.

Whilst in England, Jim had been admitted and licensed as a Lay Reader in the Diocese of Rochester and he believed it right to find a situation in Kenya where he would be able to continue this ministry. Stanley suggested that he join the team consisting of himself and Charles Tett, who had started a service in English at St. John's Church, Pumwani. Jim was delighted at this suggestion, because it was exactly what he had wanted: an opportunity to be part of a team ministering effectively to young African Christians. Much more exciting than the suggestion from All Saints' Cathedral, that he might like to help with the parking of cars at the Cathedral carpark.

Charles had realised that there was a need for this service in English among the younger, better-educated men and women working in the City. The Cathedral congregation was at that time very largely European and young African men felt conspicuous, especially if they were new Christians. These were, after all, colonial times. The English service at St. John's was popular and the congregation grew steadily into the hundreds. Members of the Contact Club were recruited from the congregation. Jim enjoyed his ministry at St. John's for many years, and only shortly before he left Kenya, some twenty years later, did it come to an end.

The Christian Industrial Training Centre (CITC)

Charles and Helen Tett were visionaries. In the same way that Charles had seen the need for a Sunday service in English, so he had seen the considerable need amongst boys in and around Pumwani. So, while he was warden of the Community Centre, he started a boys' club and concentrated his efforts on boys. Georgina Serpell was already working there amongst the women and girls.

There was not much that Charles and Helen could not do if they turned their hands to it. Charles got hold of a broken-down car and he taught the boys how to take it down and to repair it. He also made a point of getting to know businessmen and Europeans who were involved in industry in Nairobi, developing contacts with them and enlisting their support. It was not long before the boys club developed into a trade school, a place where unemployed boys could acquire basic training in carpentry and metal work. The Christian Industrial Training Centre (CITC) was opened by the Governor of Kenya on the 10th October 1958. It consisted of a carpentry workshop and about 50 boys attended daily throughout that year. The carpentry workshop was equipped with benches made by the boys out of old desks and the place was redecorated and adapted for its new purpose. The old car had been stripped, reconditioned, mechanically assembled and finally resprayed.

With the help of the Rev'd Andrew Hake, financial and moral support was gained from many people. The first offer of financial help came from a Kikuyu voluntary body, a Christian loyalist group, called "the Torchbearers". After inviting Charles Tett to address their executive committee, they formed a group to raise money for the scheme.

Easter 1958 brought Jim Thomas, a CMS missionary, to help with theoretical and practical training. He taught mechanics, technical drawing and scripture, working his way through St. Luke's Gospel.

The steering committee, which had been formed, organised an appeal to enlarge the scope of the work and the Governor of Kenya gave the scheme his patronage. The Mayor of Nairobi and many prominent citizens gave it their support and various firms and individuals helped with the fees of those boys who were unable to find money for themselves. Unfortunately, many of the boys who might have benefited from such training had no desire to learn and resented any kind of discipline.

The trade school quickly outgrew the humble Community Centre, out of which it was born. An independent board of governors was set up which included, amongst others, local captains of industry.

An early cohort of CITC trainees

CMS re-located Tony Idle, an electrical engineer and his wife Myra to Pumwani, when they were forced to leave the Sudan, and Ross and Pauline Elliot were sent by CMS in New Zealand. African staff were recruited and trained and CITC rapidly became a thriving project, regularly turning out young tradesmen who found employment without too much difficulty.

The concept mushroomed to other urban centres. A girls' CITC was started at Kisumu on the shores of Lake Victoria, where girls acquired secretarial training and Pam Wilding, a missionary from Jim's parish in Chatham, was supplied by CMS to head up this project. Inevitably, Mombasa, the port and second largest town in Kenya, had to have a CITC and Tom and Mary Fisher moved from Pumwani to do a great job at the Coast. Later Myra and Tony Idle moved from Pumwani to start another trade school at Thika.

So, four major training centres, spread across the breadth of the country, became established and flourished, having grown out of the boys' club in the Community Centre at Pumwani. From that tiny beginning with Charles and a few lads gathered around a car engine, many young men and women from deprived backgrounds were empowered through employment. Furthermore, industry and commerce were equipped with a new human resource, which had been locally trained.

Emerging financial empowerment

The formation of the Management Committee at the Community Centre did not of course solve all its financial needs overnight. It was nevertheless a first and significant step in providing financial empowerment.

Just as Pat had gone unashamedly with her begging bowl to pay for even the smallest needs of her clients, so the need to raise private donations would persist. Now at least there was a body of willing and caring persons on the Management Committee who supported the new Warden in that task.

The first fund-raising event was a concert put on at Christmas 1962 by the Elizabethan Singers. This raised Sixty Kenya Shillings. It was not a princely sum. It was just sufficient to pay for the TV licence, which was charged at a concessionary rate to charities. The gift of a Television Set by the Kenya Broadcasting Company did not, therefore, prove to be an embarrassment as had been feared, for lack of funds to pay the licence fee. The Committee was, nevertheless, faced with a big deficit in the budget submitted to it for the new year of 1963.

In addition to the encouragement afforded by the support of the Committee members, there was a further financial morale boost. This took the form of donations promised for the long-overdue extensions to the buildings. Two grants of £1000 and £2000 were made. Furthermore, the Motor Mart Trust gave a grant for the caseworkers' salaries and other social casework expenses. Finally, the year 1963 closed with a broadcast appeal for the Centre, an event to be repeated in succeeding years.

Emergence of the Centre's Governance

If in terms of financial development 1964 followed much the same pattern, a leap was made in terms of the Centre's Governance and Control.

A Board of Governors was constituted and made responsible for the good governance of the Centre. It would be accountable to the Diocese of Nairobi. Its importance was recognised by the high standing of its ex-officio members, who included the Bishop, the Archdeacon, the Vicar of St. John's Church, the representative of CMS and the Principal of the Christian Industrial Training Centre (which remained adjacent to the Centre). Its membership understandably included also representatives of the Standing Committee of Synod, St. John's Parish Church Council and All Saints' Cathedral Church Council. Significantly, the Nairobi City Council and the Ministry of Social Services were also given the right to appoint members to the governing body.

So, empowerment came to the Centre in its governance. In one gigantic step the Centre was granted the right to determine its policy, to monitor its performance, to appoint its staff and to regulate its finances. The Warden ultimately looked no longer to London for guidance but was now responsible to local people, many of whom were indigenous. The Centre had truly come of age.

Consideration and discussion took place as to whether the Community Centre should be accountable to the Diocese or the Parish. Geographically and evangelistically it would have made sense for the Community Centre to become a part of, or at least attached to, the Parish. It would naturally have constituted part of the outreach of the local church, ministering to the needs of the people in the area, be they spiritual or material. Physically adjacent to the Church, the Community Centre was ideally placed to fulfil that role.

Theological standpoints, however, made such a union impossible. The Parish Church, like the Church of the Province of Kenya (CPK) as a whole, was strongly evangelical. It placed a great emphasis on personal salvation. The faith of its people had been sorely tested during the Mau Mau uprising, when the oathing was rejected and resisted by the Church. The Church Verger at St. John's had been murdered by Mau Mau. In the face of persecution and even martyrdom, Christians had clung desperately to what they understood and they held on firmly to what they believed. Their faith was simple but strong and they were courageous in the stand that they took.

A social gospel was not a part of their experience. Around the Church and Mission complex in Pumwani stood the mud and wattle buildings of the local Muslim people. In and about those squalid buildings, the people carried on their normal way of life, much of which was centred on prostitution and beer-brewing. All of this was total anathema to the Christian church. There was no point of contact between the Church and the community. More importantly, the Church members saw no purpose in trying to forge a link with the community around them or to address the social, moral and physical needs of that community, even if they were provided with the material resources to enable them to do so.

Inevitably it was decided that the Centre Board of Governors must be accountable to Diocesan Synod rather than the Parish Church. This unfortunately led to years of rivalry between the Community Centre and St. John's Church, especially in respect of financial gifts and ownership of buildings. The Church failed to understand and enter into the co-operative relationship which the Community Centre worked hard to forge with the Muslim community.

Perhaps, in God's wisdom, He knew that the influence of the Centre would extend beyond Parish boundaries and would become a Diocesan and National player in the work of both Church and Government.

Chapter 7 – Overseas Church Support

The Anglican Church

In the early part of 1962 Archbishop Leonard Beecher told Pat that he had plans to send her to Canada for an international conference. We believe it was at a time when the world-wide Anglican Communion was thinking through the relationship between the Anglican Church in the developed countries and its sister churches in the developing world.

In fact, the trip did not materialise because in the middle of that year Pat announced her engagement to Jim, something described by the Archbishop as a pleasant shock. By the end of the year, when she had completed her initial four-year tour of service, Pat and Jim were married in Pumwani and Pat's employment by CMS had to come to an end. It would have been otherwise if Jim himself had been employed by CMS.

We believe that out of that conference came a fresh understanding within the Anglican Communion of the need for closer contact of the Churches within it and for support of the younger Churches. This had always been the province of the missionary societies such as CMS, the United Society for the Propagation of the Gospel (USPG), the South American Missionary Society (SAMS) and the Bible Churchmen's Missionary Society (BCMS). They raised money from within the Parishes in England to support the work of overseas mission. Their work would continue. It was thought, however, that the institutional church should itself be more directly involved and the result was "Mutual Responsibility and Interdependence".

Mutual Responsibility and Interdependence

The concept was, as the name suggests, one of mutuality. The established and developing churches each had a contribution to make to the well-being of the whole. Looking back, as one can do now, one sees how the established church in England could benefit from the missionary zeal and impetus, which is evident in the church in Africa today. Our waning congregations and empty pews exist in marked contrast to the vibrant church services and bulging congregations of Africa. Those of us in England need to kindle something of the fervour and zeal of our brethren abroad.

We have exchange schemes, operated by CMS and the missionary societies, whereby clergy and church workers are brought to England, where they learn more of how the church operates here and at the same time contribute effectively to its life. The Archbishop of York, the Most Rev'd John Sentamu, is an outstanding example of a man, who has come and remained in England, exercising his ministry within the Church of England at Tulse Hill, Birmingham and York, bringing with him new ideas and a breath of fresh air.

However, in the mid-sixties, it looked rather as though the younger churches saw it only as an opportunity to seek major financing of their buildings. Jim was disillusioned when the Centre Board of Governors produced grandiose schemes for the rebuilding of the Centre. This in his view was not a priority, when financial grants could be used to support workers in the Centre's activities.

The Diocese of Rochester

When we arrived in England for our long leave (three months) in March 1966, armed with the home-made movie we had made of Pumwani and its proposed redevelopment, we made contact with the Rt. Rev'd John Bickersteth, who was then the incumbent of St. Stephen's Church, Chatham, the parish in which Jim had served as a Lay Reader in the late fifties before he went to Africa. John was welcoming and was particularly keen that we should go to speak at a Deanery Meeting called to organise Mutual Responsibility and Interdependence (MRI) locally. Pat, who did not share Jim's disillusionment, went to the meeting and spoke of our plans to build a hostel for particularly vulnerable girls as well as our continuing need of staff costs. We had plans to appoint and train an African Warden. Her experience as a past Warden of the Centre and her enthusiasm clearly made an impact.

By the time we arrived back in Kenya things were already underway. By July, CMS had sent the Centre the equivalent of £1500, being raised in Rochester under MRI, which the Centre needed for the salary of the new African Warden, Ephantus Mugo, who was then appointed and ready to take up his post that October.

Competing Claims

The Archbishop of East Africa was keen that the Pumwani site should be developed in accordance with an overall plan and the needs of all bodies using it, that is St. John's Church, the Community Centre and the Christian Industrial Training Centre, should be taken into account. He asked that these interested organisations should meet with him at the end of the year.

In anticipation of that meeting the Community Centre prioritised four aspects of its work, for which it hoped MRI might assist. New Centre buildings was not one of them. The first priority was for staff, their training and a reading room. The second priority was for residential accommodation for up to a dozen vulnerable girls. The third priority was residential accommodation and facilities for the training of six social workers. The last was to be a vocational training course for girls who had reached Standard VII in their primary education.

Problems then arose. The Centre received a further £1350 direct from Rochester but CMS had not been reimbursed the £1500 they had advanced in anticipation of the MRI Grant. There was a major complication because the Archbishop considered that all MRI moneys should be channeled through him for project work. When we had asked for clarification, the Diocese of Rochester specified that their project was not concerned with capital expenditure but that their sights were definitely set on the Community Centre. So, it was decided that the matter must be referred back to the Archbishop. When Pat and Jim met with him, he decided that the matter had to be referred back again to England and in due course the £1350 was, at his request, paid to the Diocese of Nairobi and became part of the pot with other MRI money.

It was a difficult situation. The Parish Church, which was always in an impecunious state, could not understand why the Community Centre should receive money and they were excluded. The Diocese of Rochester, however, had given the money for a specific purpose and there was an obligation to use it for that. The issue became the subject of considerable negotiation. Other monies were received by the Archbishop from MRI and in December he suggested that the Parish Church and the Community Centre should build and share a "Community Church".

A Community Church

But what did he mean by this? Would the Parish and the Community Centre simply share the same building, which would be occupied by them at different times and for different purposes? Or would there be greater integration of the two bodies. Would the local Church members become actively involved in running the activities of the Centre or at least take a more active interest in them? Would the Church Council become involved in the governance and policy of the Centre? Would the Parish use the activities of the Centre to evangelise and introduce a spiritual element to the social work, which was being done there? Or would the Parish Church be encouraged to develop a greater concern for the physical needs of the community in which it was situated and to relate their religious faith and fervour to the material needs and moral well-being of the people of Pumwani.

Nobody quite understood what the Archbishop really intended. It was not for another six months that the Archbishop's intentions became clear. A committee composed of four persons, including Captain Ball of the Church Army Community Centre, was appointed by the Archbishop to investigate the possibility of carrying out this project. It was, furthermore, the Archbishop's decision that the MRI money should be used for it. There had apparently been an allegation that negotiations between the Parish Council and the Community Centre Board of Governors had broken down. This was refuted by the Chairman of the Board as no official "bridge committee" of the two bodies had been formed and so no discussions had taken place. Captain Ball then dropped the bombshell.

The Community Centre would cease to function. It would be replaced by the Community Church!

To be or not to be!

Before the Archbishop's ad hoc committee left the meeting, a long discussion ensued, and it was resolved that Standing Committee of Diocesan Synod be recommended to form a "Board of Social Outreach" to give the matter more serious and close attention

The response of Standing Committee was to constitute a Commission of Social Responsibility and the Rev'd Anne Barnett, by now ordained and a member of the Centre's Board of Governors, and the Rev'd Dishon Mwangola, the Parish Priest, were asked to convene it. The members of the Commission were very much in agreement on the recommendations they made and demonstrated a real and shared concern, reflected in their report, commending all the work being undertaken at St. John's and Church Army Community Centres and hoping this would continue.

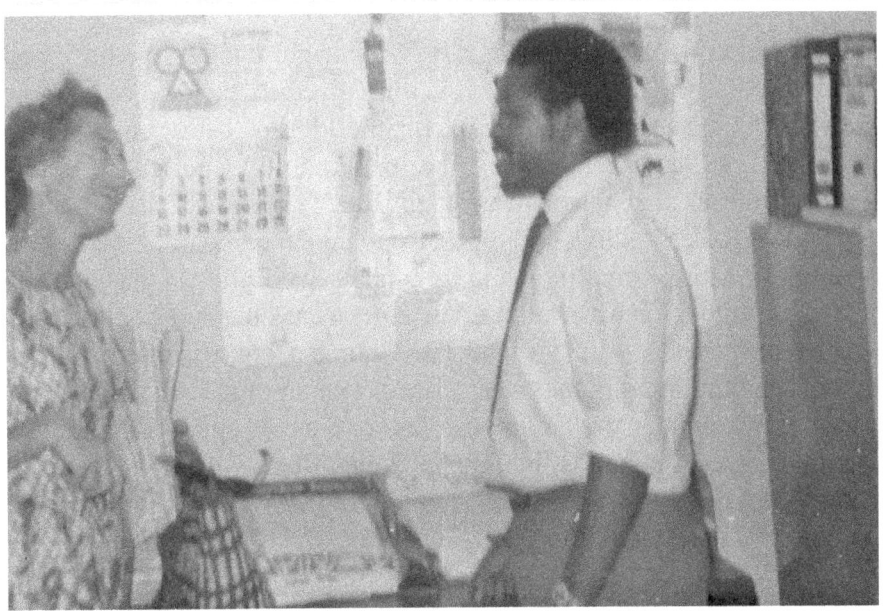

The Rev'd Anne Barnett speaking with Ephantus Mugo, the new Centre Director

The Commission's recommendations were accepted by Standing Committee in the closing months of the sixties. Most importantly, the existing work of St. John's Community Centre was to go on. There were consequential decisions taken concerning the erection of additional buildings and significantly, a review of the Centre's governance. Half the membership of the Board of Governors should be members of St. John's Church and the other half representatives of other interested bodies, including church, central and local government.

No sweeping changes took place in the Centre's practical day-to-day activities but at least out of all this came a formal recognition and acceptance of its work by the African church and a realisation, probably for the first time, of its true value. The Centre was confirmed by the church at Diocesan level in its activities. This was important, not so much in terms of financial support, as in the way it was perceived. The Community Centre no longer remained a fad of the European element in the church, started and supported by them. It was endorsed as a part of the overall mission of the Anglican Church operating in Kenya and its capital city.

The decision of Standing Committee was a right one. As we have seen earlier, the Parish Church had not been involved in the local community and its problems. It was not ready for the kind of heavy involvement envisaged by the Archbishop in a Community Church, far-seeing and laudable as that vision was. It did not yet possess the necessary theological understanding or experience to take it on board. Nor was this something, which could be made to happen overnight. The availability of a new jointly owned building would not, of itself, bring it about. Further meetings took place and the Church Commissioners were in attendance coordinating the overall development of the whole complex. It took some months, perhaps a year, before the concept of a Community Church petered out or was finally abandoned. It was, perhaps, a catalyst in bringing to the fore an understanding of what was being achieved in this sphere and a realisation of the need for social action on the part of the church nationally. To this extent Archbishop Beecher's vision was realised.

After resolving the dilemma of the Community Church, the need remained to take a decision concerning the MRI funds. The Archbishop attended a meeting of the Community Centre Board and asked it to set out its priority for new buildings. He emphasised the urgency of resolving this and to start building. He needed to inform donors in the United Kingdom, including those giving through MRI, what building had been started.

The Board of Governors revisited its priorities and decided that the Hostel for vulnerable girls remained its top priority and the Archbishop directed that the money should be used for this project, being an urgent and most pressing need. The cost of the hostel and a half of the cost of a flat for a residential warden would have been £7,500. The appetite of the Parish had, however, been whetted by the prospect of a new church building, and the Community Church continued to be spoken of. The view was expressed that the Parish Church was the mother institution and as such should be given priority. So, negotiations continued and these were further complicated by the need to develop the site as a whole.

Perhaps at the heart of the matter, the Parishioners themselves did not want a dual-purpose building: they were insistent that a new church building should be used solely for the purposes of worship. In the final result, an agreement was reached between St. John's Church and St. John's Community Centre that the available monies would be split equally between the two bodies. A spanking new Church building was erected to take the place of the corrugated iron sheets and the oldest church building in Nairobi was razed to the ground following a "Demolition Service". It was the church in which Pat and Jim had been married and our first two children baptized, but its loss did not cause us too much grief. The Community Centre received its share and applied it for the purpose it considered most beneficial to the community, the erection of the Girls Hostel.

So MRI, Mutual Responsibility and Interdependence, finally contributed to the empowerment of the Centre, the people of Pumwani and the Parish Church. It did, however, take over five years from the time that Pat had attended that meeting in Rochester and the decision of Rochester Diocese to support us, before the Board could give instructions to the

Architect to draw up plans and invite tenders for the erection of the Girls Residential Hostel. In fact, it was almost seven years before the building was completed and opened by the Mayor of Nairobi on the 13th January 1973 with pomp and celebration. In a ceremony scheduled to last two hours (it is bound to have gone on for longer) speeches were made by the Chairman, the Warden, a representative of the Diocese of Rochester, the Permanent Secretary for the Ministry of Co-operatives and Social Services and the Deputy Mayor of Nairobi. The new Archbishop of Kenya, the Most Rev'd Festo Olang, introduced the former Archbishop, the Most Rev'd Leonard Beecher, who led opening prayers and gave the final blessing. St. John's Church Choir and the Salvation Army were there to lead singing and after we had all sung "Stand up, Stand up for Jesus" the Mayor of Nairobi cut the tape and declared the Home open. Traditional Dancers entertained us and the whole afternoon ended with the inspection of the Home and a reception at the Community Centre Hall. A good time was had by all.

Matumaini Old People's Home downstairs, with the Girls' hostel upstairs (photo taken July 2019 – 46 years after it was opened)

Chapter 7 – Overseas Church Support

St. John's ACK Church Pumwani "spanking new church building"

Financial Empowerment from Other Churches – "Bread for the World"

With the passage of time, other plans for development and new building had also come to fruition, so that the opening of the Girls Residential Hostel coincided with the opening of a new Home for Old People. Matumaini House, the new double-storey building, housed not only our vulnerable girls on the first floor but also old people on the ground floor. The concept of these two divergent age-groups occupying the same building was a good one. There was both a sense of community and mutual support.

In the western world we have developed the practice of moving our senior citizens into a residential care home where they obtain the care which they require but can also be largely forgotten, and to some extent ignored, by their offspring and succeeding generations. This, happily, is not a concept adopted in African society and economic pressures would militate against it. The enormous cost of caring for the elderly in the western world, whether borne by the person concerned or the state, is prohibitive. It is not something, which Africa and its people could afford. The very real burden of development, and most especially the expense of nurturing and educating the next generation, consumes all the human and financial resources, which it can muster.

Anne Barnett had been in regular communication with Bread for the World, an overseas aid organisation of the Churches in Germany, in an effort to raise funds for the rebuilding of the much-needed Old People's Home. It was with their funds that the ground floor of Matumaini House was now constructed.

The first Old People's Home, which it replaced, had been built on a plot in Pumwani given by Nairobi City Council to St. John's Church. A joint Church and Community Centre Committee had been set up to develop the plot and raised funds through the Inter Church Action Group. The Christian Industrial Training Centre had supervised the reconstruction and furnishing of the mud and wattle building which stood on the plot and it had been opened by the mayor on the 11 October 1962 a joint operation between the Church and the Centre.

At the beginning of the redevelopment of Pumwani this building was demolished and it was necessary for it to be replaced by Matumaini House on the Church Compound, where twelve destitute old people took up residence on the ground floor.

The Rev'd Dishon Mwangola, the vicar, with Charles Rubia, Mayor of Nairobi, opening the first Old Peoples' Home

Part II – "Power to the People…"

Chapter 8 – The Concept of Community Empowerment

Neither of us were in Africa when the Community Centre was built or the work first started, so it is difficult for us to be categorical as to the mission or the aims of the Centre at that point in time. It has been our experience in other fields that the most successful projects in the voluntary sector usually begin in a minor key without too much investment into their constitutional documentation. New projects are started when people perceive an immediate need and seek to do something to meet it.

British Council of Churches

It is thought that the creation and establishment of the Community Centres in the African residential areas of Nairobi arose out of the perception of enormous need, clearly evidenced in the lives of the people living there. We have been told that they were the brainchild of Janet Lacey of the British Council of Churches, working through the Christian Council of Kenya (CCK) now re-named the National Council of the Churches of Kenya (NCCK), an ecumenical body with a liberal theological basis. This theology was very much in contrast to that of the established African churches. One of the aims of CCK would be to encourage the established churches to address the physical needs alongside the spiritual needs of those to whom they ministered.

It was, therefore, the primary aim of the newly established Community Centre in Pumwani to address the obvious physical and basic human needs of the people in that area. In doing so it became conscious of the lifestyle within the community and how best to approach the issue of change for individuals wanting something better and a future which would offer more fulfilment. The human and financial resources of the Centre were stretched to the limit in its effort to offer some relief from the suffering and meet the abundant needs of the people. Destitution, illiteracy and prostitution characterised the neighbourhood and these combined to produce a high degree of personal need.

It is not surprising, therefore, that when Pat arrived to set up social casework within the community, there was considerable scope for that activity. There was, however, little in existence to guide her in following, or even formulating, the policy of the Centre for addressing the areas of need. There was certainly no policy document.

Policy Committee & its Report

In 1965 a serious attempt was made to assess the situation. Margaret Pooley and Anne Barnett the two CMS missionaries then attached to the Centre with Alexander Shewera, who had been at the Centre before Pat arrived, sat down with the Rev'd Swailem Sidhom, an Egyptian by birth with a Muslim background, who had become an ordained Christian minister. As a small working committee they held a series of three or so meetings before issuing a Report to the Board of Governors.

A major problem in making any plans was that the policy was directed entirely by Christians but the Centre stood in the Muslim centre of Nairobi. The committee gratefully noted that the women of this community now felt free to participate in the Centre activities.

For several years there had been plans to demolish Pumwani and to build new housing. In this event an influx of a new income group would lead to different needs and demands on the Community Centre. More importantly, the lack of accessible housing for the poor and destitute who were accommodated at present in Pumwani would put huge stress on the Centre.

The committee thought that it might even be desirable to move the Centre buildings to another area where it would be appropriate to continue to offer the activities and services hitherto provided by the Centre.

In continuing its present work, the Centre would attempt to create an awareness of the existing social problems within the community itself so that the initiative to deal with these causes for concern came from the people themselves.

The Report had three principal thrusts. It will build up a closer relationship with St. John's Church so that the Christians see the Centre as an expression of the Church's stewardship of life, time and money. The Centre would invite the Parish Council to appoint a group of church people to work with the Centre and continue to invite them to special meetings, looking forward to the time when they would become one unit on one compound.

The second thrust was to get the community more involved in the work of the Centre. Religious prejudice was an obstacle for some but the Centre was now seeing greater co-operation from the community, especially from women.

Finally, it was important to concentrate on some of the most acute problems of the community and the committee highlighted destitution, old age and the need for family guidance as a focus.

How to achieve a change

The Committee then looked at these three issues and expanded upon them. They considered first the economic problem and the need to tackle destitution. They thought it important to stimulate self-help and to take advantage of the fact that the people of Pumwani were "trade-minded". As you move about the streets you are aware of the paraffin lamps burning in the "dukas" and kiosks opening out on to the streets. There is a feeling of business about it all. Quite rightly the Committee saw the potential of involving this commercially minded community in stimulating the mini economy of the area.

We have said that at this point in time, during the mid-sixties, there was much planning and talk about the redevelopment of Pumwani by Nairobi City Council. This shanty town (because this is what it was) had first started at the beginning of the century and had continued to grow and expand internally. Houses had been sub-divided into rooms occupied by whole families. The infrastructure had largely broken down, not least the roads, the water-supply and the communal lavatories and washing facilities. This redevelopment was entirely appropriate. The problem, which would arise on such redevelopment, was economic. We have seen that the new buildings would not be within the reach of the existing population to rent, let alone to buy. So, what was to be done in resettling this tight and effective community?

The Committee suggested that finance might be sought to purchase some of the newly erected flats and rent them, so as to secure accommodation for the destitute and so rehabilitate them. However, in the bigger picture, the Committee saw the Centre's task as one of support rather than provision. It should be there to help the community to find itself.

So, by the mid-sixties it was already perceived that the work of empowerment should move laterally. The relief of need and the problem of destitution would remain at the top of the agenda, at any rate for the time being, as the ensuing chapters will make clear and the projects undertaken to that end would in themselves empower the individuals who were to benefit from them. However, much more empowering would be the involvement of the community itself in planning and executing those projects, thereby raising the morale as well as the living standards of their own people. As we shall see, that would come about later: the people were not ready and the time was not yet ripe. There was preparatory work to be done.

How could the Centre make the community aware of its needs and how they could be tackled? It was the hope of this Policy Committee that one day the community itself would take over some of the Centre activities. In the meantime, we should make as much use as possible of existing channels of service within the community and co-operate wherever this was possible. We should be pro-active in this, putting out a paper explaining the aims of the Centre and inviting the village committee to come and see for themselves the Centre's work.

The involvement of the local church should also be sought. They should be encouraged to learn more about the Centre's work and to participate in it. This would involve stewardship of time and money. Most especially, there was a real need on the part of the Church and its members to develop the motive of "disinterested service". The Committee did not in its report mention the huge shift in theological thinking, which would be required to bring this about. A remark such as this in a written policy statement would undoubtedly have been counterproductive.

To bring about change the Committee made two main recommendations to the Board. There should be a training programme, especially for women workers, whether voluntary or paid. It would include social service, social research and counselling. Secondly, new staff would be recruited to work amongst young people and to do necessary research to carry the work forward. An approach was made to the Biblical Studies and Research Committee of the World Council of Churches to fund somebody for this task.

Staff involvement at all levels

Most importantly, the policy statement was to be cascaded down amongst the staff of the Centre, each member of staff seeking ways in which they might implement the ideas put forward. The staff should meet with the Church Parish Council and discuss ways of working together. After the meeting the staff were to have their own input and make their recommendations to the Board.

The stage was set for community empowerment of a different kind. It would be at a different level and it would be more far-reaching in its effect; but it would not be achieved overnight.

Policy & Governance

Indeed, it would not be overnight. The Policy Statement was circulated to members of the Board early in 1966 but it had not been finally "signed off" by the Committee. It was not until the following October that the Chairman, the Very Rev'd Raymond Harries, mentioned in AOB, rather as an afterthought, that he had agreed to go with all staff for a weekend meeting at St. Julian's to discuss their take on the Policy Statement and its recommendations. That, so far as the Board was concerned, was the end of it: well, for the next eight years at any rate.

A Second Policy Statement

At the beginning of 1972, a new Policy Statement, quite different from the earlier one, appeared in Jim's Board Minutes but it contained no date and there is nothing in the agenda papers or minutes, which would help to give it a date. With a certain amount of revision, it appeared again at the beginning of 1974 as an agenda item. The Director (as the Warden was then called) told the Board that the document had been drawn up by a sub-committee of the Board, although we see nowhere any creation of that sub-committee. It had been circulated earlier and the purpose of the circulation was to "get the Board members familiarised with the principles and broad aims and objectives that govern or should govern the activities of the Centre". So, it is clear that the vast majority of the Board members were not perceived to be conversant with the policy of the Centre or to have been involved in the setting of that policy.

The Chairman, who by then was Bethuel Kiplagat, underlined the importance of the document because it emphasised the people's or community's participation. Jim followed this by suggesting that the community should be represented on the Governing Board of the Centre but this was not accepted because there would be deeper implications requiring amendments to the Constitution. The discussion was concluded by the Chairman, who called for further study of the policy paper, encouraging us all to give it greater thought and to discuss together as Board members the ways in which it might be implemented. It was left that the Chairman and Director would arrange this.

The thrust of the new Policy Statement

So, what did this new document suggest and how did it differ from the earlier one? The emphasis in the first document had been on co-operation with the Parish Church. Whilst it sought greater involvement from outside in the planning and policy of the Centre, it was largely to come from the Parish. It was the aim then in 1965 to invite and encourage active participation of the Church members in the Centre's activities. The Centre wanted to introduce the local church to a new understanding of Christian outreach and to bring the church members on board in demonstrating Christ's concern for the whole person, physical and moral as well as spiritual. To that extent, therefore, the policy would still be dictated from within the Christian Church in an environment, which was predominantly Muslim. There was still that element of paternalism and this was understandable given that the Centre was the product of expatriate Christian initiative and national independence had been granted only a few years before. It would take some time before we would be ready for the next audacious step of welcoming our "users" (a distasteful and impersonal noun adopted in modern parlance to describe those we feel called to serve) to participate in the task of setting policy.

User Involvement

That, however, was the brave new thought behind the second Policy Statement, especially if you were to read between the lines. Hence Jim's suggestion that the Community itself might be represented on the Board of Governors.

What is to be gained by user participation at the level of governance? It ensures, in the first place, that one or two Board members can voice the views of those served by the Centre as to the desirability or wisdom of any action, which is being proposed. At a grass roots level, they can influence decisions, which might otherwise be wasteful, unnecessary, pointless or even positively harmful. Better not to embark upon a project than to abandon it later for lack of demand. Better to know the requirements of the proposed users, before discovering later that expensive and time-consuming modifications are necessary.

Most importantly user-involvement at governance level offers status to the users as a group, breaking down the "us" and "them" relationship, the "haves" and the "have-nots". Such is the nature of quintessential empowerment.

The contents of the Second Policy Statement

The first paragraph of the Policy Statement is of the nature of a Preamble, which displays an attitude of co-operation and empowerment. It manifests a desire to get alongside the community in their situation but at the same time to remain faithful to its witness to Christ and its origins:

> "St. John's Community Centre realises its task to be presenting Jesus Christ to <u>all</u> the people of Pumwani, offering in His name and spirit a disinterested service aimed at the <u>totality</u> of community life. In other words, the Centre directs its efforts so that it may achieve the one objective: **that they may have life and have it abundantly.**"

The document then goes on to expand upon the route, which would be taken to secure that objective. Strikingly, and perhaps a little surprisingly, it stresses that the initiative will have to come from the community itself. This is followed by a commitment, namely that the initiative of the community will "always be sought and encouraged to the end that ultimately it may come spontaneously." The wording, however, suggests that this will not come easily and that there is a certain reticence on the part of the community to do much to improve their conditions. There is a kind of fatalism in their acceptance of their situation, characterised by poverty, destitution and a degree of moral degradation.

The Committee realised, therefore, the difficulties in achieving this ultimate objective. Before the community would have the initiative to achieve change within itself, it would be desirable to seek and motivate an increasing measure of participation by the community, in the meantime, in planning and executing the programmes of the Community Centre. It does not suggest how this will be done but it does go on to make some very perceptive and encouraging remarks and we believe that they are so important that we should again quote these verbatim:

> "The Centre will not be satisfied with merely 'doing things for, and on behalf of, the community' nor with 'handing over tokens of help', nor still with 'creating better living conditions so that better people may emerge'. We, the family of the Centre, will endeavour to start with the people, from where they are, hoping that the people, when given the will and understanding through right guidance, will create better conditions for themselves."

Here surely are the signs of real empowerment. So far, the empowerment has been brought about at a personal level by programmes and activities conceived by the Centre. Now, perhaps for the first time, the Centre wants the initiative to come from the community itself and to enlist the participation of the community and its members in the planning and the implementation of the programmes and activities.

How would the Centre go about this? How would it draw in the leaders and members of the community and get them to share their thinking? How would it glean from them their assessment of the value of these activities and the manner of their implementation? First and foremost, the Policy Document suggests that the Centre should help the people to think over the problems and needs of their community, encouraging them to make judgments about their patterns of social behaviour. They should be helped to look at their attitudes and convictions concerning issues like health, work, community resources and social relationships.

They would need help to define their problems and to examine the social practices which lay behind them. Were they resisting change and if so why? It would require discussions on a community-wide basis and the community would themselves need to develop the desire for constructive change. Where that desire is missing it would have to be created: where it does exist, then it should be promoted.

The Centre is, however, realistic in its thinking. People in Pumwani have been accustomed to years of existence in atrocious conditions. They are aware that they are among the most deprived members of society. They believe, probably correctly, that they have no voice and if they were to make a complaint it would probably not be heard. They would need to be made conscious of their rights and to participate in civic responsibilities and take action. Indeed, it would be necessary for the first spark of vitality to be generated. What a challenge.

The Paradigm Shift

The authors, who returned to live in England in 1980, have the benefit of valuable, comprehensive documents, giving them some idea of how St.

John's Community Centre developed towards the end of that decade and in subsequent years. One such document is the report of an evaluation carried out in 2001 by CORAT AFRICA (the Christian Organizations Research and Advisory Trust of Africa), a body incidentally whom Jim had used some thirty years earlier to carry out a management and viability survey of Maridadi Fabrics, but more on that later.

Their report in 2001, in its overview of the background to the Centre, makes a clear statement which goes to the very heart of the concept of empowerment:

> "From its inception up to the end of the 70's, St. John's Community Centre adopted a welfare approach in responding to the needs of the community. However, by the late 80's there was a paradigm shift to community development approach and several reviews were done to determine appropriate responses."

The plunge had been taken. We shall see later how that had come about and the ways in which a paradigm shift evolved. It could only occur when the community itself was ready for it. During those many years when the welfare of the community had been addressed, a relationship had been established between the Community Centre and the leaders and members of the community. It took time to convince them of the Centre's genuine concern for the people. Actions speak louder than words and the faithful and systematic alleviation of people's needs, had demonstrated that genuine concern. To suggest to a community that it needs to change – to ask them to analyse what needs to change – to exhort them to make changes – and cogently to persuade them to press on and effect those changes requires the existence of a relationship of mutual trust and respect. It is a tribute to the many years of the Centre's faithful and disinterested service, that it finally became possible to motivate the community to do something themselves to improve their conditions.

The paradigm shift was part of a programme providing consistent enablement. In the case of Pumwani this had included nutrition providing energy, counselling producing understanding, education which produced capacity and finally, training which provided ability. Most importantly, this provision was made over many years of dedicated, caring service, offered in a transparent relationship and it was the generous and genuine nature of that relationship which had generated trust.

What is Community Empowerment or Development?

To understand the concept of community empowerment in the modern world and to obtain some measure of its attainment by St. John's Community Centre we have looked at a publication entitled "The Compassionate Cities" by Allan Kellehear [4]. This book is primarily concerned with end of life care and how it can be delivered in the community. It is, however, arguably relevant in other spheres of activity.

It defines community development as "any set of initiatives designed to develop the social resources of the community in order to enhance its quality of life" (p.118). So, in Pumwani, community development initiatives ought to cover, and have indeed sought to cover, such issues as welfare, health, education, prostitution, beer-brewing and alternative employment. The publication goes on to state "all community initiatives have as their main aim the desire to deepen the quality and extent to which a community may look after its own members" (p.118).

The Community Centre soon regarded itself, and sought to become, an integral part of the Pumwani community. To that extent all its activities, from the very beginning of its existence, might be classed as "community development". But the paradigm shift envisaged in the Second Policy Statement went further in seeking to help the community "look after its own members" and that we believe to be the kind of development, which Kellehear (ibid) and others envisage. It is the ultimate fulfilment of community empowerment.

---

[4] Kellehear A (2005) *Compassionate Cities. Public Health and End of Life Care.* Oxford. Routledge.

The Community Development Worker

The book "Compassionate Cities" (ibid) describes five various models of community development, one such being "the community development worker" or "community worker". This arguably is the model, into which St. John's Community Centre fits most appropriately. Its social workers and officers have successfully got amongst the people dealing with such specific matters as youth work, the social and health problems of sex workers and the homeless. They have empowered members of the community to problem-solve their anxieties and to understand their resistance to change and to supporting their neighbours. These are the hall-marks of effective community development workers suggested by Kenny[5] and Homan[6] in their respective papers, cited in Kellehear's work on compassionate cities. The Centre's workers have co-ordinated and connected people with one another and employed outreach methods by visiting people, organising meetings, enlisting volunteers, lobbying and negotiating with the Nairobi City Council and talking to the media. These have combined to constitute a grass-roots campaign, highlighting the problems of Pumwani and creating awareness of them both within Kenya and internationally. To have achieved this, the Community Centre staff have exhibited those skills which experts such as Jim Ife from Australia believe to be necessary for good community development workers, namely lateral thinking, problem solving and communication. This will be evident when later we come to examine the high degree of expertise and unrelenting effort on the part of Eunice Kamau and her staff in organising the community to dispose of its rubbish and to create a better environment. It was she who effectively demonstrated the "sliding balance" described by Holman (ibid). The community development worker assists the community to help itself. As the community becomes adept and confident in its new-found roles and activities, "insiders" take over the roles and activities formerly organised or initiated by the "outsider", i.e. the community development worker.

---

[5] Kenny,S (1999) *Developing communities for the future: Community Development in Australia.* Melbourne. Nelson. Cited in Compassionate Cities by Allan Kellehear.

[6] Homan, M.S. (1999) *Promoting Community Change; making it happen in the real world.* Pacific Grove, California: Brooks/Cole Publishing Co.

The balance slides from social action (by the well-meaning outsider) into actual community development (escalating insider control and activity). It was essential that Pumwani residents took responsibility for the ongoing clearance of rubbish once the system was established, the equipment provided and the workers recruited. Confidence was gained in this exercise leading to a much more adventurous and ambitious project to deal with the appalling sewerage and drains. But that is an exciting development, which we shall be looking at in greater detail.

Working in Special Populations

The importance of the groundwork laid by Pat, to be followed later by Anne Barnett and supported by the Kenya-Israel School of Social Work, for the professional training of social workers cannot be over-emphasised. The book Compassionate Cities emphasises this in its comment:

> "Working to persuade local government or power brokers in the community does throw significant emphasis on leadership and organizational credentials. But because most community development workers work with special populations the skills emphasis is more highly personal. The ability to be credible, and to convey empathy and rapport with those populations is crucial in enlisting the trust and co-operation of those particular populations." [7]

The reader will be in no doubt by now that Pumwani is one of those "special populations". It has attracted the attention of international agencies, which perceive the value of sending their own students for practical work within that area, fertile with almost every conceivable social problem. These agencies also appreciate the high standards of social work within St. John's Community Centre, which would be indispensable for students coming from the sophisticated educational establishments of Europe. Most especially, can we be right in thinking that there is an additional dimension to the caring "esprit de corps" within the Centre, which provides that "crucial empathy and rapport"

---

[7] Kellehear A (2005) *Compassionate Cities. Public Health and End of Life Care.* Oxford. Routledge.

of the successful development worker - the concern no less of "bearing each other's burdens".

"Bearing each other's burdens"

Swailem Sidhom's Committee summarised its main objective in the Biblical phrase "Bearing each other's burdens". You may recall that Pat used the same phrase to describe her role, when she met with Stella Purchase to discuss her work upon arrival in Kenya in 1959. She suggested that the staff of a Christian Community Centre should be prepared professionally to share the needs of clients and where necessary and possible to try to take appropriate action in response to the needs which are revealed. It is not without its significance that "bearing each other's burdens" remains the strapline of the Centre, appearing as its raison d'etre in the Mission Statement of its Strategic Plan for 1999-2003 and is central in the motif on the Plan's cover. So far as anybody knows, there was no awareness that Pat had used this Biblical quotation to describe her role when she first arrived. This Christian basis has consistently undergirded the policy of the Centre throughout all the years of its existence. Pray God it will continue to do so amidst all the demands for non-discrimination by the secular agencies and partners, with which it works. The Centre has never discriminated in choosing those whom it helps but always remained faithful to the One in Whose Name its help is offered. Such is the additional dimension, which we believe accounts for its success.

Chapter 9 – Empowerment Through Education

We have seen that when Pat arrived at Pumwani there were already classes attended at the Centre by the girls. Georgina Serpell had become responsible for them and together with similar groups in the 3C's (Christian Community Centres) they were supervised by a CCK worker.

When CMS started mission work in an area one of the first things it would introduce would be education. It is basic to any kind of progress and a prerequisite to any kind of empowerment. So, CMS had started Dr. Aggrey Primary School, but as the colonial government became responsible for education, that school was moved to Racecourse Road on the edge of Pumwani and was handed over to the Education Department of the Government.

An older girls' class in 1960 with Naomi their teacher (4th from left)

Education, nevertheless, formed a major programme of the Centre. It went through different levels of activity, according to the nature and needs of the users. Many girls had not had the opportunity of going to school for the reasons we have already indicated. If they were single mothers, they would value life skills and simple literacy and arithmetic. Pat was not an educationist, although Alexander Shewera was. He had been headmaster of Dr. Aggrey school and Pat had inherited him as a member of the Community Centre staff when she arrived.

The classes also provided a bridge between the Centre staff and Pumwani children and cases of malnutrition, sickness and lack of general care were picked up daily. So did the netball pitch and open area behind the Centre, which were used intensively by children who had no other centres for recreation. Very young girls whose job was to care for the babies of relations and employers were to be seen playing children's games with their charges tied on their backs.

The Girls' Training Scheme

By the time that Pat left at the end of 1962 there were 45 girls attending the classes daily. Georgina had returned to Australia and two new African teachers had been engaged to teach them. Funding was a problem and "Youth helps Youth" had been asked to help girls who had no money for fees, uniforms and other expenses. The Rev'd Julius Carlebach, the local Rabbi who was working for the Child Welfare Society, had visited the Centre and had been impressed with the work which was being done there. With his help a "Child Nutrition Scheme" was started in September 1962.

By this time Margaret Pooley was working at the Centre. With her co-operation, Pat was asked by the Committee of Management to prepare a scheme and a budget to present to the Nairobi City Council with an application for a grant for "The Girls' Training Scheme". By June the following year the application had not been considered and by September it was refused. The Centre was, however, invited to apply again in 1964, when a grant of £100 was made by the Council to the Centre and this was promised for the two ensuing years. Mr. Wambua, who was the City Councillor for Pumwani Estate and their appointed representative on the Board of Governors, suggested, however, that an application should be made for a larger grant.

Further girls and women also joined the classes in April 1963, suggesting that Margaret's presence and educational experience were beginning to have an effect, attracting new pupils.

Women's Classes

There was also a very informal women's class which was intended for older women and which had also been in existence when Pat arrived at the Centre. It concentrated on such domestic issues as health care, nutrition and simple sewing. Helen Tett managed this group and volunteers from All Saints' Cathedral and Nairobi Baptist Church came regularly to help. Hazel Houston, the wife of the Baptist Minister, organised singing groups and focused on traditional African tunes. More women joined the classes before the end of 1963 and a group had asked for English classes, so a teacher was found.

It was all very low key. A simple beginning but those classes would eventually develop into something much bigger and in the meantime women were finding satisfaction, encouragement and hope. In their lives and their small world, they were finding empowerment in being able to communicate better and to look after their families better, generally boosting their confidence.

First-aid Education

The aim of the girls' classes (there were some boys amongst them) was to get children back into school, if they had had to leave for financial or other reasons. It was first-aid education with which the Education Department was happy. Figures are not available for every year but of the girls attending the classes in 1964, twelve were found school places, twelve who would otherwise have had no prospect of anything better than the limited and unfulfilled life that Pumwani could offer them. The following year the number increased to seventeen. As they left the Centre classes their places were immediately filled.

Women's classes learning English – "It was all very low key. A simple beginning..."

In April 1966 the Centre lost one of its most valued teachers when Martha Wambui fell ill and died. She had been associated with the Centre for many years helping with all the women's and girls' activities. When Pat arrived, Martha had taken her visiting in Pumwani, introducing her to the people and making her familiar with her new surroundings. She had a very happy marriage with James, which was arranged by the Revival Brethren and she moved to live with him in Mombasa, where he was employed by the Railway. She returned to the Centre in a teaching role with both the women and the girls. An intelligent and very caring member of staff, she was known for offering help to clients who found themselves in difficulty.

The Board was regularly kept informed of the steady increase in numbers attending the various classes. It should not be thought that the girls' class was confined to classroom teaching. Their horizons were opened up in

Chapter 9 – Empowerment Through Education

Martha Wambui, - "one of its most valued teachers" - with her husband James

Martha & James' wedding party

different ways. At the time of Uhuru in December 1963 arrangements were made for 300 young people from the community centres to be taken to the stadium for the Independence Celebrations. Facilities were provided for playing netball on the field adjoining the Centre and the girls' team from Pumwani competed with teams from the other community centres. At the end of each term a service was held in the Centre for the women and girls attending the classes.

A new group of girls who had left school at the end of Standard VII [8] were looking for occupation and training and they were taught domestic science. Because of this development of the classes it became necessary to extend the size of the Centre. Anne Barnett raised funds from an English Trust and on 13th October 1964, two new rooms, equipped for domestic science, were opened by Miss Margaret Kenyatta.

Naomi, a Taita woman and a trained homecraft teacher, was employed: she looked very smart in her special uniform. When her husband was transferred from Nairobi, she had to leave and was replaced by a Luo woman, Gladys Chika. Anne Barnett suggested that Gladys would benefit from a community development course as offered by the government of Israel. The course would be free-of-charge but we would have to finance the airfare so it was left that Anne would explore ways of finding this. Sadly, she was unsuccessful and when the Ladies Guild of All Saints' Cathedral offered to raise the money, the Board of the Centre felt that if a considerable sum was to be raised, it could be used more advantageously.

---

[8] The following information is based upon Wikipedia ('Education in Kenya'):

East African Community 7–4–2–3 System Curriculum: In 1967, Kenya, with Uganda and Tanzania, formed the East African Community. The three countries adopted a single system of education, the 7–4–2–3, which consisted of 7 years of primary education, 4 years of secondary education, 2 years of high school and 3–5 years of university education. Children began their elementary (primary) education at the age of 7 and completed at the age of 13 (Standard VIII). Secondary education was then from Forms I-IV.

Kenya 8–4–4 Curriculum: In 1985, President Daniel Arap Moi introduced the 8-4-4 system of education, which adopted 8 years of primary education, 4 years of secondary education and 4 years of university education.

Margaret Pooley

In 1966 Margaret Pooley left following the appointment of the new African Warden. Several farewell parties were held to mark the occasion and there were many expressions of appreciation for all her work. She had been asked by the Christian Council of the Congo to work amongst Zandi refugees, her previous service in the Sudan making her eminently suitable for this new post. In contrast to Nairobi, she would be living in a remote area, hundreds of miles from any sort of civilization and her previous experience of life in the Sudan would equip her for this dramatic change of environment. A resilient person, she would, and did, cope. There is no doubt that the four years she spent at the Centre saw a marked improvement in the educational standard of the classes and the Centre derived an enormous benefit from her time there. It had also been an opportunity for her to work alongside, and in conjunction with, Anne Barnett. Both of them had years of experience in their respective fields and being two of them, they had the opportunity of bouncing ideas off each other. Their joint leadership, with their individual contacts, over a three-year period gave the Centre an opportunity to branch out into new activities.

Non-Formal Education

The first-aid education given to the girls in preparing them for entry or return to the state system continued throughout the Centre's existence. It has been of service to hundreds of children getting them into formal education as quickly as possible and changing their lives.

At the end of 1971 there were 120 girls in the classes, each class with its own teacher. The ages of the girls were then between ten to thirteen years. The average age of the girls in the classes was becoming younger and there should have been greater opportunity for the children to gain direct entry to government primary schools, without the need for prior teaching at the Community Centre. It was the view of Ephantus Mugo, while he was Warden, that these classes should be systematically phased out over the course of the next three years.

However, at the end of 1972 the number of girls in the classes had increased to 147 and of these 30 secured places in government schools. A year later the number had reverted to 120 but the Warden reported that we normally sent 40 to 50 children to government schools annually. It seemed, therefore, that the suggestion of phasing out the girls' classes was not going to materialise and, so far as we know, it never did.

Indeed, the importance of the non-formal education programme is such that a subsequent chapter is devoted to its development in more recent times.

Adult Education

From early days two evening classes were provided, staffed by two part-time teachers, offering adults education up to Standard III. The students complained because classes at a higher level were not offered.

There were, however, staffing problems. There was a lack of trained staff willing to undertake this work and records refer to the "inconsistency" of the part-time staff, meaning we suppose that they were irregular or irresponsible.

Following his return from training in the UK in 1970, the Warden, Ephantus, recommended that we should employ a teacher who was experienced in running adult education classes, which should be offered up to a minimum of Standard VII. Other practical subjects should be incorporated into the course, such as health education, civic responsibility and personal hygiene.

There were, however, other forms of training for which there was also growing demand. In the sixties and early seventies, we were not ready to embark upon intermediate and secondary education. The need then was for specific vocational training.

Commercial Classes

Ephantus Mugo had joined us as Warden in October 1966. A teacher by background and a headmaster, his penchant for education quickly became evident. It would be characteristic of his long period of service that he led the Centre forward, encouraging us to aim higher in the educational services which we might offer.

With his encouragement, Jackton Mukhwanya, our accounts clerk started teaching book-keeping classes and by June 1967 some twenty students had enrolled in them. They paid Shs.8/- per month and the Centre profited from the whole sum because Jackton gave his services voluntarily for this activity. Within six months he was joined by a young man from Uganda and by the middle of 1968 there were 15 students but it closed in September 1971 due to an apparent lack of demand.

It was also in June 1967 that Ephantus started to approach the Board to provide typing classes. He had the names of some twenty people who wanted these and the Board suggested that he seek a grant from the British High Commission to purchase typewriters. Demand for these classes continued to increase because commercial typing courses in the city were very expensive and most people could not afford them.

Other options were, therefore, considered for acquiring the typewriters. It was realised that a fund could be established from the centre's resources and would be replaced from the modest fees charged for the course, because the teachers' salaries would not be high. So, ten reliable second-hand manual machines were purchased from Business Machines, a leading firm selling business equipment. They would also offer a regular quarterly servicing contract to ensure that they were maintained to a high standard. They cost Shs.550/- each and a "Typing Class Account" was immediately opened into which the surplus from the typing classes was paid, in the expectation that the capital cost would be recouped within an estimated period of two years.

Within a matter of months, a third class was started and these commercial classes were to become an important aspect of the Centre's training programme, which would go on indefinitely. Jim recalls Ephantus' pride and satisfaction when he took him to see the new machines installed in the typing classroom, the former domestic science room, which was no longer required.

Each typing class ran for an hour daily, five days a week. The part-time teachers were replaced by a full-time, qualified member of staff and by the end of 1971 it was realised that typing of itself was insufficient. It needed to be supplemented by English lessons and tuition in office routine. The daily lessons would therefore need to be extended by a further half-hour to give time for this teaching.

When Pat and Jim visited the Community Centre in 1990, they learnt that the Centre still required additional typewriters for these classes and upon their return to England Jim made available more than a dozen manual and electric typewriters from his firm, following the updating of his office equipment. Pat persuaded the Rev'd Stanley Dakin to slip them into his container, when he returned to Kenya as General Secretary of the Church Army of East Africa. At the same time, we included sewing machines from the congregation of our church, St. John's Surrey Road Bournemouth.

Changing Patterns in the demand for education

It is interesting to discover how the Centre was able to adapt to the changing demands for education. By the middle of 1970 there were some 40 persons requiring typing classes. These classes required to be expanded to meet the demand and by the purchase of a further three second-hand typewriters the pressure on these classes was greatly reduced.

Conversely, towards the end of the same year, Standard VII girls were not coming forward for Gladys Chika's domestic science classes and only three girls were attending them. Upon enquiry, it was found that the other Community Centres shared the same experience and that pupils successfully graduating from these courses would then set up a course of their own, syphoning off the future potential students of the centres. This was not entirely good news for the Centre, which had a very able and qualified teacher employed and needed to pay her salary, struggling to do so with deficit budgets. In retrospect, however, in the broader view of things it was a positive outcome. Our purpose was to ensure that the skills imparted by Gladys should be maximised and if they were being passed on (hopefully by a competent student), and cascaded down to others, so much to the good.

One view expressed at the Board was that as the lessons for the Standard VII girls had no promise of employment on completion, the girls were not so interested, as they were very anxious to secure a job. Jim proposed that the classes for the three existing students should be disbanded and that they should be helped to join classes elsewhere.

Likewise, there was a falling away of students attending the women's homecraft classes. Mrs. Chika was also the teacher for these. They had been running for seven years and the Board felt that they may have served their purpose. In the middle of 1967 Ephantus Mugo told the Board that he intended to raise the fees for the Homecraft Classes from Shs.7/50 to Shs.10/- per month and presumably did so. Perhaps this was what led the Church representative on the Board to question whether the fees were too high for the people who would like to attend.

Ephantus felt that the need for women's classes was still there and that what might be required was re-organisation of the syllabus and the content of the course. At that moment he was not certain what pattern to follow, although he felt it important to teach hygiene and nutrition. The Chairman (then Bethuel Kiplagat), supported by Jim, felt that an association of women, meeting perhaps once a week for a specific purpose, and not being charged any fees, would be good for the community. This, however, would not keep Gladys Chika employed full-time and she should be given alternative work, at the same time being responsible for the association of women. There are no records of an association for women being started but before the end of 1970 the women's classes had closed and Gladys Chika, a valued staff member was transferred to the Home Industries project, where her experience with the women was invaluable and where there was need to provide support for an overworked Manager. Later, and until she retired, Gladys was the Manager of the Maridadi Fabrics Shop in Tom Mboya Street in the City.

Chapter 10 – Empowerment Through Employment

Early attempts to break the cycle

In seeking to empower the women of a community, whose economy was dependent on sex and alcohol, it was necessary to liberate them from the pressures, which perpetuated their involvement in these severely limited ways of earning hand-to-mouth existences. It was pointless to tell girls attending the literacy classes that they should avoid selling themselves if they could not be offered a sensible alternative. Any acceptable way of earning a living had to be an occupation, which would sustain them at something higher than a subsistence level and induce them to accept the discipline of regular work and compliance with authority implicit in employment. No mean feat.

At a very early stage in the life of the Centre the need to find employment for the women was understood and accepted. During her period as Warden, Pat had investigated possible work schemes and been advised that there was a need for the manufacture of small cardboard boxes, into which articles such as locally made jewellery could be packed. Margaret Pooley became involved in 1962 and the aluminum house, otherwise known as the tin hut, was used for the operation. People selling jewellery not unnaturally required an attractive container in which their product might be presented. Their purchasers would also look for a beautiful wrapping for what would almost certainly be a special present. Sadly, the women making the boxes did not have sufficient skills to manufacture this product to an acceptable standard.

Another possible option was domestic service. Members of the Girls Classes could be trained in domestic housework and simple cookery. A teacher trained in Domestic Science, Naomi, was employed for this purpose. The hope was that these girls would find work amongst European contacts known to the Centre. Unfortunately, although some of the girls became quite skilled they were unable to keep the jobs, which were found for them because they were irregular and unpunctual.

One girl found it difficult to understand why her new employers did not approve of her using their bath and toiletries.

When Anne Barnett joined the team, she took up the challenge again. She realised that it was a priority to secure gainful employment for our girls, if we wanted to build on the educational work we were doing with them in the Centre classes. Indeed, to lift any girl or woman out of the cycle, she would have to be prepared for, and found, work. Towards the middle of 1964 Anne raised the matter at a meeting of the Committee of Management, stressing the need for industries for the destitute. True to form, like all Church bodies, they formed a sub-committee.

When the committee reported back, a distinction was drawn between Small Industries and Home Industries. Both were to be pursued. Budgets were prepared and approaches were made to various bodies and trusts with a view to finding a worker and financial support to initiate the project.

The Break-through

It was not until the end of 1965 that we heard of the possibility of a CMS missionary to start the scheme and at the same time received a positive response from a UK trust to provide funding. A hitch occurred. The occupational therapist missionary from CMS would not be available for work in Pumwani, so the chairman wrote to the Dulverton Trust asking them to finance a scheme involving only African workers. They replied saying that they would make a grant to start the Home Industries project provided it was managed by a European. These were early days in the life of the nation and overseas donors were cautious when it came to management, because there was a shortage of able Kenyan managers. It was agreed that CMS should be asked to recruit a CMS supported missionary, able to head up the project for one tour, on the basis that she would be provided in substitution for Margaret Pooley, the teacher who was now moving to take up a position in Congo. However, by May 1966, there was no response from CMS to this request.

And then in June, Pat and Jim took leave in the U.K. and met with Mary Politeyan, a trained occupational therapist known to CMS, who was willing to offer for one year's service overseas. The budget was re-drawn on a two-year plan and Dulverton Trust agreed to provide the finance, upon the clear understanding that it would not be extended.

So, guess what? Time to form a new sub-committee. Dorothy Udall, an American woman, who had been working in a volunteer capacity with the women and girls at the Community Centre on goods for sale, agreed to serve on this committee.

Mary Politeyan

And then the great day came. Mary Politeyan arrived on 1st December 1966 and the Home Industries project was set to begin. It started in a small and varied way. Seven women in need, referred by the caseworkers, were making ten baskets per week using processed sisal. They were paid by the Centre and the baskets were later sold by Professor Wolfendale, a University lecturer, who voluntarily sold them in England, but at a loss. So raw sisal was purchased to make the project viable but the weaving of the baskets with this material was hard and the women refused to work with it. A lower amount had to be offered to the women if processed sisal was to be used. The baskets were superior in design and workmanship to those on sale through other womens' organisations or on the side of the Nairobi-Nakuru road as it wended its way through the Rift Valley. Mama Ngina Kenyatta was presented with an attractive pink basket made by the women and they felt very proud as they watched her carrying it.

Sewing also became a more enhanced activity and took on a new dimension. Sewing classes lasting eight hours each week were provided for the schoolgirls and others, while mothers were offered an hour weekly. Both the girls and the women took work home. There were four girls and two women sewing regularly and four or five on an irregular basis.

Chapter 10 – Empowerment Through Employment

Basket weaving

Volunteers played a vital role in all this. Mrs. Marshall of the Missionary Aviation Fellowship brought in ready-cut children's clothes to be made up, whilst Dorothy Udall had forged a strong trading link with Studio 66 (later to be known as Studio Arts 68), a classy shop in the prestigious centre of Nairobi. For them we were making articles such as tray cloths and cushion covers, which were sewn by girls from our classes. It was all small scale but very much what we had had in mind and like the baskets, we were learning by our experience what could be made profitably, without exploiting the girls and women who made them. This was, however, done on the backs of the volunteers, mostly white Americans.

Most important of all, the fabric used for the eye-catching articles sold to Studio 66 required first to be screen-printed. This was done at the Centre, giving expression to the artistry and designs of Dorothy Udall and her talented band of volunteers, who derived real satisfaction from this service. Moreover, the printing was done by the girls and they did it by hand. Exclusive and attractive designs were produced and the process of screen-printing by hand was labour intensive, an essential aspect of the work if we were to be faithful to our raison d'etre and produce remunerative work for the women.

Our volunteers were invaluable. There was, however, still need for additional paid staff. The decision was taken to transfer Dorothy Drury, an African member of staff from Taita, who had been teaching in the girls' classes, to be an Assistant to Mary Politeyan. She proved to be capable in her new role, good at bargaining and strict on standards of work. Standards and quality control were to be important if the Industry was to command the prices and attract the kind of market it needed.

The Home Industries project was started in the room leading into the Domestic Science room, the facilities of which proved to be ideal for the boiling and dyeing process. It had an iron and the large sinks were necessary for washing the screens and equipment. At that stage, as the Industry started, it was important that it was sited at the Community Centre in proximity to the Caseworkers, with whom a close connection was made at the outset and retained for many years. That connection was perceived as vital from the word go, as the minutes of the Board of Governors clearly recorded on 19th January 1967:

> "If an individual woman is to be helped adequately she needs the combined efforts of the caseworker and the Home Industries workers. Similarly, the girls working on the sewing call for close working together with the teachers"

That inseparable link continued for well over a decade to the mutual well-being of the Community Centre, the Home Industries project and most especially the individual beneficiaries of the Centre. At the same time, it was realised, even at this early stage, that the project would soon outgrow these limited facilities and would require to be rehoused.

The euphoric beginning of the Home Industries project was soon to be marred by an unexpected tragedy. In just over three months following her arrival, Mary Politeyan was admitted to Nairobi Hospital with a diagnosis of breast cancer. She underwent two operations there, following which she had to return to the United Kingdom for treatment. It was anticipated this would last for only six weeks and Mary hoped then to return. Sadly, this was not to be. She was not cured but died a year or so later in England. We shall always remember Mary as a kindly person, whose enthusiasm and ability won the admiration of all those connected with the project. We owe her a real debt of gratitude for it was only due to her coming that the project was able to begin and funding was obtained. It was out of her few months of dedicated service that an industry was born and the lives of many women were to be changed.

Chapter 11 – What's Brewing in The Beer Hall?

At the cross-roads

At a major crossroads in Pumwani stood a single-storey building, constructed of red brick and conspicuous by its large green double wooden doors. Geographically it was at the centre of Pumwani and for many of the older women it was also the central, focal point of their lives.

Every morning these worn-looking women waited with their five-gallon oil drums outside the beer hall, owned and run by the Nairobi City Council. Inside, the Council employees boiled up large vats of liquid which they then sold in carefully rationed amounts to the waiting women, who carried it home for resale from their rooms in Pumwani. The public was not allowed inside the beer hall but, as one passed by, it was sometimes possible to catch a glimpse of the red-hot fire burning inside. Presumably members of the City Council had decided to provide this service to the community in order to preserve certain standards of hygiene and to control the contents of the beer, which could be purchased easily in Pumwani. In fact, the women who bought this beer frequently added to its content and increased its alcoholic strength before re-sale. Women in the Community Centre often referred to a strong locally made alcoholic drink, which they called "sibiriti". It was not clear what this was made from but the state of one or two alcoholic women has been ascribed to this "sibiriti".

It quickly became clear after Mary Politeyan's arrival at the end of 1966, that the Community Centre building was too small to accommodate the burgeoning industry, with its accelerated development of the fabric screen-printing process. At just the right time the City Council decided to close the beer hall. We do not know why they decided to do this, but we surmised that this step was taken in anticipation of its demolition as part of the proposed rebuilding of Pumwani. Whatever may have been the reason and ultimate purpose of closing it as a beer hall, a request by the Centre to use the building for the Home Industries was granted.

The importance of this expansion of the Centre into the very heart and centre of Pumwani cannot be over-emphasised. What had been the focal point of the communal life of the women of Pumwani for a few hours each week now turned into a hive of activity for five or six days out of seven. The Centre had moved out into the very heart of the community, amidst the traffic and the hustle and bustle of everyday life. People going about their daily lives could not help but see the women and girls going in and out, hanging out their bright and colourful fabrics to dry in the African sun. This cheerful sight was of itself enough to raise one's spirits and provide a boost to morale in this dirty and dusty environment. We could not have hoped for a better site and we could certainly never have expected to obtain it, had we not been able to demonstrate the clear need for this community-orientated project. What is more, it was rent-free.

In contrast, St. John's Parish Church never really moved into the community of Pumwani except to occupy a house provided by the Nairobi City Council, to accommodate and care for destitute old people. Otherwise, the Church might as well have been sited in a totally different geographic location. Few, if any, of its members came from Pumwani and in all truth little attempt seemed to be made by the Church to involve itself in the day-to-day life of its people, who had little or nothing in common with the Christians and regular churchgoers. The lives they lived were poles apart from those of Pumwani residents. Symbolically, the church building stood there, isolated within its fenced compound, offering little contact with the inhabitants of the mud and wattle buildings which surrounded it.

What, one asks oneself, was going through the mind of Wambui, a dear old woman whom Pat knew so well. She would sit for hours outside her house, just across the road. Positioned on a rough wooden box, she gazed by the hour at the quaint, corrugated-iron building where people came and went, especially on a Sunday. One doubts whether even one of the many seemingly uneventful hours of her life was ever spent crossing the road and venturing inside its portals. Nor do we know whether any of the smart churchgoers ever crossed the road and went the extra proverbial mile to negotiate the open, nauseous drain in front of her house to greet her.

Part II - *"Power to the People..."*

Wambui, watching the churchgoers

The acquisition of the beer hall provided yet another opportunity to seek the active co-operation and assistance of outside bodies, which, in the process, became aware of the existence of Pumwani and the needs of its community. An approach was made to the Kenya Voluntary Works Camp Association to clean and re-decorate the interior of the building. They were joined in this task by a workforce from the Nairobi School, a private boarding school which had originally served as one of the secondary schools for European children but had by this time of course become multi-racial. They white-washed the walls, giving the place a light, happy and clean feeling.

Within that newly decorated and cheerful building a more fundamental change had to take place. An old large tank was converted because the old brewing process needed to change. The short–term pleasure produced by the alcohol, which had been brewed in the large vats of the beer hall, was to give way to more durable benefits derived from the expensive and permanent dyes to be boiled up in those vats, bringing life and meaning to the fabric.

The Christian Industrial Training Centre (CITC) also became involved. The value of the materials, dyes, equipment and finished goods would be considerable and the beer hall was situated in an area where the risk of theft would be high. The building had to be made secure and the CITC did that for us. So many people and institutions came to our assistance, generously providing their time and materials to prepare the beer hall for occupation by the industry, empowering not only the Home Industries project but also those destitute women and girls who would be working there.

The way forward

Mary Politeyan's departure was not allowed to hold up the progress of the Industry and a way forward had to be found as a matter of urgency.

Dorothy Udall with her gallant band of volunteers did a magnificent job in maintaining the work. They had provided considerable expertise and the screen-printing process had been almost entirely due to their gifts and their artistic flair. The designs had been those of Dorothy Udall herself. Her colleagues were mainly young white Americans, whose husbands were very largely in well-paid employment and who did not require to supplement their incomes. They did, nevertheless, want to use their time profitably and they derived satisfaction from knowing that while developing their artistry and their savoir faire, they were making a significant impact in lifting destitute women out of poverty and empowering them to help themselves.

At one stage, Jim believes, they were some twenty in number. They were able and powerful, full of drive as well as ideas. This, of course, drove the work forward and achieved progress: it did, however, pose a threat

Part II - "Power to the People..."

Water damaged photo of early screen-printing by hand in the beer hall

to the overall management and governance of the project, especially at a time when we were effectively leaderless. Six months elapsed after Mary Politeyan was hospitalised and Dorothy Drury had also left. Dorothy Udall in her voluntary capacity had been left alone to supervise and run the project.

In September 1967 Jim and Pat, along with Dorothy Udall and Ephantus Mugo the new Warden, interviewed five people, two of them recommended by the Kenya-Israel School of Social Work at Machakos. One of them stood out above the rest, Martha Gikonyo, a Kikuyu woman who had trained in Israel for two years. The only obstacle was the salary for which she was looking. This did not match the other Community Centre salaries and the Board felt that it could not create a large differential. This proved to be a tension which would continue to manifest itself as we tried to grow an industry and contain it within an institution, which was essentially part of the voluntary sector. The salaries of those employed in social work and social services did not reflect those paid in the commercial sphere. Nevertheless, all credit to Martha and her sense of dedication to the women and the task involved, she accepted the conditions we could offer and so started a very long career with us.

Of course, our funders, the Dulverton Trust, had to be advised that we had appointed an African manager for the project. This contravened the grant conditions, which required an expatriate manager, but under the circumstances they made no objection to the appointment.

Martha soon found that she was immersed in too much detail and there was nobody to whom she could delegate. So, six months or so following her appointment, it was decided to appoint an assistant, so that she could be freed up for work of a more executive nature.

The change in leadership of the staff was complemented by an important change in the governance. Mrs. Janie Ericsson, who had been very actively involved as a volunteer, was approached with the request that she should chair the Home Industries Committee, something which she agreed to do. Janie had provided support to the Centre, not only in the Home Industries but also in other areas. Not least she had put in an enormous amount of work on the Centre Flag Day, which had been allocated to us by the Government at short notice and the Warden explained that, without her help, it would have been impossible to organise that event.

Dorothy Udall

Under Janie's leadership and with Dorothy Udall's continued and considerable involvement, the Industry went steadily forward. It participated in the "Fahari ya Kenya" exhibition in 1967, taking away the First Prizes both for the stand and for industrial design.

By the beginning of 1968, Dorothy realised that the time was now ripe to hand over some of the responsibilities to the staff. She specified in particular the book-keeping and finances. That was to be the first step in a steady process whereby Dorothy would see the Industry take over what had been run by her rather like a personal, non-profit-making business.

All the designs were hers. So, a competition was organised through schools and colleges, with the co-operation of the Ministry of Education, in the hope of finding new designs and designers for the future. Dorothy also ensured that Martha was fully trained in the screen-making techniques. Before she left in April 1969, Dorothy held a training course, in conjunction with the Ministry of Education, on the screen-printing process. She had every intention of passing on her skills and knowledge to ensure that she left these behind when she moved away from Kenya.

The Board of Governors welcomed Dorothy Udall to their meeting on 20th February 1968 to express their deep gratitude to her for the time, money and sheer hard work she had put into this project and to congratulate her on the skill and success of her designing, dyeing and silkscreen printing process. This was to become the core business of the industry. There was a niche market for the hand printed cloth, produced by this labour intensive method. The designs were eye-catching: the quality was of a high standard: the product exclusive and expensive. Dorothy Udall's vision was to be the core-basis of the Home Industry and its success was perhaps the single most important factor in the life, not only of the Industry, but also of the Centre as a whole. The industry and enthusiasm with which Dorothy implemented her vision no doubt infected all those involved and it was not surprising that Martha inherited and displayed the same qualities.

Just as Mary Politeyan's illness had not prevented the growth and progress of the Industry, so it was with the departure of Dorothy Udall. These two talented and dedicated people had empowered their African colleagues, projecting their work into the indefinite future. Such empowerment of the staff was to become the pattern, not just in the Home Industries but throughout the Centre and its varied activities.

Management of the Business

The management of the Industry nevertheless remained a matter of concern. Did we have sufficient management and enough expertise within the management, to develop and handle growth? Martha was dealing with the production line: but what of the many other facets of running a business? It was an aspect which had obviously concerned Dorothy Udall before she left. She had reported that an organisation had contacted them with a view to purchasing the business. The Board agreed that the Home Industries Committee might negotiate with the proposed buyers and be ready to sell if the terms and conditions were satisfactory. The price offered was, however, too low and fortunately the sale never materialised.

It is easy to understand why a prospective buyer would not be willing to offer a high price for the industry. It was making a profit of approximately Shs.60,000/- per annum, a significant sum in those days in the Centre's accounts. This, however, took no account of the time given by the American volunteers, who undertook so many tasks which would otherwise have fallen to the lot of a business manager. Furthermore, they used their cars without charge, running numerous errands on behalf of the business without claiming even the price of the petrol. Last, but not least, the building we occupied was rent-free. A prospective purchaser would not enjoy these advantages. On the other hand, the Centre derived enormous benefit from this surplus, which supplemented its income from grants and donations.

One possible management solution came in the form of a generous offer of full financial support for a businessman to be recruited from the United Kingdom. It would be his task to train a local person to relieve Martha of the business administration. It would have been a personal gift from Professor Wolfendale, a Christian academic from Nairobi University, who was very committed to the Centre and its activities.

The offer was not, however, taken up. Instead it was recommended that a second person should be employed of the same calibre as Martha Gikonyo, so that the two persons could handle the business as well as the production line of the Industry.

Another possibility would have been to appoint a manufacturer's representative to boost the sales. He would, however, have taken ten per cent of the sale proceeds, having the effect of reducing profit margins and prejudicing the payments we could make to the women. Instead, it was thought to be more satisfactory to build up sales slowly through the contacts we made ourselves. So, Martha went on a business course for two weeks, bringing back and implementing fresh ideas of accounting and exporting abroad, in the days preceding computers and sophisticated information systems.

Studio Arts 68 (as it was to be called), the exclusive shop in Nairobi city-centre, continued to be our major customer and were taking 125 yards of printed material each month as against 70 yards previously. A new outlet was found in the shape of the Home Industries shop at Mombasa and significantly, a consignment was sent to Zambia and had sold out quickly.

There was a slight setback when it was found that Martha's assistant was not making sufficient effort and her employment was terminated. Bessie Kuria, an untrained teacher working in the Centre, was transferred to Home Industries to assist and Sarah Kamau, a young woman who had worked with a Tie-Dye project at Gilgil, was taken on as Assistant Supervisor.

Chapter 12 – Social Casework: Its Use & Relevance

"What are you going to do?"

When Pat first arrived in Pumwani, she was frequently asked by her potential colleagues and other CMS missionaries whom she met, what she was going to do.

Soon after her arrival, she was asked to call on Stella Purchase, who was acting as the CMS Representative in Kenya, during the temporary absence of Colonel Grimshaw. Stella asked the same question and expressed some scepticism about Pat's ability to "counsel" inhabitants of Pumwani. She was too young, unmarried, without any knowledge of the people's culture and unable to speak a word of Swahili. Pat agreed that there were going to be challenges but stressed that casework was not the same as giving advice. She suggested that the staff of a Christian Community Centre should be prepared professionally to share the needs of clients, "bear one another's burdens" and, where necessary and possible, try to take appropriate action in response to the needs which were revealed. To do this, Pat hoped to set up a social casework office in the Centre.

Visiting in the location

To begin with Pat spent her time visiting the residents of Pumwani. Martha Wambui, who was a member of the Revival Brethren, willingly shared her knowledge of Pumwani with Pat and introduced her to many families. As they visited they shared life experiences and their beliefs and drank many a cup of "chai". It was a very pleasant, carefree way of spending working hours but proved to be a valuable investment of time, as Pat later discovered that she could walk freely about Pumwani with no difficulties, being greeted frequently as she went.

Language

CMS was very helpful in providing opportunities for Pat to learn the language and something about people's lives in the countryside or "the reserves" as they were frequently called. It was arranged that Pat should make a daily visit to Ethelreda, an Mtaita, the Pastor's wife, so that she could practise her Swahili and she attended a Swahili class each week, conducted by Mary Smyth, a linguist in Nairobi.

It was a requirement, as part of her language study, that Pat take the African bus on a two-day trip to Mvumi in Tanzania, where she was to spend six weeks at the CMS Mission Station. This journey, itself, proved to be geographically interesting and culturally educative. The bus travelled hundreds of miles along dusty roads crossing a large swathe of the African savannah. It was not, however, without its privations and difficulties. Comfort stops usually took the form of the bus stopping somewhere along an uninhabited section of the road and the passengers relieving themselves at the side of the bus. A young European woman, travelling alone, did not find it easy to obtain seclusion for this exercise, in a bus full of African men gazing nonchalantly out of the window. Once she arrived at her destination, however, she found the local people living in Mvumi, the Wachagga, spoke excellent Swahili and the excursion made sense.

Finally, she spent some time with Bishop Neville and Mrs. Vera Langford-Smith at Waithaga, a village in Kikuyu country where many Christian loyalists had suffered during the Mau Mau revolt. The Bishop and his wife shared with her many stories of the bravery and even martyrdom of these Christian brethren. The Swahili spoken by the Bishop and his wife was excellent, of a standard to which Pat hoped to attain.

Relationship changes within the family

Much casework in all cultures and languages is concerned with communication and Pumwani was no exception. During that period of rapid social change there were many problems between parents and children who failed to understand each other. Soon after her arrival at the Community Centre, the local District Officer, David Lowther called, with a bouquet of flowers, to introduce himself. He referred to the many teenagers who were beyond their parents' control and whom he came across as they broke various laws and regulations. He soon began to refer such mothers and daughters to the new caseworker.

One such mother was Fatuma, a Kikuyu nominal Muslim, who had two daughters by different fathers. Kadogo was a plump Bantu-looking girl, wrapped in a bui-bui and Naili was a slim light-skinned girl, dressed in a revealing European-type dress. They were both out of Fatuma's control, often not returning at night and living with different men in either Mombasa or Nairobi. Their lack of family background and conflicting religious affiliation had resulted in a total absence of standards and values.

Poor communication often existed between parents and children and created problems within the family. Samuel and Pauline, both of them Christians and church elders, resolutely adhered to African custom in finding a husband for their daughter Ruth. They had plans for her marriage, but she wanted to marry John, the headman's son. By custom a marriage would be arranged balancing the assets of both families in a financial context. For some reason Samuel did not approve of this proposed match and the pastor therefore refused to celebrate Ruth and John's union. When Ruth eventually became pregnant, the marriage was only allowed to take place in the Church vestry. It was a matter of shame, not to be celebrated and the arrangement of a humble reception in the Community Centre by Pat and Jim was strongly condemned. It was the subject of a complaint to the Archbishop no less.

Communication between husband and wife, or the lack of it, was also the cause of difficulties in that relationship because it was constrained by tribal custom. A discussion in the Centre with Luo women led to gasps of amazement when the caseworker suggested that sex should be enjoyed by both parties and not take place solely for male satisfaction.

On another occasion, an interesting discussion arose, concerning inter-tribal marriage. The question was raised of Kikuyu girls marrying uncircumcised Luo men. Traditionally this was totally unacceptable, but the Revival Brethren encouraged their members to be free from this shibboleth.

Relationships between young persons of the opposite sex

Pat and Jim started a "Contact Club" where educated young men and women, sometimes teenagers, would have opportunity to meet members of the opposite sex. It was intended for those young people who had passed their School Certificate or attained an equivalent standard of education. However, confusion and unease between them was evident in discussions taking place between the individual men and women and it was a surprise to us to see that the nurses from Pumwani Maternity Hospital and the educated young men who attended at the Club did not converse informally with each other.

When talking to teenage girls the caseworker became aware they were very reticent to discuss their relationships with boys. They asked various questions, mainly about their physical misunderstandings. Some of the girls had sexually transmitted diseases and were receiving treatment at the special clinic. Others wanted to know about "safe periods". They were all reluctant to discuss their attitude to men and the reasons why so many of them became pregnant. Some denied that there was any problem at all and one girl, who was a member of the Church choir and the Centre youth club, insisted that she was not pregnant until a few weeks before she gave birth. This failure to tell the truth was not necessarily to escape reprimand. It was common to give the answer which would please the questioner or cause least trouble.

Fear of the law

Sometimes clients came with problems which required official action, but they were reluctant to go to the police or government officials because of the possible outcome. For example, a first wife in a polygamous relationship back in the Reserve had had her hand chopped off at the wrist by her husband. In fear she fled to Nairobi and came to the Centre for help. Pat's response was to take her to the office of a senior District Officer at Makadara, where she was provided with medical assistance and material support. She later came to discuss her situation with the caseworker on several occasions.

One young woman who drifted in and out of the casework office without an appointment was Elizabeth, a very sad alcoholic. She was dirty and unable to concentrate or hold a logical conversation. Elizabeth liked to laugh and tried to kiss Pat. She became pregnant and gave birth to a very skinny baby who was equally dirty, without clothing and malnourished. Neighbours implored the caseworker to remove the baby from Elizabeth's care, citing examples of her behaviour, such as dangling the baby by its ankles over a charcoal brazier. As she had been gazetted a children's officer by the Ministry of Home Affairs, Pat arranged to take Elizabeth, the baby and two neighbours to the juvenile court in Nairobi. To her chagrin, the two neighbours who were called as witnesses insisted they had never seen any inappropriate behaviour on the part of Elizabeth. The party travelled back to Pumwani, the neighbours continuing to protest that Elizabeth would kill that child one day. The status quo was resumed. The baby later died and Elizabeth committed suicide.

After Pat had moved away from Pumwani she was contacted urgently by one of the Centre staff, who had received news of a baby which was thought to be under the ruins of a house bulldozed by the City Council. Neighbours believed that the mother had taken this opportunity of abandoning the child. Pat immediately went to the site with the Centre staff and after the baby was safely retrieved, she took it to Gertrude's Gardens, a private children's hospital in Muthaiga. They received the child and cared for it. On washing the child, the white cotton wool turned black, but the baby was otherwise unharmed and later moved to Thomas Barnardo House from where it was placed in foster care.

Through their work the social caseworkers at the Centre became aware of many needs which the Centre tried to supply. The Old People's Home situated in Pumwani village, and later in the Church compound, was built in response to the problem of destitute homeless old people who came to their attention. Similarly, teenage girls with no suitable accommodation were provided with security at Matumaini House in the Church compound.

The caseworker's chief aim was to stimulate the client's personality growth and development. Through discussion it was sometimes possible to provide encouragement and suggest practical solutions to problems. Parents concerned about the education of their children were often pointed to suitable classes in the Centre. Unemployment was the most intractable problem, which brought many people to the office. It was possible to discuss various options and, as the Centre developed, it was able to offer training to girls and women in such things as sewing, tailoring and secretarial skills. Maridadi Fabrics provided enormous relief to many desperate women seeking to support their families.

Above all as a Christian counsellor the caseworker aimed to bring people into a personal relationship with Jesus Christ. She believed that through the whole Christian Gospel people found eternal life in heaven and a richer, fuller life on earth. One example of a young girl with a single mother living in Pumwani was Emma Owour. She had many difficulties, but she faced and overcame these. In 1962 she was singing in the Church choir and was captain of the netball team. When Pat and Jim met her by chance in Pumwani in 2004 she was a widow, whose husband had died of AIDS. She had written a book about this experience and she was involved in a revolving loan fund at the Centre. In 2014, she wrote a letter to Pat and Jim, telling us that she is now an enthusiastic member of the Mothers' Union. She also gave news of her son and daughter, both of whom had become church workers.

Stella Purchase - a prophet?

As Stella Purchase had pointed out, Pat's task would not be easy. It was Pat's opinion that her ability to converse in Swahili remained limited. Most Europeans would have envied her fluency and in any event many of her clients spoke very limited Swahili. Nevertheless, as a foreigner it was difficult to understand fully the culture and thought processes of people from different backgrounds and of different age-groups. It was certainly not easy to help clients with their own self-understanding.

The clients were interested in and puzzled by Pat's own lifestyle. They did not always believe what she told them about herself.

Emma – now an enthusiastic member of the Mothers Union

Attending St. John's Church were many Christians who received encouragement, guidance and teaching from the Revival Brethren. The members of this fellowship seldom came to the Community Centre to look for help. Nevertheless, they appreciated the professional help, which Pat provided when discussing child development and problem areas such as bedwetting and the rejection of a mother by the child after enforced separation such as a period in hospital. When this professional teaching concurred with their own experience, these parents were delighted by the new understanding with which they had been provided.

Training social caseworkers

Pat sought to train African members of staff as caseworkers, always emphasising the importance of the relationship between the counsellor and client. She demonstrated the need to understand three basic aspects of the work: the personality of the client, what he expected from the counsellor, bearing in mind the Christian setting of the casework office and, of course, his real problem.

Sometimes it was necessary to encourage and support the client but at other times to challenge and expect change, although this often did not materialise, as in the cases of Samuel and Pauline or Elizabeth. It was always necessary to listen and, as Christians, pray that they might be used by the Holy Spirit in the situation by which they were confronted.

It was obvious to the workers that careful keeping of records was essential if they were going to understand the development of the clients and the resolution, where possible, of their problems. A file was opened for each counselee and it was emphasised that the contents of the file were totally confidential to the caseworker. The files were kept in a locked cupboard in the casework office and only taken out of the office in exceptional circumstances. As historical events were recorded for all clients one or two were selected for more detailed "process" recording. As far as possible this special recording provided detailed records of conversations including verbatim accounts of the discussion, body-language and facial expressions. This enabled the caseworker and trainee to discuss the client's changes of mood and unexpected comments and with more difficulty the worker's own reactions and feelings towards the client.

The contents of the casework files would have been of great interest to the workers in the Centre years later but when Pat & Jim returned to the Centre many years after they had left Nairobi in 1980, they were disappointed to find the cupboards in the casework office empty and indeed no records of the early days in the life of the Centre.

A few months after Pat began to work at St. John's Community Centre, it was agreed that the Church Army Community Centre in Doonholm Road would send their inexperienced social worker to work with her for a short period. Raheli Aggrey was a good role model. She was trained as a teacher, married to a Church Army Captain and a member of both St. Stephen's Anglican Church in Doonholm Road and the Revival Brethren. She had several children. Raheli was an Mtaita and typical of this coastal tribe, she was smiling, warm and accepting in her attitude to other people, so she had no difficulty in making relationships. Later, St. John's Community Centre obtained funding from Motor Mart Trust to employ Mrs. Emma Obunga as a social worker. She was an equally good role model for the women and girls of Pumwani. Emma was a married mother and also a member of St. Stephen's Church. She dressed smartly and she too was always smiling. A Luo from Nyanza, she had trained as a nurse at the CMS Hospital at Maseno. Her nursing training gave her confidence and after establishing a relationship with a mother Emma would be prepared, where necessary, to confront the client in a loving manner on such matters as the cleanliness and feeding of her children. She would also challenge old tribal beliefs. One such belief, of a superstitious nature, was that preparations made during pregnancy for the expected baby would result in harm to the child. Emma insisted that such preparations were both timely and necessary and encouraged pregnant clients to prepare baby clothes before their children were born. Clients liked Emma and willingly discussed family problems with her. She was able to empathise with them and build and maintain a positive relationship. Pat encouraged her to listen quietly and then respond appropriately, coming to a decision with the client on how the problem was to be handled and then deciding upon the appropriate course of action.

A monthly meeting of social workers from the different Community Centres was established. At the meeting the workers brought examples of problems that they were facing with their clients and lively discussions ensued. Sometimes the social workers discussed their own personal problems and the general problems, which so many women in Nairobi were facing. A common theme was the unpredictability of many husbands, including their daily recourse to bars and "hotelis" after work and therefore their late return home at irregular times but expecting their food to be immediately ready. It was the responsibility of the mothers to provide food, school fees and the cost of school uniforms, whilst often well-paid husbands dissipated their wages on status symbols, such as expensive cars and even drivers or invested their income in ill-conceived capital ventures.

Some of these social workers had hard lives themselves but they were all dedicated to helping others and appreciative of any training and encouragement which they received.

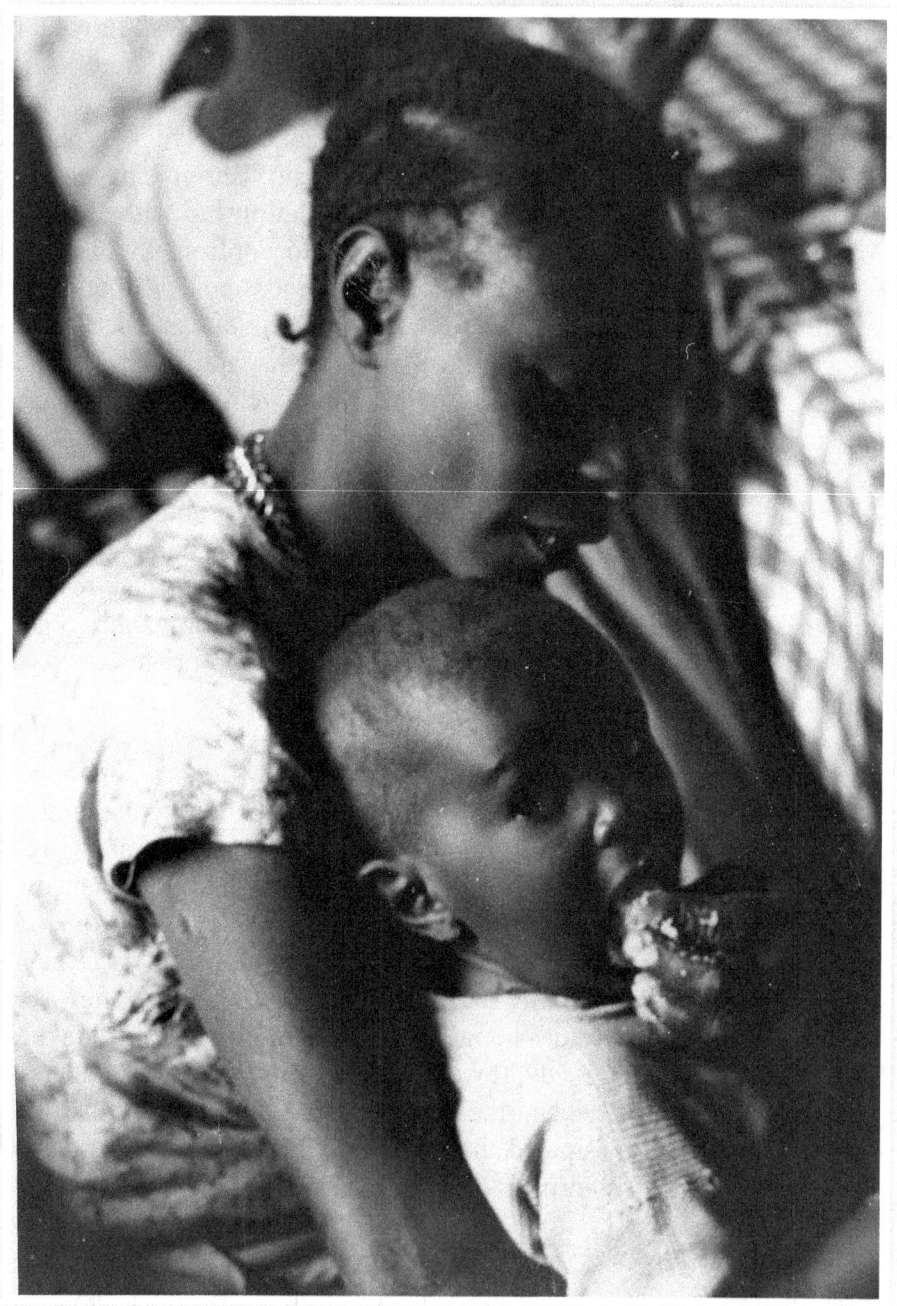

Emma provided advice to mothers with malnourished children

Outreach by Community Centre staff to other agencies

During the winter of 1960 and the spring of 1961 Kenya suffered from famine. Pat was seconded, at the request of Central Government, to the District Commissioner's office at Makadara in Eastlands, to offer some help to the District Officers who were overwhelmed with requests from the general population for assistance. Whilst she very much enjoyed working with Elizabeth Jackson and providing this assistance, it caused considerable tension because she could devote less time to the Community Centre and this was not wholly approved of by the Board of Management.

Whilst Pat was working at the Centre she also received a request from the Social Work Department of Makerere University at Kampala, asking whether she would supervise one of their degree students doing her practical placement in social work. This was a rewarding project and was repeated more than once in the following years whilst Pat, and then Anne Barnett, were in the casework office. One such student was Wilfred Oloo, who came from Makerere in 1969. After graduating, he found employment with the Ministry of Social Services, who immediately appointed him as their representative on the Community Centre Board of Governors. How rewarding was that.

Following her marriage and her return to Kenya at the beginning of 1963, Pat became involved in another agency. She was invited by Mary Ridley (who had probably been approached by Mr. Wilkinson of Nairobi City Council) to join her in evaluating the work of the Social Services Department of the Council and in making suggestions for its improvement. These experiences widened Pat's knowledge of the social work carried out by both central and local government: she in turn was able to make a contribution to those bodies in the form of lessons learned by her whilst working at the Community Centre.

Whilst still working at the Community Centre, Pat became a founder-governor of Thomas Barnardo House. This membership brought her into contact with other voluntary agencies and early benefactors of charitable bodies in Kenya, such as Charles Njonjo, the then Attorney General,

Lady Twining, the widow of a former Governor of Tanzania, Sir Malin Sorsbie and Humphrey Slade the first Speaker of the Kenya Parliament. Through these contacts she became conversant with other voluntary agencies such as the Child Welfare Society.

Over the years, while she was involved with Thomas Barnardo House, Pat became Chairman both of the Casework Committee and the Training Committee, which supervised the students working and training there for the international Certificate awarded by the Nursery Nurses Examination Board.

The Kenya-Israel School of Social Work

The most stimulating job which Pat did after she left the Community Centre was offered to her as a result of this networking. Dr. Horani-Hoffert, an Israeli psychiatrist and social worker of international repute, was sent by the Israeli Government to set up a school of social work to train Kenyan social workers. This was established in Machakos town with impressive buildings, an excellent library and very able Israeli staff. Pat worked there in the years 1965 and 1966, lecturing in child development and supervising the students' practical work placements.

The Community Centre had enjoyed a relationship with trainees from Machakos since 1963, when a student from the Machakos College of Social Studies did one month's field work with the Centre. In 1965 another student, then of the Kenya-Israel School at Machakos completed her practical training to be followed soon afterwards by three other students each spending two months at the Centre. Pumwani, with its acute and diverse social problems, was a fertile area, in which social work students could obtain hands-on experience following their theoretical training at Machakos. Here were to be found urban conditions, the like of which would be hard to match anywhere in the world. As we shall see later, social work students and their counterparts from Norway and other international centres, would gravitate towards Pumwani, where they would be introduced by St. John's Community Centre to professional social work as it should be.

Pat's work with the Kenya-Israel School of Social Work finished in January 1967 with lectures in child development to Probation Officers who were attending an in-service training course organised by the School. Both Pat and the Centre derived considerable satisfaction and expertise from this very professional institution. Unfortunately, admission to the school became curtailed and finally the School was closed by the Government for political reasons.

All Saints' Cathedral

Some years later Pat was invited to run a social casework office in All Saints' Cathedral Nairobi, where it was the intention she should primarily counsel members of the Cathedral congregation. The Provost, the Very Rev'd Roger Bowen, proudly presented her with her new office, which had been constructed in an upper floor of the Cathedral building. Unfortunately, the resignation of the Emperor Haile Selassie in Addis Ababa and the civil unrest which followed it resulted in a flood of Ethiopian refugees, who poured into Kenya. Each morning a long queue of these refugees outside Pat's office demanded assistance and it was impossible to see other clients, thwarting the original purpose of this new project. Consequently, Pat found herself consulting with members of UNHCR and, in particular, the Country Representative in Nairobi on most days. As a result, UNHCR invited her to become the supervisor of their Kenyan partner, the Joint Refugee Service of Kenya (JRSK). It was a great surprise for her to enter the education office of JRSK and find there Wilfred Oloo, the former Makerere student who had done his practical work at St. John's Community Centre so many years earlier and then represented the Ministry of Social Service on the Community Centre Board of Governors.

Joint Refugee Service of Kenya

During her time at JRSK, the overthrow of Milton Obote by General Idi Amin in 1971 led to an enormous influx of refugees from neighbouring Uganda. They nearly all came to the JRSK office, whose staff were desperately looking for accommodation and food, especially for women and children. Pat's years of experience working in Nairobi and her recent involvement with the Cathedral enabled her to find temporary accommodation on Cathedral premises and later at other churches also, including St. Andrew's Presbyterian Church, St. Mark's Westlands, St. Francis Karen and Trinity College Doonholm Road. Contacts with many other service agencies proved useful to the refugees.

Pat brought her professional training as a Social Caseworker to Pumwani in 1959. Despite the challenges envisaged by Stella Purchase and experienced by Pat, a seed of professional casework was sown in the fertile ground of Pumwani's social need. Generations of students, trainees and practitioners have used that location to develop their own vision and expertise in that caring profession and the effect is clearly seen in the national projects of the Centre, of which we shall proceed to read. Indeed, students from elsewhere in the African continent and even from first-world countries such as Norway can point to Pumwani as the place where their casework knowledge was worked out in the real stuff of life.

Part III – "More Power to the Centre"

Chapter 13 – Selecting & Empowering the New Leader

Uhuru & Expectations of the Labour Market

As one would expect "Uhuru" or "Freedom" would usher in a period of high expectations. For decades Africans had looked on as the top jobs and the top salaries had gone to expatriates, mostly Europeans. With those jobs went also power and status. With political independence that position had to change. The aspirations of the people were high and even house servants and others in low-paid employment were expecting to see a dramatic improvement in their status, prospects and standard of living. Furthermore, the unemployed were expecting that jobs would be magically found for them.

Crowd celebrating outside Legco (the Legislative Council)

The reality was that the day following independence was no different from the day which had preceded it. Life went on much the same as it had for years past and therein lay something of a "time-bomb". The aspirations of the populace would not go away but the delivery of those aspirations and the fulfilment of their dreams was a challenge of enormous proportions.

"Africanisation"

The new regime would seek to stimulate the economy but it was not a task which could be achieved overnight. Even if they were successful in doing that, it had to go hand in hand with an increased capacity of financial and human resources. Education and training of all kinds had been steadily delivered for years during the colonial administration, but national independence would prove to be the catalyst for a new impetus.

Every field of life and work was affected by it. The shift in the public sector was an obvious political necessity but equally in the private sector, there was hardly a shop, office, business or industry which was not affected. Where there was not compulsion there was strong persuasion, if not by government, then by public opinion. "Africanisation" was the flavour of the month, the year and the future.

The Private Sector

Government ensured that its policy was not ignored by introducing a system of work permits for "non-Kenyans" and although "Kenyanisation" was the official policy, one was in no doubt that the top jobs would eventually be earmarked for those of African descent. To achieve this there was an escalation in training and preparation of staff at all levels for more senior positions.

Training in the Professions

The training of lawyers was an example. It is difficult to grow a legal profession overnight, but government policy was clear that local training was required if more Africans were to be admitted as Advocates. Hitherto lawyers had qualified overseas and were admitted as Advocates after a viva voce examination following a year of practice in Kenya to ensure that they were conversant with local law and practice. In future entry would be gained by written examination within Kenya accompanied by an appropriate period of training within a Kenya legal firm and tuition at the Kenya School of Law. Jim, and the firm in which he worked, were fully involved in supporting this programme. Jim was responsible for ensuring that the firm's trainees acquired experience in the essential aspects of general legal practice during the limited time prescribed for their training period. He also worked closely with Tudor Jackson and Alan Collins of the Kenya School of Law setting examination papers in Conveyancing and Land Law, and for many years he either marked or moderated the results for the Kenya Council of Legal Education. The first few days of our holidays at the coast were often spent on this chore before Jim allowed the sun to beckon us outside to blow up the rubber dinghy.

St. John's Community Centre

When it came to training, St. John's Community Centre was ahead of the game. From the very inception the need for education and training had been recognised and addressed as the way to move people out of destitution and need. The literacy classes at the very beginning, the education classes which followed, and ultimately vocational courses were all moving in that direction and the bar of these was raised steadily as the needs of the community, and their capacity for better education, demanded. As we have seen, the training of social caseworkers had begun when Pat supervised Raheli Aggrey, from the Church Army Community Centre, in her caseload. Most especially, it was Pat who recommended that when she resigned as Warden of the Community Centre at the end of 1962, an African manager should be appointed to succeed her. That, however, was not to be. It would be four years before the funds were raised to employ a person of sufficient calibre to take on the responsibility of leading the Centre and its burgeoning and challenging activities.

"Africanisation" of the Warden's post

In the early part of 1966 the post of Warden was advertised and a sub-committee short-listed names of applicants. It was authorised by the Board to interview five applicants for the post and Ephantus Mugo from Embu was unanimously selected to start work in October. A sum of £1500 had been promised by Rochester Diocese to support the Warden as part of its MRI grant and thanks were expressed by the Board to Pat, who had attended and spoken at the meeting in Rochester, when the decision was taken to support Pumwani. In anticipation of the Centre receiving this, Church Mission Society had sent a similar sum by way of loan to enable the appointment to be made.

Ephantus came from the teaching profession and adapted well to his new role, much of the Centre's work being educational. His background would help lead the Centre into secondary education and vocational classes but to become conversant with our other activities, it was realised he would benefit from training in social work and administration. He received an application form from the Kenya National Council for Social Services for a two-year course at Swansea University. Just two places were available and competition would be nationwide.

The Board agreed to sponsor this application. They would have to support his family in his absence, pay a proportion of his salary during that time and guarantee him a job on his return. He, on his part, would be obliged to work for the Centre for at least one year following the completion of the course.

Overseas training for the Warden & his family

His application was successful and Ephantus was awarded his scholarship by the British Government under their technical aid scheme. A decision then had to be taken concerning Mary, his wife and his young son, George. It has been our experience that difficulties are frequently created within the family where men go overseas for study leaving their families behind. The experience of Western culture and lifestyle was quite dramatic, especially during the sixties and if this was not shared by the student's wife, she would feel disadvantaged and be less able to adjust to the development of her husband's thoughts and ideas.

The Church Mission Society operated a bursary scheme and if they were to award Mary a bursary to undertake a short course in England, they would pay her fare and support her during the time she was studying. This bursary would not be available in the August when Ephantus was required to travel and if the family were to go with him, other arrangements had to be made in England for Mary and George. Pat, a founder Governor of Thomas Barnardo House in Kenya, in co-operation with Anne Barnett, arranged that Barnardos in England would take Mary and George and accept them as their responsibility. It was not clear whether Mary would be working for them, because they were making a special place for her, but they had agreed to care for the family until such time as there was definite word of a training course for Mary from CMS.

Even with scholarships and grants, overseas study never comes cheaply and Africanisation, if it were to be successful, would not be less expensive than expatriate recruitment. During his absence in England, Ephantus was to be paid eighty per cent of his normal salary to help with the support of his family. A clothing allowance was paid, and Mary's and George's fares paid to the UK.

Temporary replacement warden

Most especially, a replacement warden had to be found and remunerated for the two-year period of Ephantus's course. The person, who had been initially approached, appeared not to be interested and Pat and Ephantus, therefore, approached Makerere University to find somebody else. The Board decided that an Appointments Board should be formed and they were fortunate to find in Mr. Reuben Mithamo, a teacher at the CMS Language School, a suitable person to hold the fort during Ephantus's absence.

Training for the Warden's wife

Mary Mugo found it quite difficult at first to settle into the U.K. It had been thought that she would have been with Barnardos in Cardiff, in quite close proximity to Ephantus. We cannot remember whether that transpired or not. Pat recalls that George was bedwetting, which caused Mary some embarrassment. Whatever the cause, she found the first few months very difficult and was unhappy.

She was then moved to Cheltenham, where they became very happy. She worked in Barnardos Home there and she attended lectures regularly. She and George were befriended by Professor and Mrs. Wolfendale, who had been supporters and friends of St. John's Community Centre from earlier years, when Professor Wolfendale was working at Nairobi University. Mary returned to Kenya in December 1969, having spent some fifteen months in the U.K. living, working and studying: she had acquired knowledge and experience in a new field of work, namely child-care in institutions. When she arrived back in Kenya, she joined the staff of Thomas Barnardo House. She could also relate to what Ephantus had experienced in his training overseas and share effectively the challenges of his job, when he later returned to take up his duties as Warden. Their shared overseas experience had had a bonding effect upon their relationship.

When speaking of bonding, we need never have worried about bonding Ephantus to return to the Centre. At his first board meeting he told the members that he looked forward to his work in Pumwani and would be glad to work closely with the Board being grateful for any help they could give him. His return to the Centre and its work in September 1970 was warmly welcomed by the Board, especially as the replacement warden had resigned some six months earlier and the staff had worked hard and effectively without a leader. Ephantus' first task was to interview the staff to familiarise himself with the work they were now doing. He was back and he was back to stay, at least for the next ten years.

Chapter 14 – Creating an Endowment

Sponsorship Schemes

As activities steadily increased both in size and variety, the need for more staff and administration became greater. It had been a considerable struggle to meet the needs of individual clients themselves but as we have demonstrated, when Pat took her begging bowl to the YMCA, good-hearted and compassionate individuals would respond to individual personal need, when they were confronted by it.

Sponsorship schemes have been used by various agencies and charities to raise funds for individuals requiring education and World Vision is an organisation which springs to mind. They will prepare a short dossier on a child who would benefit from sponsorship and he and his family will be enabled to send him to school, the sponsor receiving regular reports or letters, which encourage him to continue his support.

A similar scheme was operated by Geoff Griffin at Starehe Boys Centre. This had been effective in helping "parking boys" to get off the streets and into education. It was well-known and successful. We recall that many years later Princess Anne, on a visit to Kenya, became aware of Starehe and gave it a high-profile, linking it to "Save the Children Fund". Geoff went on to develop the Kenya National Youth Service for the Government, a uniformed and disciplined organisation, which was to be seen at public events acting as stewards and generally providing the manpower needed.

Pat was approached to introduce her girls to Starehe as the female counterpart. She declined to do so, because the scheme relied on producing case-histories of the individual girls. Whilst boys are unlikely to object to being named and described as "orphans" with no means of support, girls who had had a chequered start in life and were juvenile prostitutes possibly suffering from sexually transmitted diseases, would not want to be subjected to that kind of publicity. Furthermore, it was not Pat's intention that we should be selecting a few special girls as an elite but that we should offer help to a wider group of girls as part of the community. Hence our programme for "first-aid" education to get girls into the normal state schools. In later years, money was raised through sponsorship but not as I recall before 1980, while Pat and I were involved with the Centre funds.

We raised money on a limited scale by donations of all kinds. When Jim analysed the source of donations in 1971, he found 9 from individuals, 4 from trusts, 4 from the East African Women's League, 10 from churches, church bodies or the diocese, 2 corporate gifts and a grant from government.

Core-funding

The difficulty lay largely in raising core-funding to pay the salaries of administrative staff. Nobody wants really to support that. It is not appealing. It was necessary to find some way, which was more substantial and less uncertain than relying on personal donations.

Jim was working in property law and conveyancing and could see the substantial returns to be obtained from rented property. He found it possible to obtain a return of almost 20% on capital invested in residential property. He pointed out first to the Finance & General Purposes Committee, and later to the Board, that our earmarked and reserve funds had reached a point where they required to be properly invested and not simply held on deposit at interest. It was his suggestion that the Centre should use £10,000 of its funds and raise some loan capital in order to invest it in property with a safe return. The suggestion met with approval of both bodies, although Bethuel Kiplagat, the Chairman of the Board, gave Jim a knowing glance and reminded the members of the Board that, "though inevitably we should engage in fund-raising activities, we should not lose sight of our social work goal".

Eastleigh flats

Jim had found a block of six flats in Eastleigh, which had been recently constructed and was for sale through Tysons. It was let as a block to Kenya Railways & Harbours. They would produce a sure income and the title of the property would be held in trust for the Centre by the Church Commissioners for Kenya. An architect surveyed them and reported various shortcomings but approved the purchase subject to the vendor remedying any defects which might appear within the first six months. We borrowed on overdraft from our Bank Shs.50,000, the total purchase price being Shs.260,000.

We would in future be able to look forward to an annual income from the flats of almost Shs.50,000. Furthermore, by investing some of the liquid funds in property, we could offset any shortfall which might arise from the anticipated rise in building prices, in those instances where earmarked funds had been given for building projects.

Wood Avenue

This venture was seen to be a success and at the suggestion of the Warden we looked for a second income-producing property in the early part of 1973. In April the Board approved the purchase of a block of two maisonettes in Wood Avenue in the area of Argwings-Kodhek Road at a price of Shs.300,000.

The purchase was to be financed out of loan capital raised from Savings & Loan with an increased loan from the bank. After payment of loan interest there would still be a return of eight per cent income to augment the Centre's annual budget, with the prospect of capital growth. In all we had net rental income of approximately Shs.70,000 to help us meet our rising core costs.

Maridadi Fabrics Profits

Jim was somewhat concerned that the profits from the factory might attract income tax but after a little research into the taxation statute, he found that they were exempt because the industry was being carried on in furtherance of the charitable objectives of the Centre and because also the employees were beneficiaries of the charity. So, any annual surplus would be available to the industry and/or the Centre and none of this valuable financial resource would be lost to tax.

Percentage Levy on Earmarked Funds

Some charitable organisations have financed their core-costs by making an annual percentage charge for administering earmarked funds. The justification for this was that staff time and overheads were needed to ensure that these were properly protected and administered.

We never had to make this charge because we had made use of the money and by strategic investment we were able to offset the administration costs related to those funds against the income they produced. In this way we ensured that the projects and persons for whom they were intended obtained the full benefit of them.

Chapter 15 – The Role of the Volunteer

The American Contingent

We have seen in our Chapter dealing with empowerment of women through employment that Pat appreciated at a very early stage how important it was to find the girls and women a way of earning a sensible sum of money without resort to beer-brewing and prostitution. There had to be a better alternative. Pat, Margaret and Anne all applied themselves to the task and eventually a Home Industries project was launched with the support of an army of talented and hard-working American women, who gave of their time, talents and resources to make it work.

Their husbands would be working usually on fixed contracts very often for the American Government, on aid projects or for American businesses. When the time came for these expatriate women to leave, their places would be taken by others. The used to put out a packet for newcomers to Kenya and there was a page in it telling about the Home Industries project and stressing the desperate need for volunteers to do the work.

Volunteers helped in a host of different ways and capacities. They manned the sales room which opened on Tuesday mornings. They chased outstanding accounts, looked for new sales outlets, operated a quality control system and rallied around on special days when there were sales exhibitions and trade fairs. They were organised by a volunteer supervisor, a Mrs. Stade.

As with all volunteer labour, difficulties arose. Martha Gikonyo alone managed the project and volunteers would take up too much of her time. The volunteers who checked the finished products on Mondays were leaving the sales room in an "unbelievable mess; placemat and napkin sets rummaged through and taken apart." In consequence a member of staff required to restore it to order, ready for the sales people on Tuesday morning. Volunteers would cut fabric from open stock without replacing yardage labels and would allow unauthorised visitors to visit the factory on days other than Tuesdays.

These problems were voiced at a meeting of the small working committee in November 1970 and it was agreed that Mrs. Stade would carefully screen new volunteers. Martha was asked to decide whether she wanted any more volunteers and a decision was taken that volunteers themselves would no longer find substitutes to take over their jobs when they left. Furthermore, a policy was to be worked out for volunteers and procedures embodied in a formal letter. Volunteers would continue to make an invaluable contribution to the industry but it was time for the matter to be put on a more formal basis.

One difficulty had been the practice of some customers to seek help and advice from the volunteer staff without going to Martha. This would quite naturally cause resentment and it was agreed that this practice should be discouraged and disallowed. It pointed, in fact, to a more basic and far-reaching problem, namely the disempowering nature of such heavy dependence upon white, expatriate volunteers. What had started modestly as an enterprise to help women find work was fast growing into a recognised and established business. Its empowerment required that it could demonstrate it was managed and run by indigenous African staff: ownership of the project had now to be seen to be indigenous.

Kenya's Independence had been obtained in 1963 and the Kenya Government, as we have seen, was developing a policy of Africanisation in the work-place. The crunch came, and rightly so, when work permits became necessary even for volunteer expatriates. The policy behind all work permits was to produce employment opportunities for Kenyans. Whether expatriates were paid or not was, to some extent, immaterial. When, in November 1970, Jim told the Home Industries Committee that we would have to pay £25 for each volunteer work permit, the decision was taken that "we look for a local person for Saturday selling when Mrs. Michie leaves and perhaps other volunteers will automatically be eliminated as time passes." That somewhat draconian and curious phrase presumably meant that volunteer labour would be phased out as people left and that they be replaced with Kenyan staff.

Nobody pretended that this was anything but a challenge of enormous proportions. There had, of course, been huge savings in economic terms. The surpluses would not at that stage have been made without the volunteer force provided by the American Women's Association. Replacement with paid staff would be costly: more especially, senior African staff were few and far between, difficult to find and not too eager to work with a small, vulnerable business in a capacity which would carry no great prestige. Such staff could be acquired only at a premium. The ablest and most qualified were snapped up by the large, well-established organisations which could afford to pay them. We were not in that league, but we required, even more than they, the ability and experience such staff had to offer. Furthermore, as has already been explained, we tried to keep salaries in line with those of the Community Centre staff. It was all one organisation, but the Home Industries section was competing for experienced staff in a commercial environment.

Volunteers would still be needed if we were to remain viable, but they would be of a special nature. A period of rapid growth is not really the time to be shedding staff, whether they be voluntary or not.

Growth

Our Home Industry, or more properly our small industry, was now not so small. For some time, it had named itself "Maridadi Fabrics", acclaiming the beauty of its colours and boldness of its designs. Its logo, the simple, geometrical shape of a giraffe head, quickly caught on and persons seeing it would have identified it with Maridadi Fabrics. It has been a household name in Kenya, having existed for over fifty years.

In an unsigned one-page memorandum circulating with Jim's papers in 1971, it was stated that Maridadi probably ranked then in the upper 20% of registered Kenya firms, both in terms of employment and profitability. Quoting from the 1968 Kenya Statistical Abstract, the writer pointed out that in 1967 there were 12,000 registered Kenya firms. Of these only 2,771 firms employed 20 or more people and only 1,344 firms employed more than 50. Furthermore, the 1970 Stock Exchange Yearbook indicated that profits being made by Maridadi would have fallen in the same band as those of the top fifth of registered public companies in Kenya. We were anything but a registered public company.

So, what were those figures? In the six months ended June 1970, sales had totalled Shs.160,000. In Sterling terms this was then £7,800. After deduction of all expenses, Maridadi had made a net profit of £2,800, a profit of almost double the amount in the same period of the preceding year. That progress was maintained for the rest of the year and at the year-end sales had increased to Shs.347,000 (almost £17,000) and the net profit to Shs. 116,000 (£5600): a 50% profit.

We had high-class outlets for our materials and products in Nairobi, including not only Studio Arts 68 but boutiques operating in the Hilton and Inter-Continental Hotels. We were also beginning to find markets in other parts of Kenya. The prestigious Mount Kenya Safari Club, started by the film-star William Holden, had a boutique which began to give us a regular order.

This was all very encouraging and rewarding but increasing demand called for a corresponding increase in production. That was logical but easier said than done. We had the beer hall, a vast improvement on the facilities at the Burns Memorial Hall, but the increased space was still inadequate for this burgeoning industry. Only two long tables could be fitted into the main area, if there was to be sufficient circulation area for the women to move about. Urgent orders for cloth required that we install a third table.

It was not, however, just the premises and equipment which were groaning at the seams.

Full-time Volunteers

This growth and independence left the emerging industry with a massive problem: it was management. Martha was coping with difficulty, but the workload was massive and diverse. She required, as a matter of urgency, a senior management colleague, somebody who would share the load at the top and, off of whom, she could bounce her ideas and problems. That person required to have special qualities; a person who would not undermine Martha, whose effort had been instrumental in keeping the ship afloat, but somebody who would give her support and upon whom she could rely. In particular, that person would need to be somebody she could trust.

We needed also specialist help with the designs. They, perhaps, more than anything else were what sold Maridadi Fabrics. When Mrs. Udall returned to the United States, she had, as we have seen, made an effort to train people in fabric design and to ensure that Kenya was not left bereft of this skill. More work was required to build upon this preparatory foundation.

Immi Tivola

Scandinavian countries were apparently renowned for their prowess in fabric design and at their meeting in March 1971, the Home Industries Committee was informed that Afro-Arts had agreed to send us an expert from Denmark. We would be expected to provide her housing. In fact, nobody came from Denmark but instead we were offered somebody from Finland and in September we were told that we could expect her the following month. A work permit was applied for and granted. Lo and behold, at the beginning of October, Immi Tivola arrived and was welcomed to the committee.

She was every bit what you might hope for from a Finnish designer. Pat reckoned she would have created quite a stir in Jim's firm, a very formal, leading firm of Advocates filled with dark-suited gentlemen sitting in their offices at the top of the main Barclays Bank building in Queensway. In bright headdresses and very trendy, revealing outfits she would arrive for meetings with Jim, which would have lasted for an hour or two.

Immi was avant garde, not just in her sartorial appearance but also in her friendships with men. She was not recruited as a volunteer from a Christian organisation and, so far as we know, made no religious profession. We were told that she took a relaxed attitude towards visits from her boyfriends to the "tin house" which she occupied on the Centre compound. If in these matters she was somewhat ahead of her time, then we, and certainly the church members at St. John's, were lagging far behind. They would have been very offended by such behaviour; fortunately, if they were, they did not complain to us about it. Gone perhaps were the days, when, announcing his engagement to Pat, Jim was told by the Regional Secretary of CMS that he should not be seen leaving Pat's flat unaccompanied after it was dark.

Politically too, Immi held views which were far left. She believed that we were making matters worse, rather than better, by providing women with work and a modest income. Nothing short of a revolution would, in her view, bring about the change that was required to redress the social imbalance and we were just sticking a plaster over a festering wound. Indeed, in discussions with staff, she spread a scandalous rumour at the factory that Jim ran his Mercedes on the profits of Maridadi, a total misconception, because he never claimed so much as his petrol costs for attending the copious meetings and functions, which were required of him. He had no need to.

Until transport could be purchased for Immi, she was allowed to use the Centre car. Afro-Art at one time thought they could obtain or provide a grant for the purchase of a motor-scooter and it was reported that there might be one for sale by the Nairobi Christian Council of Kenya. It is difficult to recall whether this was ever obtained; we do not have any memory of Immi on a scooter, but she might well have been for all we knew.

We never really got to know Immi in the same way as the other expatriates who came to work for the Centre. We had a young family, which would probably not have interested her unduly. So, we knew very little about her background. Jim was therefore delighted when she wanted to introduce her father to him. He had come to Nairobi to attend the World Bank Conference in 1973, the occasion when the Bank President, Robert McNamara, made his famous speech, proposing a strategy for rural development with an emphasis on productivity of smallholder agriculture. Immi's father clearly had a senior role to play in the Finnish banking or financial scene. What a contrast, on this visit to the office, to see Immi accompanied by this elegant, suited VIP.

Immi was a talented designer. She got to know the designers who sold us their work. At the time of her arrival we were having sensitive discussions with them. In the past they had been remunerated on a down-payment and royalty basis. This was, however, proving expensive. Some of the designs had been used extensively. The recording of the yardage printed with their design would have involved ongoing records and paperwork, in an era when computers were not being used to any extent in Nairobi. So, it was decided to increase the down-payment and scrap the royalty. A meeting of the Committee was organised to which one of the designers, Tom Kiyegga, was invited to put his case. He came up with suggestions of recording and coding the designs. The Committee, however, decided that they would have to abide by their decision and not to re-introduce the royalties. They did however restore the previous ungenerous custom of giving a one-metre length of the printed material to the designer.

In these negotiations Immi played a part and in the same way she entered fully into the other activities of Maridadi. At an early stage of her service she was asked to research the purchase of new printing tables, in order to implement a new printing system. She found the materials required and was commissioned to hire a local carpenter to do the work. She helped in the investigation of steam boiling and took part in the negotiations to purchase a steam boiler, which had been discovered at a farm on the Kinangop. She pursued the possibility of appointing an agent for the sale of our products in Mombasa.

She was asked on one occasion to work with Jim in the arrangement of a sale of our materials one Saturday morning. It was a disappointment that she encouraged staff to claim extra money for the time they spent selling on a Saturday. Did she suppose that we were in the business of exploiting our staff? The extra money we would have taken by a special weekend sale would have been quickly dissipated by increasing our payments to the salaried staff. They, like all of us, understood the greater needs of the otherwise destitute women working on the tables and in the factory. More importantly, we sought always to align their motivation to that which prompted the rest of us to spend a Saturday morning having fun, enjoying a relaxed and friendly relationship and going somewhere different, like one of the large new prestigious hotels in the centre of Nairobi, for the good of the project.

Nevertheless, whatever may have been her political views, Immi took a full and active part in all aspects of Maridadi to ensure that it succeeded. We greatly valued her dedication as well as her skill.

Richard Hess

Immi came for a two-year period and as the time drew near for our colourful designer to leave us, our other specialist "volunteer" arrived. Richard Hess, a distant relative of the celebrated pianist Myra Hess and a cousin of the composer Nigel Hess, had completed a four-year degree course at Portsmouth Polytechnic as it then was. It has, of course, since acquired university status. Richard's course had given him training in business management and, being a sandwich year, it had included some practical experience in a workplace. On completion of his course, he made an application to the Church Missionary Society to work abroad as a CMS volunteer.

The first thing our children will tell you about Richard is that he brought them, what he called, a "bar of gold", a box of "Terry's Gold" chocolates. He had brought them from the U.K.; they were a rare delicacy in Kenya. Richard became a close family friend, visiting often and travelling with us frequently when we went away.

Richard proved to be that "special person" we really needed to give Martha the support she so desperately required. Well aware of the criteria set by CMS for their "volunteers", he arrived with the right attitude. It was desirable in a commercial situation that he should have a job-title, which carried with it some kudos, but it was important that it did not in any way undermine Martha's managerial status. So, he was called our "Commercial Manager". He did not in any way seek to take charge, but his advice was available, his active help forthcoming, never reluctant to engage in troubleshooting, often surprising in his ability to solve problems. Richard brought with him an enormous dynamism; he was able to make things happen.

So often those qualities are found only in people who want to take charge and demonstrate their ability and importance. Such a person would have created a chaotic situation, undermining the self-confidence of the manager and putting in jeopardy the respect and authority which she had amongst the staff and especially the women for whose benefit the project existed. As it was, Martha gladly took advice from Richard and developed confidence in herself and expertise in her role.

During Richard's period with us, we saw phenomenal growth. He it was who got the women onto shift working, thereby stretching our limited premises and facilities to their utmost capability. At the same time, we were able to give employment to twice the number of women, which was, after all, our raison d'etre. It might have been CORAT's recommendation that we should introduce shift-work; but if it was not Richard's idea, it was his detailed research into legalities and his planning that made it happen. As the capacity increased, we also obtained larger orders and new markets, matching our production. Richard was getting the orders, so he was always exhorting the women and the staff to keep up with the time-scales, to which we had to abide if we were to satisfy our new customers and at the same time keep our older customers happy.

Richard, like Immi, stayed with us for two years.

Chapter 16 – Voluntary Financial & Business Expertise

It is relevant, in the context of recording the value of "volunteers", to mention the total dependence of the Centre upon accountants who gave of their time to produce our accounts and ensure that our books were properly maintained. From the inception we had been blessed with the help of expatriates who acted as "honorary treasurers". They were often members of All Saints' Cathedral, where they would have been made aware of our need for the expertise of qualified accountants, whom we could not afford to remunerate.

Our first treasurer, Ralph Tattersall-Wright worked for Barclays Bank DCO and like so many young, unmarried expatriates in Kenya he adopted a robust approach to the changes he encountered in his new environment. In those days, eighty per cent of the arterial road to Mombasa was of murrum construction, without a hard tarmacadamed surface. It was his belief that the most effective way of navigating corrugated stretches was to go into hovercraft mode by driving over them at 80 mph. We valued a treasurer with a bold approach.

It would be tedious to name all our treasurers, many of whom were working for various employers in Nairobi and would return to England on the completion of their contracts. The task was quite demanding in terms of time and this became increasingly so, as the Centre's activities grew. Most especially, the formation of a commercial industry and its ongoing activities became onerous for our honorary treasurers. Stock controls and stock-taking, pricing, profit margins, indeed the whole aspect of viability was a heavy responsibility, which called for frequent advice and monitoring.

At the beginning of 1971, Don Ward came to the Home Industries Committee to present his financial report for the preceding year. He was due to leave the country in May and Jim told the committee that the time had come when we really needed two accountants "to do the books". In fact, we did have a clerk/accounts clerk and presumably at that stage he acted as a bookkeeper, but much detailed and mundane work would still have fallen on the honorary treasurer. We were certainly not in a position to afford anybody with accounting knowledge and Jim still had to use, perhaps even exploit, highly competent financial people who were willing to undertake a high level of unremunerated work. It did, however, mean that we had honest, hard-working people who found satisfaction in meeting with other like-minded folk, in a task bringing obvious relief to those whom the Centre served.

Clive Ashton

So at that meeting Jim explained that Clive Ashton, again a member of the Cathedral congregation, had been approached to help with the accounts. It was suggested that, before Don left in May, Clive could advise on the books and accounts of the Home Industries section and it was agreed that he would be invited to join the Committee. At his second committee meeting he asked to know his responsibilities on the committee and Jim set up a meeting with Don, Martha, Clive and Margaret Shaylor, another accountant who also gave us a helping hand, together with Jackton our newly employed accounts clerk. Incidentally, who would have thought that some forty-three years later Jim would find himself seated next to Margaret Shaylor at a dinner party in a marquee hosted by the Bishop of Winchester (himself an ex-Kenyan) for clergy and readers in his diocese.

Clive stayed with us two years as the Accountant for Maridadi until April 1973, an honorary but demanding job, as he wrestled with all the financial implications of a doubling of the sales figures in the final quarter of his tenure of office, compared with those in the same quarter of the preceding year.

The Dilemma

We wrote in the last chapter of the problems facing the use of volunteers and the difficulty of securing the quality of local staff we needed, both in terms of attracting them to such a small industry and paying the remuneration they could command. When Richard came to leave, after the end of his two-year contract, the issue of his replacement was discussed at the Board of Governors. Did we require a "Commercial Manager" or a top-level "Co-ordinator" of all the Industry's operations, particularly as we were then actively considering the opening of a shop in the centre of Nairobi, as a necessary outlet for our goods.

Bethuel Kiplagat, our Chairman, emphasised the fact that whether Commercial Officer or Co-ordinator, it was a top priority to make a local appointment. The minutes made the dilemma abundantly clear. "He noted however that we may face the problem of shortage of such local personnel coupled with the high salary bracket such a competitive person may demand." It was accordingly resolved:

"1. Efforts to look for a local person be explored further even through advertisement in the newspaper.

2. The Chairman should contact the German agency concerned with sending out of volunteers. Such a person should be a mature man of say middle age with experience in business administration. He should be a Christian.

It was envisaged that such agency would meet all or nearly all the costs involved in maintaining such a person for a term of about two years."

CMS to the rescue

The German agency was not prepared to meet those costs. In the final event it turned out to be our old faithful friends, CMS, who were able to deliver.

In the same month as that in which Richard completed his term of service, Jim was able to report to the Board of Governors that CMS had found somebody with a great deal of business experience who might be available sometime after Easter, just a month or so later. The Board agreed that as a CMS Volunteer would come with the usual CMS terms of service, "we should relax efforts" to search for one. Quite whom we have to thank for such prompt and efficient response to our need we are not sure. Perhaps our close friend John Ridout, the CMS representative had made clear the need of the factory at this crucial time; perhaps too he was supported in this by Archdeacon Ken Stovold, also a close friend and a member of the Board of Governors. Ken was himself a CMS missionary of long standing, wielding considerable influence and could well have lent his support.

The decision of the Board was not, however, greeted with unanimous approval. Martha Gikonyo, at a Home Industries Committee meeting in early April, said that the Maridadi Fabrics staff had not been informed of the proposed appointment. As the Manager of the factory she understandably complained that she should have been approached during the early stages of "the newcomers' arrangements". In fact, probably less than a month had then elapsed since we knew about the possibility and Jim pointed out that careful consideration had been given to the matter before any action was taken. The Finance & General Purposes Committee and the Chairman of the Board were all fully aware.

A hot potato

Martha told the Home Industries Committee that the staff at the factory were concerned about the security of their jobs. Jim told the Committee that he did not anticipate that there would be any change to their individual work or that there would be any confusion in their respective job descriptions. The purpose was to relieve them of the present pressure of work which had built up. In particular, it would be the task of the new person to manage and oversee the construction of the new factory, so releasing the present senior staff from the additional work which that would entail and leave them free to continue with their present functions without any extra workload.

The hurt created by the omission to negotiate this new appointment with the senior staff at Maridadi did not go away quickly. Some of them sent an "open letter" and copied it to most members of the Board. Jim was probably not one of them and he never recalls reading it; certainly no copy of it has ever found its way into his minutes or papers.

Bethuel Kiplagat, on receipt of the letter, called a Sub-Committee to consider it in detail with a view to making recommendations to the full Board. Jim has no recollection of those proceedings and was presumably not a participant. The Sub-Committee apparently met on three occasions. The first meeting discussed the letter, the second discussed the issues raised in the letter with the staff and at the final meeting the Chairman, Jefferson Mwadime the Vicar of the Church and a Board Member and Ephantus met with Martha "for final conclusions".

A Special Meeting of the full Board was then convened in early May and it was then reported that as matters then stood all issues had been dealt with and mutual understanding reached. Bethuel told the meeting that the proceedings of the sub-committee meetings would remain confidential and were recorded in the Board of Governors' minutes file.

The Chairman read the recommendations of the Sub-Committee and the following decisions were reached:

(a) The Board of Governors upheld the earlier decision to engage the services of a qualified person through CMS in England to work with Maridadi Fabrics.

(b) The title of the staff member so engaged should be "Acting General Manager" and he would serve for a period of three years.

(c) After the period of one year there should be employed a suitable candidate to understudy him and the person so selected subject to satisfactory performance, would occupy the position of General Manager.

(d) When the time came to fill the post of General Manager, a newspaper advertisement would be issued for any suitable candidate to apply including the person who had already been appointed earlier as the General Manager designate.

(e) The Board should try hard to nominate a new Chairman for the Home Industries Committee "as Mr. Richardson finds it really demanding to shoulder the responsibilities of the 2 Chairmanships. He is currently Chairman of both Home Industries Committee and the Finance and General Purposes Committee. He would like to be relieved of the two. Thus the Board shall have to make these appointments by September. (viz September 1975)."

(f) A full explanation of the decisions (a) to (d) would be given to The Home Industries staff by the Chairman and Ephantus Mugo.

Copies of the suggested job descriptions for the senior staff at Maridadi Fabrics were circulated to the members at the Board meeting and the main focus of discussion was on the job description for the Acting General Manager. It was observed that wording of his job description could have been made more acceptable. We do not know who drafted it, but it was decided that it should be reviewed.

It was also observed that an organisational diagram presented to the Board should also relate to the Board of Governors and that they should be shown as the supreme body "at the top". Quite right too! Finally, it was agreed that members of the Board be given more time to study the job descriptions.

So, our Chairman Bethuel Kiplagat, skilfully handled this sensitive situation of importing an expatriate to take charge of this burgeoning commercial enterprise, at a time when it was facing large challenges from every angle.

Ken Pattinson

Ken Pattinson arrived, as we had hoped, with his wife Margaret. It is pleasing that just four months after the Special Meeting, Ephantus told the Board that the Acting General Manager had settled down nicely. He had established good working relations with the staff and already got to grips with the work, especially pursuing the plans and finances of the new factory. Margaret, his wife, was already offering art lessons to the girls' school. She was also helping with Matumaini House in visiting and supporting Sister Caroline to organise activities with the girls.

Ken Pattinson came to Kenya, having spent most of his life in England in the management of a leading sewing machine manufacturer and eventually went back as an ordained Anglican clergyman, with a lot happening in between. He, in fact, fulfilled all the requirements which had been originally specified by our Board of Governors and CMS generously helped in financing the modest demands which Ken made for the upkeep of his wife and himself as missionaries.

If, when all is said and done, the reader thinks that the authors have laboured the problems in securing leadership of a small charity in the commercial workplace, we hope that you will forgive us and, if you bear with us, you might conclude that we did have some justification for doing so, as you watch the saga of Maridadi Fabrics and St. John's Community Centre continue to unfold.

Chapter 17 – Developing a New Industry

In our experience projects which start small, with relative informality, often develop more quickly than we first imagined. After several false attempts at a Home Industries project, we could not have envisaged the rapid growth which took place. We have seen some of the reasons for this, not least the flair and dedication of Dorothy Udall and her army of volunteers.

The next step would be to upgrade the less exciting aspects of the business embracing its overall supervision, monitoring and organisation of the project.

Governance

After hand-over of the business by Dorothy Udall to the Centre, it required proper governance. Two bodies met, a formal sub-committee of the main Board of Governors, which met on an almost monthly basis. In-between times an informal "working committee" dealt with day-to-day issues, composed largely of staff and Anne Barnett, the Chairman of the Home Industries. In both cases proper minutes were kept and were circulated to the Board of Governors to keep them fully informed.

On at least one occasion an ad hoc committee was formed for a specific purpose. It was commissioned to look into cloth. Its remit was two-fold. It was to consider what new kinds of cloth we might use and the prices we would have to pay for these. It would also consider what colours we should use and the suitability to the screen-printing process. Martha cautioned against a rapid switching from Nytil Jinja which came from Uganda, so four bales of that were ordered whilst twenty metres of the new cloth would be printed as a trial run. The ad hoc committee was asked to meet again to examine the samples of the new fabric, their main recommendation being that we should, in the long term, move towards local material if the customers were satisfied.

In May 1972, Anne Barnett went to England for eight months leave. She had taken over the chair from Janie Ericsson, one of the American volunteers working with Dorothy Udall, who was chairman in the early part of 1968, when Maridadi was in its infancy. Anne had looked for a suitable person to take over from her the duties of chairing the Home Industries Committee but no suitable person could be found. Ruth Waruhia had been suggested but at the beginning of 1972 she was on maternity leave. Jim was therefore asked to take on this role, although he was already fully committed as Chairman of the Finance & General Purposes Committee and he agreed to act as an interim Chairman, until a new Chairman could be found. It was expressly agreed that he should be relieved of this as quickly as possible and certainly not later than October 1972. In the end result, he remained Chairman of the Home Industries for four years, handing over to Mr. A.A.W. Awori in March 1976.

The Sewing Project

Brief mention has already been made in the earlier chapter on "Empowerment through Employment" of the place sewing occupied in the activities of the Centre. Quite apart from the employment potential of learning to sew, women and girls would be helped to develop an essential homecraft skill, which would enrich their lives and those of their families. Ella Marshall's regular visit with clothes she had already cut out for sewing by the women demonstrated also the potential of women using that skill to earn a small but valuable cash contribution to the family budget.

With the development of Maridadi Fabrics and a regular and copious supply of printed fabrics, that potential was changed into a reality. From the very beginning of the printing project, women were involved in sewing specific items.

Maridadi table mats were always popular, being an ideal purchase for gifts. Other made-up items included pot-holders, ties and dresses. However, the product-range and the quantity produced were limited.

Chapter 17 – Developing a New Industry

In 1971 Jim sent the Home Industries Committee a comprehensive paper, inviting them to consider the possibility of extending the activities of the industry by developing a sewing section. The immediate purposes of such a section would be threefold, namely to employ destitute women, to provide an outlet for the printed material when this was not fully taken up by orders from customers and to exploit and develop our existing market of private customers who came to the factory on Tuesdays and Saturdays to purchase our products.

The suggestion was to provide a versatile sewing section to take over our existing product range and to enter the clothing industry, making ready-made clothes, particularly dresses for children and adults which would be available in stock, as well as offering a bespoke tailoring service when required by our customers.

Perhaps the catalyst for this suggestion, was the availability of two skilled women who would be able to initiate and lead the project. One lady, Eva Chipenda, was the wife of someone known to Bethuel Kiplagat, the Chairman of the Board. She was highly skilled and had experience of running such a scheme in Nairobi. Most importantly she had expressed interest in Maridadi Fabrics and was prepared to help, even on a voluntary basis. The other person was a girl in Thomas Barnardo House, Esther Kalebi, who had secured a good School Certificate and was particularly proficient at needlework and domestic subjects, winning the national Junior Housewife of the Year competition in 1969. She would be the ideal person to be trained by Eva Chipenda as her successor, when the time came for the latter to return home.

Clive Ashton rightly pointed out the problems. These were lack of adequate premises, the need for independent supervision and large gaps in the control and administration of the industry as it already existed. These aspects were carefully considered and accepted but on the basis that they would be addressed forthwith, a majority of the committee decided in favour of starting the Sewing Project. A date was accordingly fixed to interview candidates and committee members were to make enquiries and ask suitable persons to attend on that day.

The selection committee duly met and it will not come as any surprise that Eva Chipenda was chosen to head up this project. She would work for five days each week part-time during the mornings because she had no transport. Her salary was rather less than she had hoped for, but it was agreed to review this after the salary structure of the whole organisation was re-organised following an external report. Esther Kalebi was not appointed as her assistant, but a Leah Chao was selected. Sadly, she did not come up to expectations and her employment was terminated six months later. A third person was also to be appointed after the project had started and it was anticipated she would have refugee status. We had received a grant from Norway for our work on condition that we offered employment to three refugee women in our Industry and it was thought we would.

So the Sewing Project started on 10th January 1972 in a small way. It was however to continue indefinitely, remaining part of the Community Centre activities long after Maridadi and St. John's Community Centre had parted company.

Developing a sewing section

Methods and Systems

It was, as we have said, a pre-requisite of starting the Sewing Project, that we should address the shortcomings of the administration. This was particularly related to Maridadi Fabrics. The industry had grown like topsy, but the management of it had not kept pace with its growth. Working as we had done with volunteer helpers and a paucity of paid staff, we had concentrated all our efforts on obtaining orders and then fulfilling them. With a workforce chosen by reference to their needs rather than their abilities, a greater deal of supervision was called for than would have been the case if skilled and able people had been originally selected. In the same way, with limited financial resources at our disposal, our supervisory and management resources were driven by necessity and developed out of experience, rather than established at the time when the business was first started.

Clive, with his accountancy knowledge, understood where we lacked essential information. He pointed to the lack of statistical information concerning our sales and our production. There were no stock records. We had no accurate means of knowing our production costs. How then could we reliably price our goods? Clive was also sympathetic towards our Manager, Martha Gikonyo, who could not take on any more responsibility than she had. He could clearly foresee the dangers inherent in working without proper systems and in his view it would take two to three weeks of a trained person's time to assess the needs and work out satisfactory methods and systems.

Rather than frighten us, he recommended that we seek the help of a Christian organisation which existed to provide this service, but they would charge a fee. They were based in England but had an East African representative, who was presently in Uganda.

So when the decision was taken to start the Sewing Project, Clive was asked to make enquiries of this organisation and also to follow up the offer made some two years previously by Professor Wolfendale to find and send a retired businessman from the United Kingdom who would establish the methods and systems which our administration required.

The need had not then seemed so apparent, but the remarkable growth in the industry proved that Professor Wolfendale's perception and forethought had been all too right.

CORAT

It must not be thought that Maridadi was totally without any procedures and when discussion arose concerning outstanding accounts, Clive told the Home Industries Committee that our accounts clerk, Jackton Mukhwanya, had sent out statements a week earlier and that the system for payment of accounts was working well.

True to form at the meeting in September 1971 Clive also reported that he had pursued enquiries of the Christian management organisation as he had been requested to do at the previous meeting. He had contacted the Director of the organisation, CORAT, the Rev'd Stuart Snell, who happened to be visiting East Africa and Clive brought him to Pumwani where he had met with Martha Gikonyo and Ephantus Mugo.

Stuart was enthusiastic about all the work he had seen and felt confident that they would be able to find one or two persons to investigate and advise on the administration of both the Home Industries and the other Community Centre activities as well. It had been the decision of the Committee at its previous meeting that the whole organisation should be advised, and that the whole administration, not merely the commercial activities of Maridadi, required this. Indeed, Stuart hoped that he might be able to carry out this exercise within the next three months and possibly find funds to finance it. The Committee decided that they wanted to proceed with this, even if they had to pay for it and the work was accordingly commissioned.

Anybody conversant with these management exercises will be aware that a considerable amount of time is expended at the beginning in learning about the organisation and the functions of the board and the staff. In order to reduce the time and expense involved in this preliminary work, Jim prepared a detailed dossier covering the governance and working of the organisation, its constitution, the agreed policy statement, a statement by each of the Home Industry's supervisors detailing their respective duties, full financial papers including the previous year's audited accounts, provisional accounts for the current year and a budget for the ensuing year, a full list of salaries, a detailed list of specific matters upon which advice was sought and a confidential addendum dealing with sensitive issues concerning the relationship with the Church and individual members of staff.

So, in the latter part of 1971, the Rev'd Dr. Rudge, who had written a paper for CORAT on the theology of Christian Administration and Michael Sams, a qualified accountant, arrived to carry out their investigation. They went away to prepare their report and an interim report was received at a meeting in January 1972. It was decided that a letter should be written to Stuart Snell to enquire when the full report would be issued and that when it was received, the Home Industries would meet at a weekend to discuss in depth and without pressure its recommendations.

Sadly, the authors do not have a copy of this document, but some highlights of the interim report were discussed at the meeting in January and certain action was agreed upon. All Home Industries accounts would in future be done at the factory. A more senior person needed to be appointed as accountant to Maridadi Fabrics and Jackton would become his assistant. A new accounting system was recommended and Michael Sams who was to come and set this up in January would be asked to defer his arrival until February.

The urgency of the appointment of the accountant was clearly appreciated. Clive and Jim had, prior to the January meeting, already interviewed a prospective candidate for the post, but it was agreed that Ephantus would obtain further information about him through a contact he had where the man had worked and that the appointment would be brought for decision to the Board of Governors. It subsequently transpired that the appointment of the man in question was "ruled out after a considerable evaluative discussion", concern being expressed that none of his previous employers was willing to give a recommendation in writing. An advertisement had also been placed in the Christian weekly newspaper "Target", which had a wide circulation in East Africa, but only one applicant had responded and he was unqualified. So nearly six months later the decision was taken to advertise in the Daily Nation, a national daily newspaper with a wide general circulation. Here was an example of a situation where this young industry was keen to appoint more senior African staff who had the ability and qualifications necessary for the task but were frustrated by limited availability of trained, reliable people.

Jim believes it was CORAT who first suggested the possibility of shift working in order to increase output. If so, it would wait for a year or two before it was implemented with the support of Richard Hess, whose marketing made it necessary.

Chapter 18 – Accommodating Maridadi Fabrics

The move of the tiny Home Industries project from the Burns Memorial Hall into the City Council Brewery had been an enormous step. It had also been a very successful step, moving into the heart of the Pumwani community at a focal point on the cross-roads of two major roads. We had the old City Council vats to boil the liquid and space, even though limited, to hang out our fabrics to dry in the hot Kenya sunshine. Visitors came to us from the centre of the town on Tuesdays and later, on Saturdays also, to purchase our "seconds" so we had made sufficient space for a small sales room. Other visitors, often official, also came from the City Council and the Community Centre, and they began to become something of a burden to Martha Gikonyo, who was busy managing the factory.

Options for additional space

However, we soon became aware of the shortage of space even within the Brewery itself and on the 6th September 1971, Jim produced a Memorandum for (inter alia) the Premises Committee, which he convened, setting out the options for the future and suggesting that one course would be to move Maridadi Fabrics to the Burns Memorial Hall and erect a new Community Centre building, probably on the Church compound as part of the proposed Community Church.

Another alternative was to build the Community Centre in a different location. For some years, as we have seen, the Nairobi City Council had intended to redevelop Pumwani section by section and a start had been made. Ephantus, the warden of the Centre, had expressed our concern in a meeting with the Town Clerk as to what would happen to the present residents, many of whom would not be able to afford to rent the new accommodation. Trying to anticipate this situation, consideration had been given to following the residents to a new location or to erect a new Community Centre in a different location where there was already extensive social need.

The reader might recall that during 1971, we were in the throes of resolving the development of the St. John's Church Compound and the competing needs of the Church, the CITC and the Community Centre for land to develop their respective work. A compromise had only recently been reached concerning the allocation of the MRI funds which had come from the Diocese of Rochester. Whilst it was entirely logical at this stage to consider the needs of Maridadi Fabrics and the possible re-siting of the Community Centre, it was unrealistic to expect to resolve those issues at the same time as the wider needs of the Church and CITC. The Master Plan for the Compound was all but agreed and it would have probably been a mistake to muddy the waters by introducing these new issues at that point in time.

Elsbeth's Report

Fortunately, the memorandum provoked a response from Elsbeth Court, one of the six remaining American volunteer ladies, who submitted a carefully prepared report to the Premises Committee of the Community Centre for their consideration. Her report fell into three sections. The first section set out in detail the specific needs of Maridadi Fabrics.

1. First and foremost was the very large printing room, to accommodate four to six printing tables, a drying area for printed cloth and an area for mixing dyes.

2. Another very large room was required for boiling fabric for setting, storage of charcoal, jikos (small cooking stoves) and large sufurias (enormous pots for cooking or washing) and drying cloth which had been boiled on rainy days.

3. A storeroom was also required to store dyes, chemicals and screens. When, later, in the early eighties many of our screens were destroyed by outsiders who gained entry in the course of a failed political coup, we came to realise what a disastrous loss that was; they were probably some of our most valued assets, which we took for granted.

4. An ironing room to accommodate ironing tables and jiko irons

5. Storage facilities for wholesale printed fabric and a sales room.

6. In addition there were ancillary areas, such as staff room, toilets, offices for manager and clerk, designers' office for storing designs and art materials, designer conferences and consultant's workroom.

7. Finally, there was need of sufficient curtilage for outdoor drying facilities.

Elsbeth and her colleagues felt it important to have all people and processes under one roof and, furthermore, to stay in Pumwani.

The second section of her report ruled out the existing Community Centre building which was too small: the required extensions and modifications would not be viable. Instead, in the final section she detailed improvements and modifications to the old Brewery, so as to allow for expansion, provided the City Council of Nairobi granted us some security of tenure and permission to make the alterations.

God's Guidance? – an unexpected solution!

It was clear that we had to address the matter and these memoranda, and the discussions surrounding them, were in Jim's mind as he was thumbing through his weekly copy of the Kenya Gazette, the official organ of the Kenya Government and a regular part of his general reading diet at the office. What should he find there? There was to be an allocation by government of small commercial/industrial building plots at the main roundabout off Landhies and Jogoo Roads. They were situated just half a mile from the old brewery in the location known as Shauri Moyo, "an Affair of the Heart". Might they become for us our hearts' delight?

A decision, however, had to be taken quickly and a commitment entered into; not something easily achievable in a voluntary organisation with several committees involved. Anne Barnett, the then Chairman of the Home Industries Committee, called a meeting, who decided that they wanted to make an application and some few hours later a special meeting of the Board of Governors was convened. A quorum was not obtained but those present decided that application should be made before noon the following day, the deadline, and ratification be sought from the next full Governors meeting. Jim also contacted our Architects and the whole matter was put in train.

In the New Year of 1972 our application was granted, not for the larger plot we had selected but for a smaller one. Jim wrote to the Commissioner for Lands asking for a larger plot if that were possible but if not, we were advised by the architect that the small plot could be used by building upwards. So, the search went on to acquire another plot on the same development, either in exchange for, or in addition to, the small plot we had been allotted.

Negotiations, Plans & Squatters

At the end of 1973, Richard Hess went to the Lands Department, who gave him details of the owner of the plot next to ours, Mbari ya Gichimu who were already on the plot. He asked Jackton to visit the owners to discover their plans for the development of the site and to enquire whether they would be interested in selling. Jacton made several visits but could obtain no definite information. The warden, Ephantus, then arranged to meet the owners in January 1974, when he was told an answer would be given but this proved to be negative. At the May meeting it was reported that the plot opposite to ours was three times the size and it would be available at £4,000. It would, however, save us at least that sum in construction costs by building on two levels rather than four. This was important because building costs had doubled since we first applied for our plot, having risen to Shs.90/- per square foot if we were to build to four storeys. Yes, we could build upwards and if we were to do this we would probably be building four storeys. This was much less satisfactory for us than having the whole operation on one floor. A lift might be necessary, not only for goods but also for the women, who would need that facility as they grew older. So, the Home Industries

Committee decided, on the strength of the previous year's performance to buy this plot and to ask Triad to prepare new plans.

New plans made provision for a mezzanine floor. On this we would site the shop and a gallery from which visitors would gain a birds-eye view of the printing operation below. It was a great concept for our PR; what we had not anticipated was that oriental gentlemen would come in the guise of buyers and carefully photograph our process in preparation for setting up a similar operation, or producing similar designs, elsewhere. Norman Howe, a member of the Home Industries Committee suggested amendments to the new plans, having studied them carefully. At the same time, it was agreed that the manufacturing process should be re-addressed to see if it could be improved, as this might affect the factory layout. A further meeting was held with the architects at which Richard and Norman discussed the new plans, but they could not be finalised until a decision was taken about the dyes to be used. In his comprehensive report, Michael Mwangi, our Technical & Design consultant was recommending that we move over to pigment dyes and this would necessitate a different process.

There were other factors which also held up immediate progress. There was usually a condition that development on the plot should take place within two years of the grant. It would take time before the grant was issued. Plans had to be prepared and approved by the various statutory bodies, governmental and local. Perhaps the greatest delay had been occasioned by the size of the plot allocated to us.

One reason holding up development was outside of our control. The land had been occupied by squatters for some years, some of them being metal workers operating small "jua kali" businesses in the open air. It was government's responsibility to ensure that they were cleared before any building work could begin. When Richard went to the Lands Department towards the end of 1973, he was told that steps were being taken to remove the illegal squatters and that it should be possible to start building in 1974.

Finance

Then there was the time-consuming factor of raising the finance. Richard met with the Archbishop of Canada who had said that the Canadian churches operated an aid scheme and might be willing to help. We applied to our own bank, the Kenya Commercial Bank but they refused a loan for the building. Richard had been in contact with the Industrial Development Bank, but they would only agree to do this if we were to become a corporate body, registering as a Co-operative or Company, which was not thought to be desirable. Ephantus applied to the Ecumenical Church Loan Fund (ECLOF) which lent money at sub-economic rates of interest; he made the application in July 1974 but over six months afterwards we had received no response from them. The breakthrough finally came in September 1975, when we learnt that SIDA, a development agency sponsored by the Swedish Government, offered a grant of Shs.450,000/- It would not be sufficient, of itself, to pay the whole construction cost but it would be the basis upon which we could think seriously about starting and Ken Pattinson, who was by now with us, would start looking in earnest for the balance.

As we have said, the time it took before we could start building had been usefully employed considering how the different processes of manufacture would best be served in the new building and there was constant liaison between our experts and senior staff and the architects. Ideas were refined and revisited. The adverse effect of the delay had, however, been the escalating costs of construction. They were Shs.36/- per square foot when we had first conceived the project. In November 1975, the architects came back with working plans and an estimate from a quantity surveyor of £64,500, based on Shs.92.83 per square foot. The Home Industries questioned the calculation but, notwithstanding their surprise, they asked Triad to invite tenders. When these were received the lowest was Shs.884,284 from Cementers Limited, a reputable company, who were confidently recommended by the architects. As yet, the title remained in the name of Mr. Kibe, the vendor from whom we had bought the larger plot and we had to press for a new letter of allotment from the Commissioner of Lands, which was forthcoming in March 1976. The matters requiring to be resolved were the services such as electricity, water and drainage but by June most of these were being processed and steel was delivered on site ready for construction to begin.

In August the steel framework was finished, the roof constructed and the floor was in the course of being laid and, by May 1977, the contractors were finishing off various snagging problems required by the architects. It was ready for the new equipment to be installed. Printing tables, finishing machines, salesroom fittings, were ready to go in, while trolleys, racks and other equipment ordered from CITC were well underway. By this time the total cost of the factory to date and the future anticipated expenditure together amounted to nearly Shs.1,350,000, not too far different from the estimate of the quantity surveyor, but it did include also land purchase costs, professional fees, other on-costs and, most importantly, factory equipment. The sums received for its construction were Shs.1,400,000 in grants and loans. Bingo!

If you wonder what happened to the first plot allotted to us, this was cleared, fenced and a temporary car park made on that site, because its future was uncertain in the light of proposed re-planning by the Nairobi City Council.

And the beer hall? Are you wondering also about that? Well what about the sewing and the Amani School of Dressmaking? Yes, we still had our central prime position in Pumwani.

Part III - "More Power to the Centre"

The new Maridadi Fabrics factory (recent photo)

Part IV – "A Decade of Disaster"

Chapter 19 – The Gathering Storm

Ken Pattinson's Final Report

Immediately prior to the opening of the new Maridadi factory, Ken Pattinson made his final report to the Board of the Centre in February 1978. It was a great report and the conclusion is worth quoting:

"The Future

The old factory has been a blessing to the women of Pumwani whom it has served but it can no longer cope with the work load and the building's very design and creaking, worn out printing tables make the task of producing precision hand printing very difficult.

The new factory is now almost completed, only final touches remain to be done before a gradual and planned transfer of personnel, equipment and stock commences. This is expected to begin towards the end of this month. Then we shall be able to locate the screens by double registration, fix the dye by intensive dry heat and treat the fabric ourselves, thus making the project autonomous. When it rains printing can be stopped so eliminating the risk of "bleeding" of the fabric and the loss of printing can easily be recovered because of the increased production capacity. We now have a factory worth K,Shs. 2 million free from rent, rates and income tax, which should serve indefinitely those for whom it was built.

Most important of all the new factory will provide modern toilets, washing facilities, a canteen and a light, pleasant working environment for the women to enjoy and from which they should benefit.

Recommendations:

I must mention however, while feeling very optimistic about the project's future, certain areas where careful vigilance is essential: -

Tourist Trade. This can no longer be considered a dependable source of income.

Financial Control. A close watch must be kept on price lists, costings, buying and especially trading and administrative expenses. During the rest of 1978 it is essential that spending be controlled.

Competition. Rivetex of Eldoret are our biggest anxiety as they have tremendous resources and are venturing into "African Prints". These are very inexpensive, the fabric is wider than ours and they have a huge retail shop in Biashara Street. The prints are inferior to ours, both the designs and the dyes, but not everyone can see the difference.

Copyright Infringement. We have one or two problems and have dealt with these threats promptly and firmly but the danger is never far away. If any firm was allowed to get away with stealing our designs the fact would soon be known throughout Nairobi and the consequences could destroy us.

Retail Shop. We should continue to try to secure a good shop in Nairobi.

Finally, I would like to say that the project will be in good hands as we have been able to build up a splendid team to manage the whole operation and if we can take as an indication Henry Kathii's early promise of fitting well into the driver's seat it would not be out of place to say that the future of Maridadi Fabrics and its part in the work of St. John's Community Centre looks exceedingly promising.

We might pray that the Lord will continue to bless that place."

Cash flow

A splendid report summarising the result of three superb years of service given by Ken to Maridadi, which was to come to an end on the 19th April 1978. Less than a month before making that report, in January 1978, Ken wrote to Jim to express concern about the cash flow of the Centre and asking that we should meet to discuss the situation. Alarm bells started to ring. Jim realised immediately that this indicated a cause for concern in respect of the continued viability of the various projects of the Centre. He agreed to a meeting but asked that work be put in hand to prepare the half-year accounts and requested Ephantus to organise a budget from all departments of the Centre for the next six months. If in those days we had had such things as computers and monthly management accounts, the cause of financial problems could have been identified so much earlier and so much more easily.

Centre Building Development

There had been considerable growth in the Centre's activities necessitating expansion of the premises. It was not just Maridadi Fabrics which had outgrown its accommodation. In February 1976 Ephantus had brought to the Board proposals and architect plans for new offices and toilet facilities. Two new classrooms were also required and a library/reading room and the Board confirmed that this additional accommodation was required as the "work had expanded while original space remained the same." We do not doubt that the extra space was necessary, but an observation made at the meeting is not without its significance. "It was also observed that while the surrounding area was renewing and talks for the redevelopment of this area extended, the Centre should not remain behind as this would not be good planning". Who knows what was in the mind of the person making that observation. Were we concerned about losing ground to another institution? Was it the green eye of the little yellow god speaking to us and the thought that we had to keep up with the Jones's? Whatever, the Board urged the Director to take quick action as some of the materials which had been granted by the Nairobi City Council might be withdrawn if no work was going on.

However, the erection of this block, contemporaneously with the construction of the new factory (though of course on an entirely different site), required an enormous amount of extra administration and would have overloaded the accounts staff. The operation of a single bank account for Maridadi and the other Centre activities, whilst it had been a considerable boon in the past, was undoubtedly, at this stage, a major stumbling block. Vast sums of money were flowing in and out of it.

At a meeting of the Finance & General Purposes Committee in April 1977, it was reported that we had received total grants and loans for the new factory of Shs.1.4 million but only Shs.850,000 had actually been spent on the factory. When all the available cash resources were added up there was a gaping hole, a shortfall of Shs.300,000. Needless to say all bills for the factory were ultimately paid and all the grants and loans received for the factory were properly expended on it. It was, however, a nasty moment and the discovery demonstrated that we were spending money we had not got.

The Nursery School

At that same meeting Ephantus reported that the toilets, nursery school and new offices were due to be completed at the end of May 1977 and that the total cost for the nursery school and the offices was Shs.115,000. He also made the comment that "The Nursery School should be asked to repay the Centre all the money it owed after completion of the School. When work was completed valuation should be made to include voluntary labour and donated materials to get real value of the building." Then a special meeting was called a month later, with the architect present, to discuss payment of the final costs amounting to Shs.75,000. Jim pointed out that although the Board had authorised some of this work, they had not specified the cost. Perhaps more important still, the Nursery School had never appeared as part of the authorised work. So why had it been built contemporaneously with the offices, classrooms and toilets? Had the free materials offered by the City Council been specifically given for the Nursery School? Who knows? What is more, for whom was the Nursery School built?

Although it was built and financed by the Community Centre, the Parish church always laid claim to it. The Church had themselves always had a nursery school which had been demolished to enable the Church Commissioners to erect new student accommodation for letting to the Christian Hostels Fellowship, a body formed by Kenyan members of the Lee Abbey Fellowship. Hence the comment of Ephantus in the earlier meeting that the Nursery School should be asked to make repayment.

Everybody anticipated that the project would belong to the Parish Church and the Vicar, Canon Leonard Mbugua, reassured the Finance Committee that the Church had agreed as a matter of principle to reimburse the Centre for all the costs incurred.

The Last Straw

It just never happened. Financially, it was almost certainly the catalyst, which wrought havoc with our cash flow and brought the Centre to its knees. The project was to have been valued and charged to the nursery school or whichever body owned it. It would be an income generating project, providing a full day's care and education for 160 children. The capital cost should be borne by those who were to receive the revenue. At the February 1978 meeting of the Board, it was reported that the project was completed apart from snagging.

At the October meeting, the Chairman reported that the building accounts were finalised; it was possible to see what was then owed by St. John's Church to the Centre. He then handed to the Vicar a copy of the building account showing a detailed breakdown of the expenditure and asked him to make due reimbursement to the Centre and help ease it out of the current cash flow problem. The Vicar responded saying that the Church were quite willing to refund the Centre the money spent on the Nursery School, but he needed time to present the matter to his Finance Committee for approval of such payment. He requested that the Nursery School be allowed to occupy the premises while his committee considered repayment, but the Board unanimously decided that it was a better arrangement that the

Church should commit themselves to the amount of repayment before occupation of the premises was approved.

The matter came before the Board at its next meeting some three months later. The Vicar again asked the Board to allow occupation of the new premises since it was the beginning of the New Year. His Finance Committee had not been able to meet as soon as he had promised, to authorise reimbursement to the Centre. There were too many holidays in the month of December and a majority of committee members were on leave. He would nevertheless convene his committee meeting "as soon as possible" and he had "no doubt" they would authorise due payment. After some discussion the Board acceded to the Vicar's request to take occupation of the building on condition that he ensured the Church made due payment to the Centre at the earliest convenience. It was strongly felt that the matter of the repayment should not be delayed any more in view of the financial strains currently being experienced by the Centre.

Alas, it never happened. Empty promises with little likelihood of fulfilment. Jim cannot recall or ascertain why it was that the Centre ever undertook the rebuilding of the Nursery School. Maybe the building had to be upgraded if the Nursery was to be allowed by the Nairobi City Council to continue. Maybe the offer of new materials by the Council was specifically for the Nursery School rather than the toilet block offices or classrooms. Maybe the Centre perceived the demolition of the old building as the loss of an important facility of the local community or the possibility of a new income-generating asset. Had the rebuilding of the project been brought before the Board, we would have known the answer to these questions: but no reference to it can be traced until it was well on the way to completion.

The writers do have a subsequent balance sheet showing a cash input from the Church of Shs. 20,000: it does not specify the cost of building the Nursery School or any indebtedness on the part of the Church. The building costs were, however, a significant sum of money which would have gone a long way to pay off creditors, provide working capital to purchase raw materials for Maridadi Fabrics and give further time to assess its viability. The warning of Ken Pattinson was not without cause:

the steady growth of the industry had come to an end. It was no longer the cash cow from which a certain amount of social work and welfare had been financed and any outside perception, by the local church or others, of the Centre as a cash-rich organisation was soon to be dispelled.

Financial Control and Management

Lack of funds to employ highly-experienced commercial management may have been a contributing factor. Henry Kathii, previously head of the Kenya Scripture Union, did not have the background of cut-throat competition in the commercial environment enjoyed by his predecessor. Ephantus Mugo was stretched, in terms of time, experience and staff, to handle the phenomenal growth in turnover and project management and to control the expenditure. Most importantly, as an organisation we embarked upon a sizeable building programme, which necessitated close supervision of materials and progress, and this put an even greater strain on the human and financial resources, which were struggling to cope. There were even allegations of dishonesty and misappropriation.

Whatever may have set in motion this financial crisis it would get deeper with dire consequences for both the Centre and Maridadi Fabrics.

Part IV - "A Decade of Disaster"

St. John's Church Nursery School (above + below)

Chapter 20 – Struggling to Survive

Information Sources

The minutes and records of the Board and the Finance & General Purposes Committee held by Jim came to an end in 1979. These were comprehensive and detailed and have been of incomparable value in compiling the material of this book. So far as we recall, they mark the end of our personal involvement with the Centre and Maridadi Fabrics. Following the discovery of the problem with cash flow, Jim alerted the Diocese, to whom we were accountable, to the difficulties of financing the Centre's activities. Ken Ashton, the Diocesan Accountant, then came to make investigations and recommendations and to the best of Jim's recollection the activities of the Board and the Finance & General Purposes Committee were brought to a close. Jim is not entirely sure of the composition of the Committee which assumed their responsibilities.

In dealing with the history of the next decade, the authors are grateful to Ken Ashton and to Mike Nunn, the Accountant to the Church Commissioners for Kenya. They also received from Margaret Pattinson a letter some time later supplying information about the early period following the disbanding of the Board.

A long and particularly well-informed letter covering a much longer period was also sent by Marjorie Oludhe, whose association with Pumwani has been so long that it preceded Pat's arrival and continued long afterwards. She became secretary of the Parochial Church Council of St. John's Church; so more about her and the information she was able to provide of the period which she occupied in that role.

Marjorie Oludhe Macgoye (nee King)

Marjorie Oludhe Macgoye was born in Southampton in 1928 and attended Royal Holloway College London University where she obtained an M.A. in English Literature at a time when women with post-graduate degrees were rare. In July 1954, at the height of the Mau Mau Emergency, she went to Kenya as a Diocesan missionary to work at the Church Bookshop in Nairobi. Soon after Pat arrived in Pumwani in January 1959, she found herself in the middle of preparations for Marjorie's wedding, which took place on 4th June at St. John's Church with the reception in the Burns Memorial Hall. Her fiancé was a young Luo medical dresser named Wellington, Mr. D.G.W Macgoye. The inter-racial marriage was the subject of many conversations and much disapproval amongst Europeans in Nairobi. Most European settlers knew Africans only as members of their labour force or servants. They rarely had the opportunity to meet educated and sophisticated Africans and found it hard to envisage a happy marriage between a white woman and a black man. The couple were both very brave and the Community Centre was privileged to host an event which typified one of its most important aims, to bring together people of different backgrounds.

Through her marriage Marjorie became a member of an extended Luo family and at first hand she has been involved in its tribal traditions. The wedding took place as the Emergency was coming to an end, and so, during her marriage, Marjorie has observed Kenya's development from a colony ruled by Great Britain, to a young independent country establishing its place in the international community and shaping its way of governance. A well-known writer, Marjorie expresses in her work the confusion and frustration still experienced by African women today. In her poems and novels, one detects both her intellectual ability, derived from a first-class university education, and the rare experience of living within a social group, which is only beginning to feel the vibrations of modern society whilst holding on tightly to the past.

Marjorie taught at Dar-es-Salaam University for four years but has spent most of her time in East Africa living in Nairobi. To celebrate the fiftieth anniversary of her arrival in Africa she had a special service at St. John's Church Pumwani.

Marjorie has been called "The mother of Kenyan literature". She published novels, essays, poetry and children's stories. During her later years she was handicapped by her poor sight which must have caused her immense frustration in continuing her writing career.

She died in Nairobi on the 1st December 2015 and is survived by four children.

Information source provided by Marjorie

As the secretary of St. John's Parochial Church Council, Marjorie could throw some light on the confused history and relationship of the Church and the Community Centre during the eighties. She said that the Church saw the Community Centre buildings as part of the parish but there was confusion as to which building belonged to which organisation. It was her recollection that Archbishop Kuria "gave" Matumaini House to the Parish Church but the Parish had believed it was theirs already. There was an element of truth in their understanding, but it was only partly true. As has been seen earlier, the original Old People's Home was a mud and wattle building erected on a plot in Pumwani, which had been given to the Church by the Nairobi City Council and was operated jointly by the Church and the Community Centre. When that sector of Pumwani was demolished in anticipation of redevelopment of the area, it was replaced by the ground floor of Matumaini House with money raised by Anne Barnett from Bread for the World. On the first floor there was the Community Centre's accommodation for twelve girls which was financed by MRI. So, in a sense it was partly given to the Church and partly already owned by them: hence the confusion which Marjorie describes.

Marjorie's letters have also confirmed important facts and incidents which we have gleaned from various minutes and reports. Marjorie tells us that in 1984 and 1985 the Parish Church had two sub-committees which dealt with the (job-description) work of the Centre and the chain of financial control of the Centre. As Secretary of the Parochial Church Council, Marjorie was asked to provide an inventory of the Centre's assets, but she was then prevented from doing so by the Centre Warden, the Rev'd Sasaka, with whose appointment we shall be dealing later in this chapter. She also confirmed the date of the departure of Canon Leonard Mbugua, which we shall see had a dramatic effect on the Centre and its future.

Marjorie stated that after 1985 the Community Centre did not appear in personnel or financial records of the Church and this would be consistent with the appointment of the new board or committee by Diocesan Synod to govern the Centre. Thereafter, the situation became such as Mrs. Eunice Kamau found in 1989, when she became Manager.

Caretaker Committee

Apart from the letters which we received from our friends and colleagues, our information has largely been provided by the staff of the Centre from their records of the supervening years following our departure. There is, however, a gap in those records from 1979 until the 15th September 1981 when a caretaker committee was convened at Imani House, not at the Community Centre. This committee appears to have been set up by the Church of the Province of Kenya possibly at the instigation of the Bishop. Timothy Ramtu, a respected businessman and a member of All Saints' Cathedral, was appointed Chairman. The Committee included also Justice John Mwangi Gachui, who was a High Court Judge and a member of St Stephen's Church. He had, incidentally, been an old friend and legal colleague of Jim's. In attendance, were Mr. Katembu, who was employed by the Community Centre and Mrs. Martha Gikonyo of Maridadi Fabrics. This small committee was very concerned with the financial state and the governance of the Community Centre and Maridadi Fabrics.

Some of the Community Centre activities, whose finances were reviewed, were the High School, Adult Literacy Classes, Typing and Shorthand Classes and the Amani School of Dressmaking. It was reported that the High School and Amani School of Dressmaking were self-supporting, but it was agreed that the fees charged for Adult Literacy, Typing and Shorthand Classes needed to be increased to cover their running costs. Mr. Katembu described how the fees were paid into income accounts but then items of expenditure were paid from wherever money could be found and not necessarily from the appropriate account.

The committee discussed the future sale of the Community Centre car. Staffing also required to be discussed. It was agreed that the discussion of the salaries of the staff and their contributions to the Provident Fund should be carried forward to the next meeting. Furthermore, replacements were required for the social worker and caretaker positions. Elizabeth

Mulatya had been working as a social worker for the Centre since October 1974, a total of seven years. The caretaker, Mark Shiundu had retired after 21 years of service. Everybody who used the Centre knew Mark. He joined the Centre in Pat's early days and his reliability and willingness to tackle any task made him much more than a caretaker. It would not be easy to find a replacement.

It was noted with concern that members of the Matumaini House Committee were not attending the meetings which had been arranged.

The caretaker committee next met a month later the 13th October 1981 and further consideration was given to the financial situation of the centre. Mr. Katembu presented full accounts of the expenses incurred by all the programmes during the period July 1980 to July 1981. One very interesting item of income was "Sale of assets for Shs.500,000" The authors can only think that this represented the sale of the Wood Avenue flats which had been bought in 1973 at a cost of Shs.300,000. If that was the case, it seems that the main, if not exclusive, source of funds for maintaining the Centre's work was income derived from, or the capital realisation of, the Centre's investment properties. This sale, although desperately necessary, was indicative of the Centre's financial ill-health.

The committee arranged for the interview of candidates for the positions of caretaker of the Community Centre and the messenger for Maridadi Fabrics. There was further discussion about the appointment of a social worker.

Mr. Ramtu advised Mr. Katembu that the Nursery School was built on the site of a former church building and that the Vicar, Canon Mbugua, could give him all the details about the school.

It was reported that the old ladies at Matumaini House were getting too old to cook for themselves. However, the committee agreed that it was not possible to appoint a cook, presumably for financial reasons. When the money was raised to build Matumaini House, the original vision was for a hostel which would accommodate 12 old people on the ground floor and 12 vulnerable girls on the first floor. To begin with the Church Army provided Sister Caroline, who was a loving matron to all the residents;

the girls did physical chores for the old people, who watched over these needy "grandchildren". The house was a very useful resource for the Community Centre social workers.

Re-organisation of the Centre's governance

At the following meeting in February 1982, Mr. Ramtu was able to suggest that the Community Centre was gaining stability and the time had come for it to break away from the caretaker committee. He suggested that the Diocese should appoint another committee to manage the Centre and the Caretaker Committee would then concentrate on Maridadi Fabrics.

The next meeting of Mr. Ramtu's committee was held 3 months later in May 1982, when he reported that the appointment of the suggested new committee for the community centre was under discussion in the office of the Archbishop. It seems, however, that the new committee was not appointed until September 1983.

It was agreed at the May meeting that Mr. Katembu should ask the Church Commissioners for a loan to improve the Community Centre's financial situation, but we do not know whether the request was ever made or what was the outcome.

The interview of candidates for the position of Matron for Matumaini House was discussed. There had also been a request for an increase in the salaries of the teachers in the Centre and it was agreed that this would be discussed at the next meeting.

The final meeting of this caretaker committee took place on the 6th July 1982. Dates were set for the interview of candidates for four vacant positions, namely the matron of Matumaini House, a watchman and a cleaner for the Community Centre and a marketing officer for Maridadi Fabrics. A new salary structure for all the staff of the Community Centre was agreed.

It was reported that Canon Mbugua had written to the Archbishop stating that the Community Centre would be handed over to the Church at the end of 1982. His authority for making this proposal is not explained and one questions why this would be appropriate if the Diocese was in the process of discussing the formation of a new committee. There is no record of any further meetings of the caretaker committee and there is nothing in its minutes or those of the inaugural meeting of its successor as to how, or by whom, it was appointed. However, the very fact that the caretaker committee ceased to exist and the nature of the make-up of the committee meetings which started in April 1983, would suggest that the Archbishop or Diocesan Synod had passed control of the Centre to the Parish. So, tedious though it is, we need to see who attended those committee meetings.

It was a further nine months following the final meeting of the Caretaker Committee before any committee met to govern the Centre. Then, on the 7th April 1983, a preliminary meeting of an "interim committee" of St. John's Community Centre Pumwani was held at the Centre. The Chair was Mr. D. Waweru and another member was Mr. Holla, both of whom had been members of the caretaker committee. Mr. Katembu was now Warden of the Centre. No minutes of this meeting were recorded, but Mr. Katembu made notes of proceedings. He gave the committee all the information which he had previously given to the caretaker committee on the items of the Centre's income and expenditure. He said that he would prepare a list of all the assets of the Centre including the buildings.

Mr. Katembu also made mention of "Children Incorporated of USA". He explained that this organisation had been partnered with St. John's Community Centre and a committee had been appointed to allocate the funds received from it. This, incidentally, is the first time that the authors have seen any mention of the organisation; the handling of this money and its distribution remained a matter for debate.

The then curate of St. John's Church, the Rev'd Sasaka, who is not known to have had any earlier contact with the Centre but who was presumably present at this meeting, asked for an office with a telephone and suggested that the Church telephone be incorporated into the Centre switch board. This was agreed and later implemented but when Mrs. Eunice Kamau became Warden in 1990 she reviewed and reversed both the decisions concerning Children Incorporated and the telephones.

The next meeting of a committee known as the 'Board of Management' was held a week later at the Centre on the 15th April 1983. Once more, the meeting concentrated on the financial and other assets of the centre and the regular payments which needed to be made. The warden Mr. Katembu submitted bank and cash balances and detailed a list of the income, namely fees, rent, donations canteen profits and the sale proceeds of materials. He also provided a list of Centre payments including wages and salaries and was asked to prepare a list of all outstanding accounts.

Management or Merger?

A decision was made that the Centre vehicle should not be used for private travel but only for Community Centre and Church business. The Rev'd Sasaka explained that the office he was occupying had no phone, which he found unsatisfactory. It was again suggested that the Church telephone should be incorporated into the Community Centre switchboard so that the number of extensions could be increased using the same switchboard.

At this meeting, without any clear overriding decisions, the physical assets and financial liabilities of the Church and the Community Centre therefore became confused. The car, originally belonging to the Centre would also now be used by the Church, the telephone would be used by both organisations and paid for by the Centre and the curate would use an office in the Centre.

All this would be consistent with an organic merger of the two bodies, if that had been the intention of the Diocese rather than control or management of the Centre by the Parish. This would only be clear from the Diocesan Synod minutes or some letter emanating from the Archbishop's office. Whether it was merger or management, the manner of its implementation was hardly professional or likely to assist in resolving the financial problems faced by each of the two bodies. Furthermore, the mention of the sale of materials would seem to indicate that there had been no formal separation of the Centre and its activities from Maridadi Fabrics. If that were the case, then a third body operating a commercial enterprise was also included in this re-organisation. There is no mention of accountants or professional financial advice in the operation and the way in which it was conducted, so the viability of all or any of the institutions must have become even more difficult to assess.

New Committees

The next recorded committee of St. John's Community Centre was entitled the 'First interim Committee' and was held one week later, on the 22nd April 1983.

The reports and statements which had been produced by the Warden at the previous meeting were accepted as Appendix 1 (not available in any records). These had been set out in the minutes of the Caretaker Committee in July 1982 and in minute 1/ 83; at this meeting they were accepted as a starting point for the taking over of the Community Centre by the Church.

The committee discussed possible donors to be approached by Mr. Katembu, but it was realised that audited accounts would be required by such donors.

The Rev'd Sasaka reported that he had moved to his new office.

The next Management Committee minutes are entitled "St. John's **Church** Community Centre" and the title of the meeting is "The **First** Management Committee of the above Centre" [9]. The meeting was held in the Church vestry on the 17th June 1983. This was to be a kind of re-branding, with a new image, a new constitution, new governance, a new executive head and a new leader. The Vicar, the Ven. Canon Leonard Mbugua was Chairman; the former warden, Mr. Katembu, who had been "in attendance" or "Secretary of the Caretaker Committee" since

---

[9] The underlining and emboldenment are those of the authors.

Part IV - "A Decade of Disaster"

October 1981 was not present at this meeting and the Rev'd Sasaka was there as "Curate-for Warden". It was agreed that he would take over the management of the Centre on the 1st August 1983, replacing Mr. Katembu, who was to be made Education Adviser. It was noted that the Rev'd Sasaka could not receive payment from the Community Centre for his services as Warden as he was paid by the Church. Instead, it was decided, that the Community Centre would reimburse the Church.

At the formation of the interim committee in April 1983, one of the members had been Mr. Gachira, the Parish Assistant Treasurer. At this meeting in June, it was decided to ask him to provide accounts for the Centre on a professional basis.

Canon Mbugua suggested that the High School should be moved to a more appropriate place "because of the Nursery School and no playing ground". What this meant, we do not understand. Does it mean that the High School did not have sufficient playing fields; if so, what had happened to the football pitch? Or did it mean that the Nursery School had no playground? Whatever may have been the reason, one questions how easy it is to pick up an established High School and put it down in a different location without a good deal of forethought and years of advance planning. At the same time, Canon Mbugua said that qualified teachers should be sought for the High School.

At this same Committee meeting, it was resolved that the bank signatories should be changed. The two mandatory signatories would be the Vicar and the Church Treasurer, neither of whom had been involved with the work of the Community Centre during the period since Mr. Ramtu's Caretaker Committee was formed in 1981.

There appears, therefore, little continuity in the governance of the Community Centre by the Church with that developed by the Community Centre following the meetings of the interim Caretaker Committee which started in November 1981. No reference to any of the social outreach, which the Centre had developed over so many years, was made at this important meeting at the beginning of a new chapter in the life of the Centre.

Chapter 20 – Struggling to Survive

The second meeting of this "Management Committee" was held in the Vicarage on the 26th July 1983, when just four members attended, only one of whom, Mr. Waweru, had been a member of the earlier committees running from September 1981. The other three were the Vicar, the Curate and Mr. Gachira, the Assistant Parish Treasurer, all officers of the Church.

The Rev'd Sasaka, whose involvement with the Centre appears to have begun only three months earlier, produced a chart showing future staff management plans which he had prepared for the Centre, based presumably upon the knowledge he had derived by working there during that brief period. One wonders what induction he had received when he began. More especially, one questions what experience he had in the field of social work or social outreach to qualify him for the role of Warden of a Community Centre, with a long history of professional and dedicated service to the community.

Mr. Gachira reported on the Centre's accounts, which appear chaotic. No reference was made to the reports made to the Caretaker Management Committee by Mr. Katembu on the 15th September and the 13th October 1981 or at the meeting on the 22nd April 1983 at which Mr. Gachira was present. It might have been helpful if Mr. Katembu had been present at the meeting to explain how he had been able to produce all the figures at earlier meetings.

The last meeting of St. John's Church Community Centre Management Committee was held on the 2nd November 1983: we are not sure of the venue. A discussion took place on the terms and conditions of service of the Warden and other members of staff. Requests had been received for these from the staff since 1981, a further example of the lack of any accountable management for some time.

From the minutes of the interim caretaker committee it appears that Mr. Katembu was originally working as the administrative secretary and then acted as Warden, becoming known sometimes as Director. In July 1983 he had been appointed Education Supervisor so that the Rev'd Sasaka could assume his position as Warden on 1st August 1983. At this final meeting in November the Committee was advised that Mr. Katembu was not giving any assistance to the new Warden, nor making any suggestions for improving the Education Department. It was, therefore, agreed to terminate his services immediately.

In July 1982, Messrs. Katembu, Malinda, Waweru and Holla had been appointed to deal with the money associated with Children Incorporated and the first two had been operating the relevant bank account. At the meeting in November 1983, it was agreed they should be replaced by the Vicar, the Rev'd Sasaka and Mr. Holla.

Chapter 21 – Back to Square One

More change

Following the apparent merger of the Parish Church and the Centre in 1983, a new and even more dramatic change took place the following year. On the 28th July 1984, the Parish dismissed, or purported to dismiss, the Vicar for allegedly embezzling church funds. He also held the office of Vicar-General or Archdeacon of the Nairobi Diocese. The Archbishop was not convinced and suspected anti-Kikuyu prejudice. So, he sent the Vicar on leave, appointing a new Parochial Church Council. Whatever may have been the position, and whatever the outcome, there followed within months a complete reversal in the governance of the Community Centre.

A new Board of Management

Just a year after the last meeting of the Church Community Centre Management Committee, another new body emerged and the 'Board of Management for St. John's Community Centre', rather than 'St. John's Church Community Centre' held its inaugural meeting back in the Centre on the 14th November 1984. It would seem that the interim Committee meetings and indeed the so-called "First Management Committee" of St. John's Church Community Centre had all been of an interim nature, and that this further "inaugural" meeting was to be the substantive one. Was it perhaps convened pursuant to the new constitution awaited since Mr. Ramtu's advance report in 1982? If so, by whose authority, one wonders, were all these interim meetings held and why did their mandate cease so abruptly?

The new Chairman, Mr. James Chege, had been at his first meeting in November 1983, when he explained that Diocesan Synod had passed a minute in 1983 by which the Constitution of the Centre had been suspended and replaced by a new constitution drawn up by the Diocese. Mr. Chege himself had been made Chairman of the new committee. Amazingly, he was not present at the inaugural meeting in November 1984 and we have no further record of his activities after he attended a meeting on the 1st March 1985. At the meeting in 1984, the Rev'd

Sasaka was present as Secretary and **all other committee members** were new.

So, four months after the inaugural meeting a second meeting was held on the 1st March 1985 in the Warden's office. The new chairman Mr. Chege proposed that new members should be co-opted to the Committee and appropriately nominated three women; Elizabeth Macharia, Mary Wanjiku and Millicent Opiyo.

We can find no reference to previous decisions taken at the meetings of the interim committees or of the First Management meeting of St. John's Church Community Centre. Instead the new Committee became seriously involved in investigating what happened to the Ecumenical Church Loan Fund (ECLOF) loan which they suspected to have been absorbed by Maridadi Fabrics but for which repayment was being sought from both the Community Centre and Maridadi Fabrics. To the best of Jim's recollection, it was a loan to Maridadi to complete the erection of the new factory premises and if that is the case, it would have been a joint liability of both Maridadi Fabrics and the Centre, which was all one entity at that time. Three committee members were chosen to investigate this matter and file a report.

From the minutes of spasmodic committee meetings there does not appear to have been any close connection between the Centre and Maridadi Fabrics after the time when Mrs. Martha Gikonyo attended the Caretaker Committee in 1981.

Budgets for the various activities of the Centre were then discussed. It appears that there was a serious shortage of money and it was suggested that the Diocese could assist in raising funds. It was also agreed that the Church Commissioners for Kenya should be able to pay the social worker, Mrs. Onyango, her gratuity of Shs.7,200 which had become due when she finished her contract the previous December.

The Warden reported that Age Concern England had visited the Centre and agreed to finance a lunch scheme for elderly people. Funds for this scheme were being held by the Kenya National Council for Social

Services. The new Vicar of St. John's Church, the Rev'd John Ndungu, asked questions concerning the Nursery School being handed over to the Church. It was agreed that he and the Warden (viz the Curate of the Parish) should look into the financial viability of the school before any decisions were made.

It is difficult to be certain who signed off the minutes of the meeting of March 1985 and chaired the next meeting on 20th September 1985, which was less than a year after James Chege had become Chairman. It is significant that it was held some six months following the previous meeting. The rapid succession of different committees, meeting at irregular and often infrequent intervals and frequent changes of Chairmen left the organisation without effective leadership or control in a period when it was challenged by depleted funds and any real expertise in turning it around. It is little wonder that it lacked real direction or policy.

The next meeting appeared to be that of St. John's Community Centre Board of Governors held on the 16th July 1986. The meeting of the Board was attended by eleven people including five heads of departments and the Warden of the Centre, three of whom were women. Apologies were received from five governors, who included Johnson Muchira, Principal of CITC. The Rev'd George Mambo introduced the new Warden, Mrs. Mary Mbiu Koinange to the Board and remarked that she had been working with a Christian organisation for the last 14 years. The Vicar, the Rev'd John Ndungu, noted that since Mrs. Koinange had been at the Centre during the last one and a half months there had been a remarkable change.

The Board once again discussed the Centre's financial situation. Mrs. Likalama, the head of the secretarial section, explained that her equipment was in very poor condition, ten out of thirteen typewriters being out of order and there being no tables or chairs. Many students enrolled but left immediately because of this pathetic situation. The School did not make any financial profit or support itself. Ways were suggested of injecting money into the project and of seeking financial help from overseas.

Mr. Lucas Mpita, the acting head of Dressmaking and Tailoring, reported that their sewing machines were very old and kept breaking down, they had no stools on which to sit and they needed tables for cutting materials. The point was made that this should be an income-generating project if properly advertised and properly managed. The standard was very high. He also reported that they had no toilet facilities and that they had to walk all the way to the Centre (from the old Brewery where it was based). It was decided that enquiries should be made of the City Commissioner whether a toilet could be provided for these premises or, if this were not possible, whether the Centre could provide suitable facilities at its own expense.

Mrs. Koinange informed the Board that the only other source of income was the Eastleigh flats. The whole block was rented by the Kenya Posts & Telecommunications at a rent of Shs.7,500 per month. The Church Commissioners for Kenya had proposed a rent increase and the Board raised the total rental to Shs.9,000 from the 1st January 1987.

'Children Incorporated' of USA

Mrs. Onyango, a social worker employed in family and child welfare, told the Board that the monthly sponsorship income from Children Incorporated was US$909. Sometimes extra money was sent as special gifts from the children's sponsors. The money was sent through the office of NCCK and then paid into St. John's Community Centre account. Mrs. Onyango found it difficult to access the money for distribution to the children as it was diverted to other projects. It was suggested that a new account should be opened with the Standard Bank and that Mrs. Onyango, the Rev'd Samuel Nderitu and the Warden should go ahead and regulate the programme. The Rev'd Mambo suggested that after everything was properly organised he should approach the Archbishop to arrange with the Richmond office of Children Incorporated for the money to be deposited straight into the new account, rather than going through the NCCK office.

This is the first reference the authors have found to the Rev'd Samuel Nderitu, who became Chairman. His involvement became important because he clearly remained dedicated to the Centre and ensured that its existence and work continued.

Chapter 21 – Back to Square One

Mrs. Onyango's contract had ended in November 1984. Her bonus had been mentioned at several management committee meetings but after the lapse of a year and eight months the bonus had still not been paid. A small committee was appointed to find a solution. The Board also discussed the Warden's house, which was still occupied by the Rev'd Kabiru and the Chairman agreed to check with the Chairman of the High School Governors, who, we understand, was the Rev'd John Ndungu, the Vicar of the Parish. Presumably the High School had at that stage been separated from the Community Centre.

Matumaini House & Centre Buildings

A reference was also made to "Matumaini Old People's Home". Why, one asks, was there no reference to girls in this title? The first- floor accommodation for vulnerable young girls no longer existed and it is understood that their accommodation was being used as a rented property by the church to generate income for church purposes. If this had not been the case, why did these minutes record the Warden as saying that Centre staff did not feel free to visit the Home and why did the Chairman agree "to do what he could about that". It would seem therefore that Matumaini House had become the exclusive province of the church and was no longer a resource for the social work of the Community Centre.

A large part of the agenda was adjourned until a later meeting. It included the maintenance of the "Community Buildings" such as the Centre, the High School, the Nursery School, the Canteen and the Hall. The lack of financial control and accumulated debts were items adjourned for further consideration. This is no small wonder because the meeting which had commenced at 5p.m. concluded at 9.45 p.m.

The Executive Committee

This meeting of the Board was soon followed by an "executive committee" held two weeks later on the 29th July 1986. The chairman was the Vicar, the Rev'd John Ndungu, and the new warden Mrs. Mary Koinange was the executive secretary. Reference is made to the last meeting on

1st July 1986, and one imagines this must have been a meeting of the executive committee, but no minutes were read. The present meeting was an emergency meeting to look into the theft of more than Shs.15,000 which a teacher had stolen from pupils of the secondary school. He was therefore summarily dismissed.

The appointment of two new teachers, to replace two who had left, was agreed. The two new teachers both appeared to be more qualified in Christian religious education but were willing to try other subjects. The sentiment of Canon Mbugua for qualified teachers, to which we previously referred, does not yet seem to have come to fruition.

The next Minutes of the executive committee, held on the 18th November 1986, are headed "St. John's High School and Community Centre", the new Chairman being the Rev'd Samuel Nderitu. The first Agenda item was Laboratory and Workshop but this was deferred at the suggestion of the Rev'd John Ndungu, Chairman of the High School Board of Governors, as he had not been consulted about it.

Following the discussion at the inaugural meeting of the Board of Governors of the Centre on the 16th July, the Warden had reported that she had agreed that Mrs. Margaret Onyango, the social worker, could live temporarily in the Centre house. The Board members discussed the principles upon which Centre and Church housing should be allocated and the rents charged to employees. Mrs. Onyango was required to write an application to the Chairman. Further discussion involved Mrs. Onyango's contract as it had expired and not been renewed. A small committee was chosen to study her file and make recommendations.

Other items on the agenda included debts, working capital and leaking roofs and the possibility of organising a Harambee. A serious matter had arisen because all members of the management staff had written to the Chairman of the Board concerning their remuneration and he believed that their requests were genuine. A further financial problem was reported by the Warden: she said that Form 4 leavers had left without clearing their outstanding fees and recommended that in future leaving certificates would not be issued until fees were paid.

Chapter 21 – Back to Square One

It was mentioned that a report had been written on the re-organisation of the School and the Community Centre: a suggestion was made that a copy should be obtained by Board members so that they could inform themselves and implement it.

Whether the Board members, or any of them, ever obtained a copy of the report the authors do not know because we now enter a lacuna during which no further papers related to the governance have been available and, to be honest, even if there were any to be had, they would probably be of little consequence or interest to the reader. It was about this time that Mrs. Mary Koinange had found it necessary to retire due to ill-health, apparently due to the conflict between the Parish and the Community Centre. Following the departure of the Vicar and Archdeacon Leonard Mbugua in the middle of 1984, the governance of the Centre seemed to get back on track but meandered along without very much direction or vitality. If it had not had the endowment, comprising the Eastleigh flats, it may well have been wound up in an insolvent state. The condition of equipment was lamentable and the staff disillusioned by stagnated pay scales and poor standards.

It seems accordingly appropriate to fast-forward during the period of the next three years, which are something of a vacuum in the governance. What a relief that must be to the reader. During that time, the Chairman, the Rev'd Samuel Nderitu, took on the position of Warden. He not only held the fort, he moved things forward strategically and financially, bringing to an end the decade of disaster and paving the way for a decade of Renaissance and new birth? Please turn the page and you will not be disappointed.

Part V – "The Paradigm Shift"

Chapter 22 - Renaissance

New Leadership

On the 1st July 1989 Eunice Kamau was appointed as "Manager" of St. John's Community Centre after a career as a High School science teacher for the previous eight years. Eunice had a Science Diploma (S1) from the Kenya Science Teachers' College but her earlier academic career had been repeatedly frustrated because of her family commitments, not least of which were the responsibilities following the births of three sons. Her studies at Delhi University came to an end prematurely and later offers of places at Kenyatta University and then in England by the British Council could not be taken up. A scholarship to a medical school in the USA could not be pursued because of the birth of her third son. She did, however, find it possible to study for a degree in Business Administration and Community Development from Daystar University, whilst working at the Centre and she started this in September 1989.

A parishioner of St. Paul's Anglican Church, Eunice saw an advertisement for the Community Centre post and she realised that this was where her aspirations had been leading her. She looked forward to meeting the not inconsiderable challenge which the job offered.

The Induction

During her interview with the Chairman of the Community Centre Board, the Rev'd Samuel Nderitu made clear the assets of the Community Centre and the territorial boundaries of the Community Centre plot. He informed her that the Centre had commissioned a baseline survey of its activities which had been paid for by Norwegian Church Aid with a view to its future funding. The new Manager would be expected to develop the Centre's programmes along the lines proposed in the survey.

Samuel explained the composition of the Board, part of which was made up of the Vicar of St. John's Church and several members of St. John's Parish Council, each of whom was responsible for looking after the interests of the High School, the Nursery School and Matumaini House respectively. No mention was made of Maridadi Fabrics and it was with surprise that one day Eunice saw a van pass in the street bearing the signage "Maridadi Fabrics – a project of St. John's Community Centre". The remaining members of the Board represented other interested bodies or areas. There was the director of CITC Mr. Johnson Muchira, a representative of Nairobi Diocese, a Muslim living in Pumwani, a representative of Norwegian Church Aid which was a major stakeholder, a resident from the Community who lived in the new Pumwani called "California" Mrs. Elizabeth Malatya, and a representative of African Evangelistic Enterprise, the Rev'd Daniel Serwanga. Elizabeth and Daniel had had connections with the Centre for many years

A poisoned chalice!   A rich inheritance!

It was also made clear to Eunice that at the time of her appointment the Centre had very few activities. There were two groups of old people who came regularly to collect their monetary allowances. One group was paid by Centre staff from money provided by Help the Aged Kenya and another group of "grannies" were paid directly by the Mill Hill Fathers who made the distribution alongside the Centre social workers. Another sum of money came regularly from Children Incorporated. This, as we have seen, was a sponsorship scheme enabling needy Pumwani children to receive money for their education from families in the United States. Finally, a few girls were coming to the Centre for secretarial training.

The High School, the Nursery School and Matumaini House were no longer governed by the Community Centre but had been taken over by St. John's Church.

The Rev'd Nderitu gave Eunice a potted history of the Community Centre, as he understood it, explaining that it was started by CMS Missionaries.

In the seventies, the first African warden Mr. Ephantus Mugo had a continuing disagreement with the Parish, who accused him of mismanagement of funds. They disagreed with his insistence on developing the High School. The Diocese intervened and Ephantus was required to tender his resignation, although he protested that the allegations made against him were untrue. He and his wife had built, and were running, their own primary school.

Following Ephantus' departure, the Rev'd Mwangi was appointed as interim warden until Archbishop Manasses Kuria made a substantive appointment, in the person of the Rev'd Sasaka. It appears that the motive for this appointment was more to provide work for the Rev'd Sasaka than to provide the Centre with a Warden who had particular gifts or relevant training. When the Rev'd Sasaka was later removed from office, Henry Kathii who was the General Manager of Maridadi Fabrics, was asked at the same time to give oversight to the Centre, until Mrs. Mary Koinange was appointed Warden. Sadly, the pressures caused by the political conflict between the Parish and the Community Centre were too great to withstand: she became ill and this forced her to resign.

During the intervening period between Mary Koinange's resignation and Eunice's appointment, the Chairman of the Board the Rev'd Samuel Nderitu assumed the role of Acting Warden. He distanced himself from the political bickering with the Parish and focused his attention to finding financial support for the Centre. Through Daniel Serwanga, who had been involved with the Centre since the 1960's, he established contact with Norwegian Church Aid and as a result funds were raised from that body and channelled through African Evangelistic Enterprise to the Centre. This paid for the baseline survey and supported the Centre staff through 1988 and 1989.

Eunice was told that the ownership of, and responsibility for, the High School, Matumaini House and the Nursery School had been transferred from the Community Centre to St. John's Church. It was explained as a kind of deal which sought to compensate the Church for the transfer to the Diocese of the land on which the Community Centre had been built.

If this was so, then it was either a fudge or a genuine attempt at compromise to re-allocate the ownership of land formerly held by CMS. It took no account, however, of the cost or use of the buildings erected on it. It had been Jim's understanding that when CMS relinquished ownership of its land and assets in favour of the autonomous Kenya Church, it passed the legal title to the Church Commissioners for Kenya, to hold it in trust for the respective bodies who then assumed control of, and responsibility for, the activities then taking place there. At the time of the handover, the Community Centre Board was established and as we see elsewhere in this book it became a Diocesan institution. Logically, therefore, the land on which its activities were carried out should have been held by the Church Commissioners for the Diocese, who in turn operated the Community Centre through its Board. The Centre operated out of the Burns Memorial Hall, which clearly belonged to the Centre. Adjacent to the Centre was the football or games field, which the Community Centre understood was theirs, although others also used it. It stood between the Burns Memorial Hall and the Church building but the Church would have never had occasion to use it. The High School was built upon it with funds raised by the Centre.

Matumaini House, on the other hand, stood in grounds on the other side of the Church on land which the Church conceivably believed should belong to them, although the building had been erected with funds raised by the Centre for occupation by the larger community.

Most, if not all, of this land, had been unused and unattended but the beneficial ownership of it started to become an issue when the various Church bodies started or wanted to develop it, either to expand their activities or, more significantly, for income generation. The Parish never had funds to carry out any development but wanted to generate income, as they could see the Centre was doing to expand its work. The re-allocation of the land between the Centre and the Parish Church had the effect of divesting the Centre of buildings which had been expensive to erect and depriving it of vital income in the form of school fees.

Perhaps, in God's larger scheme of things, this financial set-back was a preliminary requirement. To divest the Community Centre of these localised projects, would set it free to concentrate upon the empowerment of the Pumwani community to help itself. More importantly, it would later be liberated to set its sights on national programmes designed to

Chapter 22 - Renaissance

combat the problems associated with HIV/AIDS, which was taking hold throughout the country with such a devastating effect.

The Financial Challenge

At the time of Eunice's appointment, the Community Centre had very large debts and she was told that one of her chief duties would be to clear this indebtedness. The only liquid asset of the Centre, of which Eunice was made aware, was a sum of Shs.3000/-, although the Eastleigh flats still belonged to the Centre and these were income-producing. She was advised that Archbishop Manasses Kuria had regarded the Community Centre as a liability and that he had considered giving it to the Nairobi City Council. He had met with the Board to discuss this situation and Nderitu asked the Archbishop for an opportunity to turn the situation around. The Archbishop agreed that he could have a period of one or two years in which to do so.

Before making any plans for new programmes, which would transform the Community Centre along the lines suggested in the baseline survey, Eunice needed to understand in more detail the Centre's current financial situation. To establish the Centre's liabilities she requested an audit by the Centre's accountants, Carr Stanyer Sims, who discovered that these totalled nearly Shs.1,000,000. She examined the payroll only to find that a large sum was paid regularly to the High School staff and the Warden of Matumaini House. All telephones serving the Parish, including the Vicar, the High School, Matumaini House and the Nursery School came, as we have already said, through the Centre switchboard, and the charges found themselves on the Centre's invoice from Kenya Posts & Telecommunications. Other expenses included of course the salaries of the Centre staff, the utility bills for the Centre and the cost of running the few programmes.

The Centre's income was diverse. It consisted of rental from the Eastleigh flats, a small amount made up of fees from the secretarial school, the donations sent by Children Incorporated, money from Help the Aged to support the Old People living in Matumaini House and money paid directly by the Mill Hill Fathers to other elderly people known to the

Centre. A quarterly payment from Norwegian Church Aid came through African Evangelistic Enterprise and sometimes the Centre obtained ad hoc grants for specific purposes. No income was received by the Centre from former assets, such as the High School and Nursery School, the fees of which were collected by the Parish.

The new Manager sought to understand how debts of nearly a million shillings accrued. She discovered that the auditors had never been paid for their previous audit, the Nairobi City Council water bill was outstanding and the Centre owed money to the Church Commissioners, which they had paid towards loans taken (inter alia) for building the High School. Eunice discovered a loan was made by the Ecumenical Church Loan Fund (ECLOF) and it is Jim's belief that this loan was taken to assist Maridadi Fabrics complete the erection of the new factory.

As the new warden gained a clearer picture of the Centre's finances, she took several steps to remedy the situation. In the first place she wrote to the Vicar indicating that with immediate effect the Centre would cease payment of the salaries of staff not directly employed by the Centre. She then called Kenya Posts & Telecommunications requesting them to disconnect those telephone lines which were routed through the Centre switchboard to the extensions on the Church compound, as the Centre would no longer be responsible for bills incurred by these other users.

Eunice also re-designed the child sponsorship scheme. She had discovered that some of the children benefiting from these sponsorships did not come from the slum area but were relations of, or known to, staff members. Eunice therefore decided that the only children to benefit from the scheme in future would be primary school children who attended the Community Centre classes, to whom the whole of the funds coming from America would then be entirely devoted.

Mounting opposition

These actions caused consternation among the members of St. John's Church. The Vicar preached a sermon about "the demon who has come to the Community Centre". When he knew himself to be within Eunice's earshot, he sung a hymn in Kikuyu about his new creation in Christ and his consequent freedom from attacks by the devil.

The Parochial Church Council (PCC) met and chose representatives of their number, who would go to see Archbishop Manasses Kuria, complaining about Eunice's behaviour. The Archbishop arranged to meet the representatives of the PCC but, unknown to them, the Archbishop called to the meeting the Chairman of the Community Centre Board, the Rev'd Samuel Nderitu, and Paul Kang'ori, the Dean of Students at Kenyatta University, who was also on the Board. When the Archbishop asked the PCC representatives to outline their complaints, they remained silent and he accordingly took no action on them.

Rather more serious was a later deputation, composed of high-powered individuals, who went to the Archbishop voicing their concern. The robust stance assumed by Eunice created wider resentment and Johnson Muchira of CITC, the Vicar and Joel Buku, the Secretary to the Church Commissioners, went to discuss with the Archbishop the action she had taken concerning the access of construction lorries through Community Centre property when building CITC property. He refused to support their protests. It was his view that Eunice had been given the task of resolving the problems of the Community Centre and she should be allowed to get on with this.

A time for rationalisation: Territory - Staff – Governance

Eunice re-designed the physical boundaries of the Community Centre. She wrote a letter to Johnson Muchira and then closed the gate through which CITC students had regularly passed to gain access through the Community Centre to the Church compound; this had been disruptive of the Centre activities.

Likewise, she built new offices and classrooms for the Centre's use within the Centre's grounds and vacated the premises within the High School which the Centre had been using as part of the Centre's premises. This enabled her, in turn, to discontinue the use which was still being made by the High School of the Centre's premises as a reception centre and for some of its activities, which were taking place in the Burns Memorial Hall.

More importantly, and quite illogically, the Community Centre had been left to bear the expense of activities, which it ceased to operate and from which it had ceased to derive any revenue. It became Eunice's necessary, but difficult, responsibility to ensure that this situation did not persist.

In the same way, the staffing situation required to be rationalised. Following the transfer of activities to the Church, there had been no formal separation and redeployment of the staff. It was unclear as to which members of staff should remain in the employ of the Community Centre and those who should properly be transferred to the Church or other bodies to whom they should have to report. Eunice wrote to all staff making clear who their employers were.

Finally, she turned her attention to the governance of the organisation. She came to realise that the Board of Governors was very largely composed of members of the Parish Council. So, Eunice persuaded the Archbishop that it was necessary to constitute a more professional body, which would be competent to give direction to the work of the Centre.

St. John's High School

It is perhaps appropriate to mention here what has ultimately become of St. John's High School. Although built by the Centre at its own expense, it became, as we have seen, an asset of the Parish, and the management as well as the ownership became the responsibility of the Parish church. It generated income in the form of fees and this must have been very welcome. But by about 2004, it began to experience challenges in management. Is this surprising? How would a parish church expect to have the expertise to manage a high school?

The Bishop of Nairobi at that time, Bishop Peter Njoka, requested the Centre to assist the school in getting back onto its feet. Whilst the School remains under the Diocese, it has the benefit of oversight from a sub-

Chapter 22 - Renaissance

*Mrs. Eunice Kamau -
"She looked forward to meeting the considerable challenge
which the job offered."*

committee of the Centre's Board of Governors. They promoted Quinter, a member of staff, to become headmistress. She is both visionary and dedicated and has been successful. The school is only now showing real signs of recovery. Debts had accumulated and most of these have now been cleared: the student population has increased three-fold. Confidence has been restored among parents, guardians and the general community.

Honorine Kiplagat, whom we remember meeting with her late husband Bethuel when he was Chairman of the Board, played a large part in the recovery of the school. Now, a member of the Board herself, alongside Canon Jane Mwangangi who is also a Centre Board member, she has mobilised resources for a sponsorship programme to assist needy students and raised funds to refurbish and equip the library and school laboratory. In this, they have involved St. Mark's Church in Westlands, which had several fund-raising events.

Although it has been repainted, the school's infrastructure is badly dilapidated and its performance is still wanting because it recruits those students who have performed poorly in their primary education, especially from the Non-Formal Education programme of the Centre. For them it is a last-resort school, but they gain much more than an academic education.

The Centre has a Youth Programme, which is working closely with the school to establish vibrant student activities, such as a debating society, music and drama clubs, that do not presently exist. They are planning after-class discussions offering life-skills and spiritual nurturing. It is noteworthy that the Muslim population in the school is increasing and this is great, although it will present additional challenges. Although the school is now out of the woods, it still needs a lot of help to stand on its own and the Centre remains in charge to enable it to do so.

Chapter 23 – Strategic Planning

The Baseline Survey Report & New Programmes

The baseline survey report, which had been funded by Norwegian Church Aid (NCA), resulted in their giving financial support for new programmes of the Centre. At the beginning of her term of office the new Manager called together representatives of the local community, all staff members and members of the Board, with a representative of NCA to a meeting which lasted two days. She asked them all to consider, and to decide upon, the priorities of the Centre's work and they concluded that these were fourfold.

First, it was agreed that there should be a programme which would address the current high incidence of dropout from primary schools and therefore the serious rise in the number of street children. The "structural adjustment programme" of the World Bank had resulted in cost-sharing between parents and schools with the consequence that poor parents encountered difficulties in paying school fees.

Secondly, the appalling environmental conditions in which the people of the local area lived were obvious to all and we have already seen what these were. It was agreed that the Centre should try to improve these.

Thirdly, there was an urgent need to expand vocational training for the many high school dropouts. The clear need, which had been seen and addressed some thirty years earlier by Charles Tett, resulting in the establishment of CITC, still remained.

Finally, the widespread poverty pointed to a need for income-generating projects. The Home Industries project of the Centre and Maridadi Fabrics had symbolically made a dent in the tip of the iceberg. A differently pronged attack on this problem was now called for.

A New Strategy

Neither the report nor the stakeholders' meeting recommended relief-orientated activities.

The Parish Church was asked to take responsibility for feeding the old ladies who were living on the ground floor of Matumaini House. They would have available the rent then being earned by commercially letting the rooms originally intended for young girls in moral danger, who had been housed on the first floor of that building.

The second-hand clothes received from donors in the U.K. were directed to the Diocese for distribution, as was the assortment of food given by East African Industries and the congregations of other Anglican parishes. From 1989 relief through the Centre was phased out and development by the people of Pumwani was phased in. Such was the nature of the "paradigm shift" which we have referred to earlier.

Upgrading of staff and activities

At the time of her appointment Eunice was disappointed by the quality of staff working in the Community Centre. There appeared to have been no understanding of the special qualities required in these people nor of the professional training which was desirable.

In her first proposal to Norwegian Church Aid the Manager requested help in expanding the dressmaking school. She hoped to be able to appoint more qualified teachers and buy more sewing machines. Together with financial assistance from outside, Eunice planned that the pupils would themselves contribute by paying fees.

Likewise, it was suggested that the secretarial school should be expanded with a wider and more sophisticated syllabus, teaching shorthand, typing and office practice. The purchase of new typewriters was also required. Mr. Peter Njuguna joined the staff of the Centre as Head of the Secretarial College. He had recently qualified as a graduate at Kenyatta University with a B.A. degree in business studies and brought much higher standards to the organisation.

Financial Correction & Re-arrangement

Financial resources had become depleted and it is not difficult to see why that was. Equipment had become tired or fallen into disrepair and the upgrading of staff and renovation or replacement of essential equipment would bring higher standards to the Centre, which would in turn generate income. Whether or not Maridadi Fabrics was again producing a profit is not known but even if it did, it was no longer a part of the Centre and any surplus would not be received for Centre activities. Perhaps more serious was the way in which the slender income with which the Centre had been left was being syphoned off to pay recurrent expenses, including salaries, which should have properly been passed on to those who acquired the assets. Nice arrangement if you can get it and bearing in mind that most of the board was constituted by Parish officers, there would have been conflict of interest, calling in question the probity of the organisation and the Parish.

Corruption had crept into the sponsorship programme, which was no longer used exclusively to benefit the most-needy children in the community but also those known or related to Church members. It is noticeable that the Mill Hill Fathers themselves came to distribute their financial assistance to those in need. Could it be that the financial integrity of the Centre was in question in the selection of beneficiaries or did the Fathers themselves, as part of their own discipline, want or require to participate personally in this charitable distribution?

Eunice ensured that corruption in the sponsorship programme was eliminated and the programme was redesigned to enable school dropouts to acquire practical skills. The new education programmes covered language, mathematics and practical skills such as crafts, masonry, painting, carpentry, welding and mechanics. The Centre asked Kenyatta College and the Kenya Institute of Administration to assist in developing the curriculum for the school. Social workers were put in place to follow up individual children and the families from which they came.

Work took place on the Burns Memorial Hall and it was sub-divided to form additional classrooms. This development of the informal school attracted money into a building fund, which was used to provide non-vocational classrooms and at the same time facilitated the re-location of the Centre's offices.

To top it all, and most importantly, parents were empowered and involved. A parent-teachers' association included parents who represented different villages. The local community along with the teachers participated in the selection of children for the school.

We have seen, therefore, that the problems of the Centre were superficially a lack of finance and more immediately a cash-flow problem. In the short-term an attempt had been made to meet the material needs of the Parish, but this could not be continued indefinitely at the Centre's expense. More importantly, it was necessary to address the root cause of the problems. The vision and mission of the Centre had to be clarified and a return made to basic standards.

Eunice had made some far-reaching and robust decisions, which had inevitably brought her into conflict with those who were adversely affected, but they had rescued the Centre from inevitable bankruptcy and probable closure. They were decisions which had the support of stakeholders and staff, whom she carried with her. They went beyond financial liquidity: they embodied a vision of the future and took the Centre in a different direction, leading it into a challenging and successful long-term future. This change in direction, when it came to be recognised, was significantly entitled a "paradigm shift".

Deeper needs

New values required to be inculcated into the ethos of the Centre, its workers and its activities. As a Christian Community Centre those values should be set according to the teachings and the life of Christ. They would, nevertheless, be values acceptable to persons of any faith or, indeed, no faith at all. It was, moreover, agreed to request the Diocese to supply an evangelist, who would be paid by the Centre and who would take responsibility for the spiritual life of the Centre.

Part and parcel of those values would be the importance of raising the hopes and aspirations of the members of the community. A decision to abandon relief-related activities meant that the community itself required motivation into taking the action necessary to lift itself out of the morass, which it had come to accept.

Already, a dark cloud had appeared over the national and international scene, which would have a big effect on the nation's morale, not least that of Pumwani. The incidence of HIV/AIDS was growing in the community. An urgent need, which the Centre tried to meet, was to make people aware of the disease. They had to understand the ways in which it was spread and the need for treatment. The Centre staff became aware of HIV sufferers. They arranged for them to be linked to either Kenyatta Hospital or a Roman Catholic organisation for treatment.

Growing unemployment and frequent dropout from schools had resulted in a high incidence of crime. As an attempt to remedy the situation a very well qualified youth worker was appointed. The youth were involved in games such as football and vocational activities. When the environmental project began, they were recruited to take part in such work as cleaning and maintaining the lavatories. The resulting safety on the streets was a total transformation.

Water supply

All slum areas in Nairobi find a problem in securing a sure and sufficient supply of water and Pumwani was no exception. Water had been supplied to this location by Nairobi City Council, but it was inadequate and the water pipes required replacement. To deal with this Eunice had obtained from Danida, the international development agency of the Danish Government, a grant of Shs.4,000,000 for the improvement of Pumwani's infrastructure including the water supply.

It was, however, necessary to connect the new water-pipe infrastructure to the main twelve-inch supply main and this was not usually allowed in a slum area, where there would be nobody to pay for the water. When Eunice made her enquiries, she was told that only the Town Planner, Mr. Kuria WaGathoni, was able to give permission for such a connection and she was advised to "come early in the morning" if she wanted to see him. She did just that and, furthermore, persuaded him that against the loss of revenue for the enhanced supply of water the City Council would be able to offset the savings which would be achieved by fewer persons attending the health clinics.

Eunice's approach to the Nairobi City Council formed a fresh link between the Council and the Pumwani community. Apart from the all-important connection for the water project, this contact established a line of communication between the local community, the Community Centre and the City Council. Eunice believes that hitherto there had been little contact between the City Council and the members of the community for many years. Once this was opened up, it was a route or channel, which Eunice continued to use, indeed exploit, for the benefit of Pumwani and its people.

The environmental conditions

When visitors came from outside of Pumwani they were struck by the smell of open drains and rotting garbage. Heaps of rubbish were piled up between the houses. Eunice set about making the local people aware of the need to remedy this situation. She divided the area into grid-like sections and found volunteers who would undertake to keep their section clean. She worked with these people and, with money she raised from external sources, she bought the articles which these cleaning teams thought were necessary. She purchased Wellington boots, protective hand-wear and basic tools such as brooms, shovels and wheelbarrows. They encouraged one another to heap up the rubbish and when they were ready, Eunice arranged with the Nairobi City Council to send a lorry to collect it. When Pat visited the area, after this exercise had started, she was amazed by the change in the appearance of the streets.

Chapter 23 – Strategic Planning

Lamu Road - a current street scene without rubbish

The concerns of the community were then directed to the appalling condition of the eighteen lavatories, which had been there since the area was first set out for development. When they were newly constructed, they were not of a kind that would be acceptable today for public lavatories. There was no privacy. People would squat over an open drain in company with others.

Next to most of the lavatories were water standpipes, the sole source of water for the people living in Pumwani. The standpipes were, however, providing even less water than they had done when the Centre was first concerned about them in the 1960's. While their mothers waited for the water to drizzle out into their jerry cans, the children would play in the surrounding mud, an area cheek by jowl with the lavatories and faeces. A recipe, if ever there was one, for contamination, infection and sickness.

The Tudor Trust

It was at this time, soon after Eunice began work in Pumwani, that Pat and Jim made a visit to Kenya, visiting the Centre for the first time after leaving the country in 1980. The environmental project was already being discussed by the Centre staff and the community. All they needed was funding and Pat was able to put them in touch with Roger Northcott of the Tudor Trust, who happened to be in Kenya at that time and immediately made a visit and prepared a report for his organisation. The Tudor Trust provided £40,000 sterling for environmental improvement work. It included the rebuilding or refurbishment of the lavatory blocks, the installation of new water standpipes, and the construction of storm water drainage. There were plans to clear out and channel the open drains into a gridlock of ditches, which would carry the contents to the Nairobi River.

The blocked drains used to cause the water to spill over on to the footpaths between the houses, making them dangerous, so the footpaths and the potholes in the roads also required to be addressed. But equally well-trodden was the route which Eunice had made for herself to the City Hall, because once again she was in need of funds to employ Pumwani people to carry out the necessary work.

What was it that induced the Tudor Trust to go outside their normal remit to provide help for Pumwani? It was the empowerment of the community which they perceived to be of supreme value. The hygiene and environment were important, but the overriding consideration was the commitment to training young people to do work under the supervision of Nairobi City Council and, once completed, to monitor the facilities. Here, supremely, was an opportunity for Christian and Muslim to work together for the benefit of the community. Young people would be enabled, across the face of dialogue, to become involved themselves and to provide an enduring source of income generation. It was only after such dialogue and after full discussion, that agreement was reached to pay the youth and selected members of the community were chosen to do the work.

Tudor's hopes were realised when Roger returned with Pat on a subsequent visit to photograph the young people laying foundations for the storm water drains to be constructed in cement. Its insistence upon the keeping and producing of accounts was also respected and observed and the young people were taught the essence of community leadership and the need to become good leaders.

As we have seen, some of the young people took on the continuing jobs of cleaning and maintaining the refurbished lavatories taking small payments for their services, which remained income-generating projects. In return, they took pride in their cleanliness and when Roger took photographs of these edifices, their custodians were insistent that they themselves should pose for inclusion.

We found that amusing, as of course it was, but not realising just how important to the young people themselves was their new role. We shall look at this again when we come to consider the position of youth empowerment, because the staff of the Centre today see the Environmental Programme initiated by Eunice as one of the most outstanding empowerment initiatives for the disadvantaged youth. She it was who negotiated on their behalf with Nairobi City Council, to allow them officially to manage the facilities and she, herself, could not have envisaged at the time just how far-reaching the effect of that decision would be.

Pat showing Roger Northcott of Tudor Trust around Pumwani - 1998

Authors' Note: when Pumwani was set out originally in 1919 there were 12 blocks of lavatories & ablutions. This increased in subsequent years and when the Centre became involved, 18 blocks were renovated. The government has since been able to construct additional facilities and a few toilet blocks have been erected by private community groups for commercial purposes.

Stinking foul water from the lavatory in a pub

*Lavatory block 34 - Wanaume lipa 10 (Men Pay 10) –
"taking small payments for their services"*

Chapter 23 – Strategic Planning

Lavatory block 32 with its proud custodian

"In return, they took pride in their cleanliness and when Roger took photographs of these edifices, their custodians were insistent that they themselves should pose for inclusion"

Chapter 24 – The Paradigm Shift

Answers to prayer

Throughout her time as Manager, Eunice and the staff made the financial needs of the Centre a constant topic for prayer.

One Friday afternoon she was astonished to receive a telephone call from the Danish Embassy, asking her to receive a visit from the Danish Minister for International Development, with a television crew from Denmark, the following morning. Yes, a Saturday morning. Rapid telephone calls. Staff alerted to come in. Eunice telephoned the Centre's social workers requesting them to come in to pray and discuss what needs they should emphasise to the Danish delegation, who wanted to see the areas for which Danida, the Danish Government Aid Agency, had made their grant.

This unscheduled visit had come about because the Danish Minister had an appointment with President Daniel Arap Moi, which had been cancelled and then an appointment with the Kenyan Minister of Health, which was also cancelled. The resulting benefits of that unscheduled visit were inestimable. The international connection with Danida was strengthened and was supplemented by a link to MS Kenya, the Danish Volunteer Service, who sent volunteers and social workers to the Community Centre. They also sent professional sportsmen to train the young people in games. Finally, on the Monday following the Minister's visit, Eunice was to her amazement given a cheque by the Danish Embassy for Shs.256,000 so that she could pay her fees to do an MBA degree at the American University in Nairobi.

The unbelievable improvements in Pumwani brought the Community Centre publicity and approval. The self-help nature of the work became a model for the much younger Kibera slum and for the new shanti communities in the City Centre. Here was a model of empowerment spreading out beyond the small confines of Pumwani itself.

A new positive inter-faith relationship

The Pumwani community took ownership of the newly-restored lavatories and water standpipes and took pride in their new, clean surroundings. As a result, the Muslim inhabitants began to identify with St. John's Church, whom they saw represented by Eunice. On one occasion some Muslims planned to burn down the Christian church building of St. John's. However, some of their number protested that they should not burn down "Eunice's church". Ironically as an alternative target they selected the Roman Catholic Church in Nairobi South "B", which happened to be the area in which Eunice lived.

Very successful programmes, which were entirely new to the area, were the micro-finance programmes run by the Centre. At first the aim was to help small businesses to expand but they were difficult to organise and not always successful. So, they were curtailed and the appropriate staff concentrated on identifying and funding suitable women and advising and supporting them in small businesses.

The fees from the newly re-organised Secretarial College and the rental income from the Eastleigh flats were used to liquidate the Centre's debts and slowly the Centre began to make a surplus. The task given to her by the Archbishop was completed.

Eunice also trained the Board to know how it should function effectively. She developed a proper financial manual, human resources manual and a training policy manual.

When the Diocese realised that the Centre was no longer in debt but making money, they asked it to make a donation to the work of the Diocese. Eunice, however, declined insisting that it was, conversely, the responsibility of the Christian church to support the work of the Centre.

Time to move on

After eight years of hard work as Manager of the Centre, Eunice believed that something had gone out of the dynamism which had characterised her early years in that role. She had already begun the work of staff empowerment. Peter Njuguna had been employed as Head of the Secretarial College and from 1997 Eunice began to groom him as her deputy. She had started to hold staff meetings to discuss the Centre's programmes and these took place for two hours every Tuesday morning.

In April of the same year Eunice began to study for her Master's degree, which she completed in June 1998. This was a heavy programme with the classes running from 5 pm to 9.30 pm every week-day and 9 am to 1 pm every Saturday.

In December 2001 she became aware of an advertisement for the post of Programme Manager by Skills for Southern Sudan, an organisation which sought to equip suitably qualified and able people from the South with experience and training to take up responsible positions in the New Sudan, if, as and when that might be created. She knew immediately that this was the task which God was calling her to do; she collected the application forms the following day and submitted them on the 13th December and she heard on the 14th that she had been successful.

When she told the Board of her new appointment, Eunice recommended Njuguna as the new Manager. She left St. John's Community Centre at the end of February 2002, with a staff, which was skilled with training and relevant experience. She had established exciting programmes and bequeathed a solvent Centre with a balanced budget.

The "Paradigm Shift"

The impecunious condition of the Centre which she inherited on her appointment, stripped of its assets and burdened with debt, opened the way for drastic change. So, it was during her time as Manager that a paradigm shift took place in the aims and activities of the Centre – the paradigm shift to which we have referred in an earlier chapter in greater detail. It moved from a relief agency to a community development agency. She found a Centre, which in her words "was not working with people but for people". Eunice was convinced that continuity and sustainability of development in the community required the goodwill of the inhabitants and their governing bodies. This would only come about from community ownership. This clear policy and these new working methods also gave confidence to the donors, who were supporting the Centre's work.

It was the experience of Eunice that as the community was given the right to choose the changes to be made and to participate themselves in these programmes, the rate of progress within the community itself accelerated. A noticeable drop in youth crime and drug-taking came with community ownership and participation in reforms. Water pipes and other equipment were not stolen. Negative social attitudes, demonstrated at the beginning of Eunice's time in Pumwani, were often due to people's frustration in life generally and these attitudes changed noticeably as they sensed that they were appreciated and loved by the Centre staff, something they experienced as they met and planned together.

Eunice instituted a time each Monday when staff would meet to pray for the work of the Centre. There were other ad hoc times of fasting and prayer and these activities brought cohesion among the staff and a high level of commitment to their tasks and determination in their work. Answers to prayer included the acquisition of a very useful and expensive van in 1994 and new sewing machines and computers.

Continuing Opposition

The opposition which Eunice encountered soon after her arrival, never really went away. Her uncompromising honesty and high standards of integrity were bound to create enemies. Her introduction of Christian values and lifestyle and the rooting out of corruption resulted in personal attack, criticism and complaint. Undoubtedly, a certain amount of jealousy arose from the success resulting from her honest practices and clear-thinking strategies.

Allegations were made that Eunice and her colleagues were using the Centre's money for their own gain. On one such occasion, Eunice was summoned to a meeting by the District Officer and at that meeting leading Muslims alleged corrupt behaviour on the part of the Centre staff. Fortunately, Eunice had already purchased an expensive accounting computer package and was able to demonstrate that the monetary grant of the Tudor Trust had been fully utilised for the water project. Following this explanation, a Muslim woman present at the meeting decided to own up and she confessed that she had attended meetings at which she had been urged to make false accusations against Eunice.

Eunice's motives were also suspected by persons in authority. While the repairs to the lavatories and water supplies were taking place, the local Member of Parliament and the local City Councillor both opposed this work because they believed that Eunice had political aspirations and that her purpose was simply to seek popularity in the community.

When Eunice first came to the Centre as a new manager, she was anxious that Christian values, to which the Centre was committed, should be transparently adhered to. Before her arrival the staff had indeed practised some deception. They experienced pressure from their families and succumbed by supplying them with benefits in kind such as rice and other food. This was another reason why Eunice was disinclined to continue with the relief programmes which had made these fraudulent practices possible.

The "mind-set" created by poverty

It was the experience of Eunice and the new staff that it was very difficult to eradicate poverty. It sometimes appeared that those whom the Centre was trying to help, strangely wanted to remain in a state of deprivation. She was led to the conclusion that the Centre required more than money and resources to confront poverty. As she saw it, it would be a moral, even spiritual exercise "fighting out" poverty as a disease. This, she believed. was the difference between the approach of Christian organisations and that of secular international bodies in their face-to-face battle against poverty. That moral and spiritual battle would be carried out by empowering the community, persuading it to recognise and abhor what it saw and to set about eradicating poverty and deprivation itself.

Eunice's perception of the perpetuation of poverty by a mind-set is not without a sound basis. Years of living in poverty can cause stress and other negative emotions such as anxiety and fear. These negative emotions will in turn guide people in the making of decisions and those decisions will determine whether they can climb out of poverty. They may be reluctant to make a decision which involves risk. They may look only to the short-term and see only the need for day-to-day survival rather than investment of time and effort in the long-term, such as the benefit of education and life-time change. There is a saying "Better the devil you know than the devil you don't know". Vulnerable people may feel safer in habitual behaviour rather than goal-directed ambition. Perhaps that is why only five years ago more than 1.5 billion people were still living on less than $1 per day.

The inhabitants of Pumwani are largely women and girls and, unlike their male counterparts, they have lived their lives almost exclusively in Pumwani village pursuing their time-honoured occupations as sex workers and beer-brewers. For them to step out of this lifestyle into a brave new world would demand a psychological leap. It is, however, a leap they must take before they can climb out of the poverty which is all that they and their parents have known. The creation of Maridadi Fabrics, for instance, did enable the women employed there to make the change because they could continue to live in Pumwani, with no travel expenses. They had their families and neighbours to care for their children and their work-colleagues were well known to them. More especially, they were treated with concern because the factory existed for them and their welfare – they did not exist for the factory.

Whether we agree with Eunice's diagnosis that this mind-set is a moral and spiritual ailment or whether we see it as a psychological barrier which inhibits deprived people from stepping out of their deprivation, we realise that it is a mind-set which might just be overturned with help and encouragement, a process requiring empowerment of and within the community.

The psychological effect of "Livelihood Training" given to the Youth Groups

Immediately following the millennium, the Centre became heavily involved setting up and developing "Youth Groups" to maintain the refurbished lavatories. We have noted that it was Eunice who persuaded Nairobi City Council to allow the young people of Pumwani to manage the toilets and to be involved with the environmental development. After she had left, the Community Centre continued to work with the Groups and their members to the extent of influencing their constructive households and encouraging community and political participation.

Importantly, the Centre found it necessary to convince the Group members of their self-worth and the need for them to acknowledge their skills and to discover their capacities. It was a process of building self-confidence. The Chair of the "Young Mothers' Group" lacked confidence in public speaking and doubted that she had any attributes to offer, which might be of any value to herself or to society. After joining a savings group and interacting with the other members, she gained confidence and found herself elected as the chair. To use her words: "This was further enhanced by the livelihoods training (given by the Centre) that reinforced the idea that I had a lot of capacities and resources which I can use to improve my life and the lives of my relations."

It was the same with a member of the DIGO youth group, who had been an alcoholic addict, spending most of her time on the streets before joining the group. After undertaking the Livelihood Training of the Centre, she now attends all meetings of the group and regularly goes for her prayers five times daily in accordance with her Muslim faith. Past challenges had produced in many people of Pumwani a warped view of themselves, leading them to believe there was nothing they could do to change their situation.

A report written for the Centre evaluating the Livelihood Training programme describes this condition. It cites, in support, a book "Walking with the Poor" edited by Bryant Myers[10] which supports the need to

---

[10] Myers, B. Walking with the poor. Principles and practices of transformational development. 2011. Orbis Books. NY.

establish self-esteem in those whose estimation of themselves has been adversely affected by poverty. People living in poverty are vulnerable to a web of lies, which have grown up over many years in their minds or been induced externally and they struggle to break free from their condition. They wrongly accept that they are impotent to change the situation and resort to heavy drinking and other forms of temporary relief, which is harmful, serving only to exacerbate their problem.

Furthermore, a lifetime of suffering, deception and exclusion is internalised by the poor in a way that results in them no longer knowing who they truly are, or why they were created. They are led to believe that they are valueless, without gifts, talents and abilities and it is specifically the understanding and recognition of those attributes within themselves which the Livelihood Training restores. Accepting that they do possess these attributes will help disempowered people find and use their gifts and propel them into a life of well-being.

Independent assessors evaluating the Livelihood Training given by the Centre in their Integrated Youth Development Programme (sponsored by Tearfund[11]) walked into a house of one of the Young Mothers' Group where they were meeting. They were immediately impressed by the atmosphere that greeted them. There was a very joyful mood, punctuated by laughter as the women engaged in their weekly activity of remitting savings, drawing loans and catching up on events of the preceding week. This communicated strong interpersonal relationships between the members to express themselves even in the presence of the evaluators.

Sammy Kymana

We cannot move on from the youth programme interventions without mentioning Sammy Kymana. He became a participant in this programme around the year 2000. He is someone with the condition Albinism and when joining the programme, he was rather shy and conscious of his condition. He was among the pioneers of the programme which became fully fledged in the year 2000.

---

[11] Tearfund is a large Christian Charity & Aid agency, based in the UK.

Sammy became very active and took part in numerous empowering trainings, becoming a key facilitator for the weekly youth Coffee Bar. This is a forum that brought together over 100 young people to discuss their dreams and aspirations. His active engagement earned him a scholarship for a diploma course.

Some years later, he assisted a couple from the UK to settle as volunteers. At the centre they were impressed with his character and funded his university education, something which he had been praying for. Sammy studied hard and graduated. All the while, he was an active member of St. John's Church Pumwani and led the drama unit.

Sammy was among the first of his peers to marry in Church. This impressed his sponsor Jacky Batten who flew out from the UK to witness it. When Sammy and his wife had their first baby girl, they had no doubt about the name – they named her "Jacky".

Sammy went on to get a great job with the government. He is the Head of Team in the Department of Immigration, a very senior position. He was therefore able to sponsor himself for a Master's degree and has since graduated.

Sammy is a real inspiration to other young people and to the Community in general. Today he gives back to the Community by helping them obtain essential services where he works. This includes arranging for street children to obtain their entitlements such as national identity cards. He has been instrumental even in organising the availability of some Government services from the Community Centre, such as the issuance of certificates of good conduct for young women, who are frightened of going to a government department. Without such a certificate they would be unable to secure employment.

Sammy is a beacon of light and the Centre is very proud of him. He has accepted his albinism and by making others aware of it, he helps to reduce any stigma attached to the condition.

Chapter 24 – The Paradigm Shift

Sammy Kymana –
"a real inspiration to other young people"

The Spiritual Dimension

There is a way out of the psychological impact of poverty but is there a spiritual aspect which requires to be addressed, as Eunice and her staff believed? The Centre, a Christian organisation, seeks to achieve a spiritual transformation by enhancing the spiritual assets and capital of the poor following its Livelihood Training. The Centre's catchment area in Pumwani is almost equally populated by Christian and Muslim communities and it is the hope that with the alleviation of poverty, members of the groups and inhabitants of the community, whatever their beliefs, will experience a new freedom from the oppression and restriction to which poverty had subjected them and a corresponding enrichment of their spiritual faith, whatever that might be. Some young members of Majengo Digital, Pumwani United and Digo groups indicated their commitment to their roles in their respective churches.

The current Director of the Centre, Njuguna, who has been in office since Eunice's departure, does not share Eunice's belief that poverty and deprivation are spiritually induced. He does, however, see that lifting those who suffer from poverty and deprivation, out of that condition, can produce spiritual awareness and spiritual growth. The Centre has witnessed to the community around it what it understands to be the real basis of life and has extended the hand of friendship to all its inhabitants, whatever their religious faith or denomination.

In consequence the youth groups who have found help and transformation from the Livelihood Training programme, whether they be Christian or Muslim, exhibit a deeper commitment in their religious observance. Negativity is replaced by positivity in a holistic way, with more energy going into matters both material and spiritual.

Eunice: A personal appreciation

It was Pat who first met Eunice at the Community Centre, when she visited there for the first time after we had left Kenya. Pat was enthusiastic about what she had found at the Centre and the transformation which had taken place. She said that Eunice would be sending a vehicle to collect us so that we could share with her our earlier involvement and learn at first-hand what was being done. Eunice has since told us that that first meeting with us was an encouragement to her in her work because she properly understood for the first time how the Centre had begun and its aims and purposes at that time.

Our first return visit coincided, by chance, with a visit being made by a representative of Water Aid. We were amazed at the searching and intrusive questions being asked by the representative of that body as to the involvement of the local community in the improvements being carried out. We realised that this was normal and in principle we have every sympathy with user involvement. Jim was used to it in the voluntary housing activities with which he had been involved in England. We were, nevertheless, a trifle embarrassed by what we thought to be aggressive questioning of somebody who had clearly demonstrated herself to be a champion of community involvement and representation. Eunice quietly and patiently gave Water Aid the assurances they needed, but she did not receive the funding from them for which she had hoped.

We have now known Eunice and her family for many years. She loves a challenge but in taking on the job with Skills for Southern Sudan, she could not have foreseen what a difficult task it would be. Not being a Sudanese was in itself a disadvantage. All African countries are fiercely nationalistic and she had to win the confidence of the leaders of the Sudan People's Liberation Army (SPLA), because the country was then still in the grip of civil war. Her visionary and organisational skills impressed her new bosses and her loyalty and dedication to the organisation for which she worked is obvious for all to see. It is no wonder that she was eventually appointed to be its Director.

Like St. John's Community Centre, Skills for Southern Sudan was no sinecure. She required diplomacy in maintaining good relationships with the political leaders. She needed persistence and foresight in raising funds from demanding and high-powered donors. Not least it called for considerable self-sacrifice when the time came to relocate to Juba, involving a large measure of privation and separation from her family, friends and fellow countrymen. When the time came for her to leave

Skills for Southern Sudan, she left behind the legacy of a successful and well-managed organisation, which made an undoubted and significant contribution to the civil society of South Sudan.

When we left Kenya in 1980, we left a Community Centre which was struggling to keep its head above water. The situation, as we have seen, got worse rather than better. When we returned some nine years later, we found an organisation with a new vision, a new strategy, new values, new staff and new hope. It was the faith, ability, courage, hard work and determination of one woman, Eunice Kamau, which brought this about with her Chairman the Rev'd Samuel Nderitu and in later years with her well-chosen successor Peter Njuguna, who has built upon the new foundation which she laid.

Peter Njuguna

Peter was no stranger to Pumwani when he came to work at St. John's Community Centre. He had been supported throughout his secondary education by his uncle who has been an Imam at the Pumwani mosque since the 1970s. He trained in Business Studies and obtained a degree in Business Administration. When he came to work at Pumwani it was as an untrained teacher at St. John's High School. He taught business subjects and was made head of the Business Education Department. When the post of Principal of the High School became vacant, he was promoted to that position.

Eunice was impressed with Njuguna throughout his time with the High School and she promoted him to become her Deputy Director and trained him in that role. She told Jim that if she were to take the position with Skills for Southern Sudan, she had somebody ready to take over her position at the Centre and, upon her unqualified recommendation, Peter was appointed the next Director of the Centre in 2001, a position which he still holds today.

Part VI – "The Bigger Picture"

Chapter 25 – HIV/AIDS Orphans & Vulnerable Children

Just put yourself for a moment in this position. You receive the news that your mother has died; your father had predeceased her two years earlier. You are eighteen years old and are still at school. You have three siblings, all at school. You are not only an orphan; you are a CHH – the abbreviation given for Child Head of Household.

What does that mean? You have no means of support and neither do your three siblings. There are no savings upon which you can draw, no welfare state upon which you can call for support. Further schooling for you is not an option. Forget your aspirations as a teenager; forget your ambitions for a full and successful life. It is all now a matter of survival; survival not only of yourself but of your three brothers and sisters for whom you are now suddenly and frighteningly responsible.

What are you to do? Yes, you have, first and foremost, to provide food. You all have to eat. If you are in the rural areas, you may have a shamba or kitchen garden, where, given time, seeds and the right weather, you might succeed in feeding the family. If, however, you are living in an urban situation, you are unlikely to have this facility. Even if it is possible, you will struggle to grow sufficient to provide a balanced diet, let alone raise a meagre cash income to pay your siblings' school fees and clothe them.

So, you are not only an orphan but also a vulnerable child. Vulnerability comes in different shapes and sizes for a child household living on their own. Not everybody is kind and helpful to those less fortunate than themselves. Some might be compassionate: others, however, are opportunistic. So, children in this kind of need are often exploited, used as cheap labour, if nothing worse.

You are not, however, alone. You are just one of 110,000 households where there is no adult in occupation or to give support. Due to no fault of your own, you and your siblings are hungry, destitute and without any real hope. Worse than that, you are stigmatised. Your parents died of HIV/AIDS and that is a cause for shame. There is little understanding of the disease and its causes. There is not only ignorance but also a lack of sympathy for those who suffer as a result of this disease.

Pumwani

St. John's Community Centre, working in Pumwani, was soon made very well aware of this situation in the homes and lives of the people there. The lifestyle there made the inhabitants more susceptible to HIV/AIDS than in other areas. Prostitution is still rampant in the location and ignorance or reluctance to have safe sex make the women more vulnerable. So, when the pandemic struck, the Centre had to grapple with the social problems peculiar to it, not least the orphans and vulnerable children who are left behind. Is it any wonder that the Centre workers soon built up considerable experience in facing these problems as they went about the daily work of the Centre? This experience soon developed into expertise and, given the compassion undergirding their work, they reached out for solutions to the considerable social problems which they now found on their doorstep.

Partnerships & the Larger Scenario

It is not surprising that, given this expertise, understanding and caring compassion, the Centre soon found partners to work with it in seeking solutions to this enormous problem. This was important. It is one thing to have all the know-how; it is quite another to have the financial and other resources to apply it.

For many years St. John's Community Centre have had a long-term partnership with the German charity Kindernothilfe (KNH), which in English means 'Children's Emergency Help'. It was founded in 1959 and is currently one of the largest Christian organisations in Europe focused on children. The overall goal of KNH is to achieve a world in which children and young people can live a life of human dignity, develop personal talents and, together with their families and communities, take their development into their own hands. KNH supports more than

600,000 children and young people in 29 countries in Africa, Asia, Latin America and Eastern Europe.

Funding came through KNH from the United States and, more specifically, from the President's Emergency Plan For AIDS Relief (PEPFAR). It was channelled through an organisation called the New Partners' Initiative, which had been developed to expand the reach of HIV and AIDS prevention and care programmes. It provided funding opportunities to organisations like St. John's Community Centre, which had an established presence in local communities but no prior experience of managing United States Government funds. It all sounds very bureaucratic and demanding. It certainly was demanding. The Centre, however, derived help from New Partners' Initiative in building its own capacity, enabling it to implement high quality HIV and AIDS programmes and the size of the financial support for those programmes justified the demands which were made.

This funding found by KNH and the Centre was given to support a much larger programme than that which pertained in Pumwani. It started on the 1st December 2008 and was to last for three years. It was widely spread geographically, embracing different ethnic or tribal groups, extending over five Kenya provinces and implemented in 31 districts.

Small Community Projects

To enable the Centre to implement the programme over such a vast distance, it appointed 29 Small Community Projects. This fitted in admirably with the way in which the Centre would want to work. It was essential to involve local people to participate in the project and to have hands-on control and supervision of it. This would ensure that it enjoyed local support: it also dealt with the issue of stigma, which we have seen characterised the attitude of others towards AIDS sufferers. Any feelings of stigma towards the children or their deceased parents was immediately confronted and dealt with.

Local knowledge would also be important when it came to revolving funds and the beneficiaries who would seek loans. Local expertise would be invaluable in appointing committee members and obtaining their active involvement. If the benefit of this programme was to endure beyond the three-year period then it would be up to local people to secure resources, both human and financial, to ensure its longevity. Most importantly, the Centre was primarily concerned, as it always is, to empower others and it was in line with their overarching purpose that they should enlist others in their mission of bearing each other's burdens.

The Community Centre acknowledges the value which it obtained from working with its long-standing partner KNH and their regular field visits. These enabled the Centre to spot unnoticed problems or shortcomings at the community level and to review what steps had been taken to overcome these during the monitoring and evaluation system put in place by the New Partners' Initiative. Both the Centre and KNH benefited from New Partners' Initiative's Technical Assistance and the Centre was pleased to introduce new standards and operational manuals which it learnt: indeed, it applied them across the whole of the Centre's work, not just this project.

Furthermore, the learning and improving process cascaded down to the 29 Small Community Projects, who were of course the local partners responsible for implementing the project. It was a capacity-building journey all the way, which began at the appraisal level where the local bodies' capacity strengths, or lack of them, were assessed. Any gaps which were identified, were quickly addressed and rectified. The training provided by the Centre included the care and support to be given to orphans and vulnerable children, child protection guidelines, stigma and discrimination guidelines, how to motivate volunteers and how to provide psycho-social support.

The project was not only extensive in area; it was also comprehensive in the way in which it sought to solve the complex problems experienced by the children and young people. Six basic programmes or interventions were provided to achieve this and some or all of these were used with different children as appropriate, or as they were willing to take part.

Apprenticeships

The first programme targeted the needy 15 to 17-year-old teenagers who were out of school and did not stand any chance of joining the formal education system in future. They were carefully vetted before being placed with local artisans to undertake a course of their choice for a minimum period of six months, after which they would automatically join the job market.

Jacob Karani was identified by a volunteer who raised a concern about him. His father had died when he was eleven and his mother was unemployed. The small income she derived from working as a casual labourer was insufficient to pay his school fees and meet his other basic needs and those of his siblings. So, he had dropped out of school at Standard V.

The volunteer recognised that Jacob had a strong will to be independent and to support his mother in raising the other children. During the career awareness training, Jacob chose to pursue a course in welding and was placed under a welding artisan. Following the successful completion of his course, he was taken on by the artisan as an employee. As a result, he can now meet his basic needs and comfortably support those of his family without much struggle.

Valary Ouma can tell a similar story, although she calls herself unique. She is the fifth-born in a family of seven children. Her father died, leaving her mother, who was sickly, to care for this large family and when Valary was fourteen, she had to drop out of school to look after her. To earn some money to take care of the family, Valary would do casual jobs but the money would barely make ends meet.

She was recruited to pursue an apprenticeship and decided to train as a mechanic, an unusual course for a girl. She trained for a year with an artisan, who retained her following completion of her training. The income she receives enables her to support her family more easily than before. She happily says "I am now being called a unique mechanic girl".

It is a fact that, after completion of their training, many of the trainees are retained by their artisans. Others become self-employed or find employment. An evaluation from eleven of the Small Community Projects revealed a high success rate of this programme, ninety-eight per cent of the apprentices completing their training and an average of seventy-five per cent of those finding immediate employment, while another two per cent start their own businesses. The apprenticeship scheme has been cost-effective, the apprentices usually completing their training within a year and starting to earn some form of income even before they complete. As a result, most of them can earn sufficient to get their siblings back into school and provide for their basic needs including school fees and materials.

Revolving Funds

There is a second main programme of this project, which aims to empower orphans and vulnerable children economically. It is a Revolving Fund scheme, which works on the basis that whilst poor families have insufficient money with which to achieve anything or even to make ends meet, they can pool their savings and collectively their wealth will help them do things which they could not do on their own. Micro-credit schemes have worked well in Kenya, but they are often denied to those most in need of them.

The project, therefore, made available a Revolving Fund scheme, which was implemented by 21 of the Small Community Projects who were partners. It sought to promote the economic empowerment of the guardians of orphans and vulnerable children, to help them meet the needs of the children in their care. Some of the Small Community Projects used this Fund to strengthen already existing savings and loan groups. Others initiated new groups whereby guardians were carefully vetted to ensure that the group members met established criteria of socio-economic vulnerability.

Guardians usually started with saving small weekly amounts of Shs10 (10p) to Shs100 (£1), depending upon the members' financial capabilities and a general consensus reached within each group. Gradually they started to borrow small loans from their own savings. This enabled them to develop a savings and loan culture and promoted cohesiveness within the group. The next step would be to obtain a "table loan" from other members of the group.

The guardians were helped to develop group "constitutions" comprising rules and regulations to govern the savings and loan activities of the members. The role of the Small Community Projects would be crucial to this. It would also help establish sound record keeping ensuring that the concept of the Revolving Fund was properly understood. Vetting criteria for group members were also adapted to meet the local situation, so that the most-needy guardians were targeted to join. A prolonged orientation and "savings only" first phase, followed by a gradual increase in loan amounts could help guardians develop business skills and confidence, minimizing the risks involved in loan taking. Finally, training in business skills and thorough preparation and vetting of business plans were vital to prevent guardians running into debt.

After a period of five to six months, "mature" groups would have developed sufficient experience in handling their funds and were provided by the project with a "seed fund" which enabled the guardians to increase their borrowing capacity. They were then able to access bigger loans to start or scale up their businesses. At the same time guardians underwent training in the management of revolving funds and business skills to equip them to run businesses, keep records, scrutinise business plans and ensure that loan contracts fixed repayments.

In the closing months of the project, gaps were identified and addressed in the expectation that all parties would remain accountable to each other and that the schemes should remain accessible to the guardians after the project ended. With that in view, memoranda of understanding were signed with each of the Small Community Projects, involving also the provincial government administration and guardians who will oversee the further running and management of the revolving funds in the communities.

To give some idea of the scope of this programme, some 264 guardian groups were formed during the life of the project serving a total of 4,538 group members. Only a very small percentage of these received training in management of revolving funds and business skills. They all benefited from access to group savings loans and about seventy per cent of them went on to access seed fund loans. In all, about half of the guardians were expected to benefit from an improved income by the end of the project and more than 17,000 orphans or vulnerable children benefited indirectly as members of the guardians' households.

In effect, most orphans and vulnerable children were economically better off. Most older teenagers who would not be able to benefit from further education in the schools and their families were empowered economically from the apprenticeship scheme. The basic needs of younger ones and others were better met through their guardians by the revolving loan scheme.

Sensitisation of the Community

In this project the Centre saw the fulfilment of one of its objectives, namely the economic empowerment of those whom it seeks to serve. Furthermore, through the Self Help Group it also achieved another major objective, supporting no less than 87,390 orphans and vulnerable children through education by providing basic learning materials, education scholarships and economic empowerment of their guardians to provide their basic needs.

However, we know that "man does not live by bread alone" and children's needs are deeper than food in their tummies, clothes on their backs or even the education of their minds. Children deprived of their parents need care and protection, love and help. In order to protect child headed households, the Community Centre used a community based fostership approach. The foster parents were volunteers and how, one wonders, were volunteers persuaded to take on such an onerous, long-term and time-consuming responsibility?

Whilst writing this book, we have watched several instalments of a UK television programme entitled "Corrie goes to Kenya". It is a documentary demonstrating a two-week visit to Kenya by the cast of Coronation Street, the long-running soap from the North of England. The cast and their supporting team went to Kenya to select and train Africans to present theatre shows, demonstrating the dangers of HIV/AIDS and suggesting ways of preventing or reducing the incidence of the disease. Following the performance, there was to be a discussion. They used a combined bus and mobile theatre presented by Daniel Craig, the James Bond actor, complete with the high-tech gear one associates with Bond's vehicles and were amazed when an audience of 850 turned up for the open-air performance at Msambweni on the Kenya coast.

It was precisely the same kind of media used by St. John's Community Centre, to sensitise the communities in which this project was to be launched. The Centre facilitated the training of twenty-four theatre groups in what was called "participatory education theatre" and some 327 young people took part. Following the training, they presented 438 shows within the three-year life of the project and in the course of these, they developed messages with different themes on community fostering of orphans and vulnerable children. These shows were given in strategic locations in the community, such as the chief's baraza, churches or marketplaces.

Christine Adhiambo, a 45-year-old widow, attended one of these shows in her local church and when she went home, she had taken on the burden of fostering two child headed households realising the need for her to take care of these children. It was a responsibility which she pursued consistently, visiting the two households on a weekly basis and, at the same time, providing spiritual support and encouragement. She also gave them advice on health matters, trained them how to keep the house clean and assisted them to do household chores, such as washing clothes. She assisted in farming and ensured that the households had kitchen gardens. Her major achievement, she claims, was to establish poultry farming for both households. From this the children could raise a small income which they used to buy food and other small needs. She also used her contacts, sourcing old clothes from well-wishers. She even obtained funding from a politician for one of the children's college fees.

A total of 2,600 orphans and vulnerable children were fostered, almost half as many again as were planned at the commencement of the project. In one of the Small Community Projects, the foster parents have formed a group which meets once a month to share experiences and challenges and provide mutual support and supervision. In other instances, foster parents have been able to mobilise resources from the wider community to provide the orphans and vulnerable children with additional food, clothing, school fees and scholastic materials. Community members have also helped repair and improve the children's home. These examples demonstrate how community ownership and sustainability has been promoted and achieved in the AIDS crisis and seemingly catastrophic effects have been ameliorated.

Child Protection

Foster parents have acted as protective barriers to the households ensuring the children were not abused or exploited and that they attended school. Children without parental protection were very vulnerable to predators from their communities. Their lack of money meant that they had no bargaining power and were exploited by those wanting to use their services. Sometimes they were sexually abused.

Legislation existed to establish Area Advisory Councils, the purpose of which was to provide protection in cases such as these. They did not, however, exist everywhere and even where they did, they were not always effective. The Centre, therefore, through the project, enabled the Small Community Projects to identify existing governmental structures for child protection in places where they existed and to assess their capacities, because some were found to be dormant. It even created new Councils where they were non-existent or new child protection committees where they were ineffective,

It was the function of these Area Advisory Councils to fight for child rights, identifying cases of child rights violation in the community. It was their responsibility to refer such cases appropriately and subsequently follow them up to ensure that they had been solved. These Councils are usually chaired by the Area Chief but also comprise community members and representatives of institutional stakeholders.

The project arranged for all the structures, whether they already existed or were newly created, to receive comprehensive training on child protection issues and this was conducted or chaired by the District Children Officer appointed by the Ministry of Gender or Social Services. The training focused on child abuse and how to detect it: it also dealt with procedures, such as the formation of linkages and networking. The Area Advisory Councils and child protection committees developed action plans to respond to and report identified cases.

As a result of all this activity, prompted by the Community Centre if not driven by it, an amazing number of 5,691 cases of child rights violation or neglect were identified by the Area Advisory Councils or the child protection committees, who themselves addressed them or, where this was not possible, referred them to an appropriate legal authority.

Health and Hygiene

Orphans and Vulnerable Children required guidance in safeguarding their health and maintaining hygienic living conditions and the project sought to provide instructions and help at a local level, so that it would be easily accessible to them. There were several ways in which this was achieved, and one very impressive programme relied again upon the enlistment of volunteers. It trained 648 volunteers as Community Health Workers in primary health care and more specifically in areas of hygiene, disease prevention, nutrition, immunisation and family planning. After their training, these volunteer workers were each assigned a maximum number of ten households, which they visited at least monthly to support them through the skills and knowledge which they had acquired. The Small Community Projects also linked these Community Health Workers with local health facilities to which they could refer individual cases of illness beyond their capabilities.

Through these Community Health Workers, needy families would be encouraged to establish kitchen gardens to improve their nutrition and to adopt domestic hygiene and sanitation practices to reduce infections. Indeed, some of the Community Health Workers got to work with a jembe helping to dig pit latrines for needy households.

These Community Health Workers brought back with them to their communities, fundamental life skills which would enure not only to the benefit of the children and families in their care, but to themselves, their own families and all with whom they would be in contact for the rest of their lives. It was an intervention which will hopefully outlast the project itself and continue indefinitely for the communities in which they operated.

Four village pharmacies were also established, which made drugs available at subsidised prices or free of charge. These were either stationary or mobile. Where stationary pharmacies existed, Community Health Workers could refer cases in need of treatment. In the mobile form, the Community Health Workers were provided with a small drug supply in the form of a medical kit which they took with them on their household visits for treating the children. Akin to this was a specific provision for treating jiggers in areas where there was a high prevalence of jigger infestation. Community Health Workers were themselves provided with kits which they used to treat households infested with jiggers and to prevent re-occurrence.

Psycho-social support

It was particularly pleasing to note that this project was not only extensive in its geographic and ethnic outreach but at the same time intensive in its holistic approach. It would be easy and tempting in cases of extreme physical hardship, such as hunger or exclusion from school for lack of school fees, to concentrate only on the relief of those physical or material needs.

However, the negative impact of HIV/AIDS on children's development and their emotional wellbeing was understood and also addressed. Long-term illness and death of a parent are traumatic events and the stigma and discrimination associated with this disease, and not infrequently social exclusion, will often leave children showing signs of withdrawal, depression or aggression. They might develop eating, sleeping or learning disorders.

We have seen how the foster-ship scheme was aimed at offering domestic care and affection within their homes. Children, however, spend much of their time in school and caretakers and teachers often fail to detect the symptoms of psychological distress, sometimes ignoring or punishing the child in response to behaviour changes they see.

The project therefore sought to provide support at school through the medium of school clubs. It trained club "patrons" to run the clubs and co-ordinate activities at their weekly meetings, providing a guidebook for their assistance. The local Small Community Projects negotiated with the Ministry of Education and head teachers and in all these Projects school "peer educators" were selected and trained to identify the problems of their peers and to give them support. These clubs were opened-up to membership by other children to avoid further stigma and discrimination. They provided specifically peer-to-peer counselling and club experience sharing sessions, as well as more general activities such as inter-club competitions or sports, drama, debates or devotional meetings. These helped to boost the children's self-esteem and self-confidence.

Other young people, who were no longer attending school and who had been helped with vocational skills training, also had the opportunity of psycho-social support through one of 61 newly formed community clubs, meeting monthly. There they could share experiences, discuss problems and give each other mutual support.

Over 30,000 children and young people benefited from psycho-social support through the clubs, either school clubs or community clubs and more than 780 teachers or community representatives were trained as club patrons, supported by 1,100 peer educators. Stigma and discrimination reduced as a consequence, alongside an improved sense of belonging and inclusion.

The children developed self-esteem and confidence. Some were helped through the grieving process to deal with the loss of their parents. In fact, everybody benefited because an interesting by-product of the clubs was the platform they created for comprehensive sex education. Stakeholders' forums were held by the Small Community Projects at the end of the scheme in the hope that ownership of the clubs will be maintained in the future.

Continuing effectiveness

The good news is that the Small Community Projects continued to operate after the end of the three-year contract period. For a while the Centre continued to monitor their activities. Indeed, more than half of them have been able to access other funds and resources to continue the work. They have achieved this, partly through the support which they have derived from the contacts obtained through the Centre and partly by virtue of their own enhanced capacity developed by them during the life of the project.

At the same time the Centre Committee which was co-ordinating the Small Community Projects continued to meet regularly while performing its monitoring role. This caring attitude and persistence on the part of the Centre, along with successful impact of the initial project, rightly produced its own rewards. The Centre itself received funding for another three-year phase, enabling it to establish ten new Small Community Projects.

Chapter 26 - HIV/AIDS "Springs of Life"

If readers found encouragement from, and could sympathise with, the psycho-social aspect of the project for Orphans and Vulnerable Children, they will hopefully understand the value of this other project, which St. John's Community Centre pursued contemporaneously to complement its relief work. This project took a further step away from the relief of physical and material disadvantage created by the HIV/AIDS pandemic. It looked at the root causes for the rapid spread of the disease and sought to find a Christian solution to the ongoing devastation which it was causing.

Its purpose was two-fold. It challenged the Churches in their attitude towards victims of the disease and it endeavoured, through the Churches, to move society forward to seek prevention rather than cure. The Centre reached into its Christian roots to engage society in a spiritual battle against the forces which have wrought havoc in this developing country by this devastating disease.

Stigma

One would expect the Church in Kenya to have adopted a strong line in its attitude towards HIV/AIDS. It had always taken a strong stance in relation to sexual immorality, including pre-marital intercourse; in consequence, unmarried mothers used to find themselves excommunicated. African Revival Brethren, fanatical about sexual morality, had challenged European Christian missionaries in the 1960's about sleeveless dresses and the temptation they constituted. One wonders what they would make today of plunging necklines in modern Western culture. Unsurprisingly, the Church saw the contraction of HIV/AIDS to be a consequence of extra-marital sex. It understandably had little or no sympathy with those who were suffering presumably as a result of this behaviour, which they regarded as sinful.

Society today, in the Western world, has moved away from this ideal and would find this attitude strange. It has to be remembered, however, that the moral standards of the African Church grew out of those held by

Christian missionaries, who had been coming out from the established churches of Western Europe since Victorian times and had brought with them the established ethical standards of the Church at that time. African church members would, therefore, adhere strongly to the principles they had been taught and handed down over many years and would treat seriously any deviation from them. The strong cohesion of church membership and fellowship would cement and uphold those values, especially in relation to sex.

These issues were seen only in colours of black and white with no room for shades of grey. So, the hardened attitude towards those who suffered from HIV/AIDS made little or no allowance for the way in which the individual had contracted the disease. The sins of the fathers were visited upon the children and even, ironically, upon the faithful spouses of those whose partners had been less faithful. There was, and is, a stigma associated with HIV/AIDS which is widespread throughout the Churches and, understandable though it might be, it has devastating consequences not only for those who are suffering from the disease but for society at large.

Nobody owns up readily to being infected. More importantly, those who suspect that they might be infected do not seek help, because they do not want others to think badly of them. Indeed, many will not even submit to testing, for fear that they might discover that they are HIV positive. In consequence, others with whom they come into sexual contact, are at risk. Within the Church, then, those affected by the disease are handled with a lot of secrecy, stigma and discrimination and therefore denial on their part. It is an attitude which serves not only to isolate those affected but also to contribute to the spread of the disease.

The Centre's Response

We have already seen how the Centre obtained funding from the New Partners' Initiative Fund of USAID for the Orphans and Vulnerable Children's Project, and they were to be the ultimate source of the considerable financial resources which would also be needed, if the Churches were to be educated in the matter of HIV/AIDS. In this separate, though related, project, which was inspirationally entitled "Springs of Life", Tearfund became the lead partner with six other Christian organisations called the Christian Partnership on AIDS in Kenya, of which St. John's Community Centre is one.

As soon as the funding had been obtained, the Centre approached the then recently retired Bishop of Nairobi, the Rt. Rev'd Peter Njoka, to lend his name and support to the project and sensitive handling led to an invitation allowing the Centre to address a Clergy Chapter meeting on the subject. At this meeting, sixty clergy were introduced to the project and twelve selected parishes in Nairobi were announced in which the project would operate.

The next step was to visit these parishes and to induct the Pastors in the objectives and targets of the Project. Each Pastor in turn selected three leaders to form the "Springs of Life" committee in their parish. They would be the key people in implementing the project and they were fully orientated on what the Church's role should be. It would be their responsibility to sensitise their congregations, enrol volunteers and inform them of the role they would perform. By the end of 2008, twelve parish committees had been formed and over 230 volunteers enrolled.

To try to bring about stigma reduction, three of the Centre staff members were appointed and trained as "Channels of Hope" Facilitators. It was their task to train 108 Pastors and church leaders using a manual developed by World Vision and they did this in four workshops. Following this there was a noticeable change in the Pastors' attitude, who promoted HIV/AIDS testing in their sermons and, leading by example, they themselves submitted to the test. In consequence stigma levels were drastically reduced.

Unfortunately, due to several problems there was no follow-up on stigma reduction initiatives and the New Partners' Initiative Office at Tearfund decided to halt the stigma reduction process. As a result, parishioners who received positive results from HIV/AIDS testing resisted joining support groups within the parishes because they could not afford to be discriminated against by their fellow church members.

How sad is this! It does, however, demonstrate clearly that the stigma factor remains to be dealt with because it is significant in the spread of the disease. If one views the three-year term of the Project as a pilot, then it proves the need for continued promotion of this aspect of the programme. Most importantly, a key lesson learnt from this project is the same as that learnt from other projects. It is essential to ensure that the churches develop ownership of projects before effective implementation is started. It also indicated that religious institutions were yet to come to terms with the reality of HIV/AIDS.

The value of the Community Centre's involvement in the Project was highlighted when the Centre decided to redeploy three regular staff members from their normal Centre activities into the work of the Project. This more than doubled the original number during the last year of the project term and it had a dramatic effect. The outreach work was more closely monitored and, what is more, the Parishes were helped in their planning and started to reach the community outside their congregations. During that third year alone they reached nearly 18,000 people. This has something to say not just about numbers but also the quality of the Centre's regular staff.

An interesting by-product of the Project was a requirement that each of the participating parishes should complete a more general needs assessment. They had difficulty in doing this and the Centre had to assist three-quarters of them with this exercise. The parishes had also to develop action plans to address the needs identified. Interestingly, poverty was regarded as the biggest problem by more than half of those responding to the survey, unemployment by a further quarter of the participants and HIV/AIDS came in as the third contributory cause of social problems. The community living in Pumwani was, therefore, not alone in experiencing major poverty and unemployment and not surprisingly the long experience of the Centre in dealing with those problems was relevant to other parishes in Nairobi with whom they were now coming into contact.

Behaviour Change – Abstinence

The other major thrust of the Project was to encourage behaviour change. In the case of young people and children, there would be an emphasis on abstinence. To obtain a balanced view of the outcome of this initiative, it is important to understand that 62% of the youth who were reached had already engaged in unsafe sex and a further 32% in behaviour exposing or leading them into that possibility, including kissing and caressing, viewing pornographic material and alcohol misuse.

Training was given by the Centre to church leaders in youth counselling and 26 of them completed the course. The training, which lasted 200 hours, was conducted by the Kenya Association for Professional Counsellors. The role of the trainees was to provide confidential counselling to young people and to enable them to sustain their choice of abstinence. By the end of the project term, the youth counsellors had provided counselling to 221 individuals, both on a one-to-one basis as well as in groups, on issues such as drug abuse, family conflict, alcohol addiction and those concerning children.

The youth programme centred on choice. Entitled "Choose Life", it invited young people to change their behaviour, ideally by complete abstinence. They were encouraged to engage in constructive leisure, such as sports, and they became assertive and gained confidence as a result. The Centre supported young people by providing equipment and at three sports events it provided for HIV testing with one of its mobile testing units. The reader may think that this was simplistic: probably it was, especially for those who had been sexually active. Some young people did not go the whole way and abstain, but they curtailed their sexual activity in ways which involved less risk.

Abstinence was also at the heart of the programme for children, those under the age of 14. They were reached by "Jehovah Jire peer educators", over 1100 of them in all, and with good effect. Most of them were able to maintain their commitment to choose life and of those who had chosen to maintain their virginity, 84% had succeeded when the project term expired.

Faithfulness in Marriage

As one might expect the approach to adults was more difficult. The challenge offered to married adults was to "Be Faithful in Marriage" but trainers were not listened to by older members of their own congregation due to their young age. It did not matter that they might be married. This surely was to be expected in Africa, where age and seniority in years are given greater respect than in the western world. This hindered participation in the forums and some trainers were discouraged. As one might also expect, women were more committed than their menfolk, who were more interested in matters of "business" than those of a social nature. However, some allowed their women to attend and waited to see if something "beneficial" would emerge, in which case, they too would attend. Interestingly, more men than women took the HIV test.

Dialogue forums were an important part of the process adopted to educate and inform participants and these were held in all three age-sections. Some of them were called "Coffee Bar Forums" and they gathered momentum towards the end of the project term, so that at the end almost 2,500 people had attended 61 Forums.

HIV Counselling & Testing

Volunteers, some 39 of them in all, were trained for a week to become counsellor aides. It was their task to persuade parishioners to take up counselling in HIV matters and to go for HIV testing. This was provided by the Centre, who had two permanent testing sites, one at Pumwani and the other at St. Andrew's Church in the Zimmerman location. Furthermore, it had three mobile units, which were particularly valuable as they could be set up temporarily in individual parishes, when "camps" were organised.

A date would be negotiated with a Parish and once this was set, the Pastor and the Springs of Life Committee within that Parish would make announcements and invite the congregation to come forward to be tested. The Parishioners in turn would display posters and distribute fliers to publicise the event across the wider community. Camps were held in all the selected pilot Parishes.

Nearly 12,000 people took the test, a considerable overachievement of the project target. The combination of the Abstinence or Being Faithful campaign on the one hand and the Counselling and Testing on the other proved to be very important as a prevention tool because the participants took the necessary prevention step.

Conclusions

We believe that this was a very audacious programme and we are not surprised that many challenges were encountered. The realisation that the stigma had first to be reduced struck at deep-rooted cultural and moral convictions. Furthermore, church members, especially those who are prominent in the Church, ran the risk of exposure if they had been involved in risky sexual activity.

Many lessons were learnt in this pilot project. The Centre now knows better ways of working and how to tackle the problems it faced. Indeed, the real success of the project will rely upon its replication in the other parishes of the Nairobi Diocese, when corrections can be made to the policies and procedures.

Targets were met, even exceeded and the Churches have benefited, because they have been seen to be meeting at last the real needs of people, reaching out to them and giving them hope. That, of itself, is vital, an integral part of the overall mission of the Church. What is more, the perception of the Church's involvement by the community at large, has invoked a spontaneous response from those who were outside, even from the youngest members of society. "For a long time, very few children used to attend our Sunday school. But after the outreach that was conducted by the peer educators, the numbers attending Sunday school multiplied and the attendance has been consistent." The same was true of young people. Those in the churches increased in number due to the feeling that the church was now addressing current issues that concerned them most. Even adults who had stopped attending church had "finally found the church attractive."

Viewed from the Centre's perspective, this project has helped it to achieve its major objective. It has stimulated the Church to address a major social need, the fight against HIV/AIDS and to do so reaching many thousands of people. It has itself at last received due recognition of that achievement. At the ceremony celebrating the close of the project the Bishop of Nairobi applauded the part the Centre had played. "St. John's is one of the most outstanding ACK (Anglican Church of Kenya) institutions, delivering transforming services to our community effectively".

However, it is questionable how far there has been any lasting effect of the project. The Parish Projects did continue for a while to remain active following the close of the project, but it seems that this may no longer be the case, at any rate in Mathare and Mukugu slums. Two church representatives from those areas reported that some pastors and church elders were not in support of the project, while counsellors, who had been trained, demanded to be paid if they were to provide psycho-social support to the Orphans and Vulnerable Children. How far this was the case in other areas we do not know. Furthermore, we do not know whether any Nairobi parishes other than the twelve originally selected, have independently sought to replicate the "Springs of Life" project themselves.

A key lesson, which was learnt from this project, is to ensure that the churches develop ownership of projects before effective implementation is started. It also indicates that religious institutions are yet to come to terms with the reality of HIV/AIDS.

"Springs of Life" was followed by four further projects: "Hope", "Aphia Plus", "Dreams" and "Nilinde".

"Hope"

"Hope", an acronym for "Health Outcomes through Prevention Education" was working with some of the parishes. It was, once again, funded by USAID. The project was interestingly scheduled to last four years, a year longer than that allowed for Springs of Life, but only lasted for two years due to reduced funding. "Hope" aimed to achieve its main purposes by intervention in the schools and the community, intending to work through 400 primary and secondary schools within Nairobi informal settlements and its environs, introducing the children to HIV/AIDS prevention activities.

135 school health teachers were trained, and 125 schools formed school health committees. However, USAID cut financial support so there was no opportunity to establish more committees and those which existed lacked necessary support, including the creation of linkages for the care and support of the school community,

A spin-off from the project was the distribution of almost 3,000 bags, bearing a behaviour change message, as an incentive to "peer educators". Their task was to encourage their fellow pupils to do just that, namely to change their behaviour. Even more interestingly, more than 4,000 parents, almost exclusively women, sought training, and were empowered, to communicate sexual health and substance abuse prevention messages to their children.

Barolina, a grateful parent had this to say: "Before I participated in Families Matters Programme (FMP), I did not know that it was okay for me to discuss sexuality with my children especially my 11 years-old daughter. I used to think that my girl was still very young to be taught about this issue. Since I joined FMP however, I have realised I was doing the wrong things that could impact on my relationship with my daughter. So, I started drawing her closer and making time for her and advising her. I also got to know her more, the changes she was going through and challenges she is experiencing at her young age. Today, she has opened-up to me about her physical changes and her views on sex, drugs etc. I am very grateful to Family Matters Programme."

Part VI - "The Bigger Picture"

Barolina – "Grateful to the Family Matters Programme"

"Aphia Plus"

This is another funding organisation and it was anticipated that it would produce complementary financial resources to support work analogous to that of the Orphans and Vulnerable Children Project. The hope was that as many as 10,000 children would be reached, all of them living within the same parishes as were targeted by the "Hope" project, the aim of the Centre being to see how the two simultaneous projects would interact. Would the joint approach to HIV/AIDS within the same area be more dynamic in its total impact than the OVC and the Springs of Life projects had been individually?

Significant challenges, including late disbursement of the funds, doubts concerning the sustainability of the development strategy, insufficiency of staff and other resources required to meet the needs of the beneficiaries and a breakdown in communication between the Community Health Workers and the parents all combined to militate against the success of this project.

"Dreams"

Nobody in their wildest dreams would want to dream about HIV/AIDS, especially girls and young women aged between 16 and 24 years. Any such dream would be a nightmare. It became just that for the 16-year-old girl seated in front of an adviser. She had gone with two of her friends for testing for HIV/AIDS and her test had turned positive. Alarmed and upset, her immediate and persistent question was "Am I going to die?"

DREAMS, however, gives hope for the future for thousands of adolescent girls and young women who are very vulnerable but still uninfected by the virus. It is an acronym for "Determined, Resilient, Empowered, AIDS-free, Mentored and Safe" and it describes the kind of lives this HIV/AIDS programme in Kenya was intended to produce. Moreover, those adjectives describe the wide-ranging and comprehensive processes by which these lives will be attained.

Sadly, the group of people who are most vulnerable to the HIV/AIDS virus are those in the age group we have mentioned, and they represent 74% of all new victims of the disease. The adolescent girls and young women of Pumwani would fall largely within that group because they have limited education and come from poor households. Furthermore, if they are by choice or necessity earning their living as sex workers, they are obviously the most at risk.

Funded by a consortium of big donors, headed by the U.S. President's Emergency Plan for AIDS Relief (PEPFAR), Global Communities and its two partners, St. John's Community Centre and the Kenya Girl Guides Association are implementing the two-year Dreams lives programme in Kamukunji and Starehe sub-counties using a two-pronged approach. It combines customised individual support with the girls and women on the one hand, and system strengthening aimed at family/community/sexual networks and government entities at the wards, sub-county, county and national levels on the other.

St. John's Community Centre with its long-established expertise in education, formal and non-formal, its equally well-established vocational training programmes, and its social outreach and sustained compassion and support is clearly suited to promote this project successfully and it has two years in which to do so.

To date, the programme has reached about 8,000 Adolescent Girls and Young Women with the knowledge, skills and competencies that have empowered most of them to live healthy, fulfilling and HIV-free lives. It has been instrumental in ensuring that the boys and men in their communities see the value of healthy, educated and empowered local women.

For Pumwani slums, where the majority of the young women have very limited opportunities to improve their livelihoods, the DREAMS programme has been a miracle. Today, hundreds of these formerly vulnerable women are breaking their glass ceiling and venturing into all sorts of constructive and productive ventures, whether they be economical, social, spiritual or even political. Their levels of self-esteem

Dream girls graduating from vocational courses celebrate as they throw their mortarboards in the air

and confidence have significantly soared. The Centre has had occasions at which the adolescent girls and young women have shared platforms with the U.S. Ambassador to Kenya and made amazing presentations. They can now be found owning profitable businesses, organising outreach events, filling leadership positions and so on.

In the past, young mothers seeking advice or help found that the response was piece meal, reactive and disconnected. The DREAMS project has shown itself to be a well-conceived programme, capable of successful implementation, which even includes evidence-based interventions around women's reproductive health concerns, namely screening for sexually transmitted infections and for tuberculosis as well as testing for HIV/AIDS.

"Nilinde"

Immediately preceding the time of going to publication, both DREAMS and Nilinde were concurrently and successfully running together. The Centre was, however, told that Nilinde would come to an abrupt end by the end of March 2019 rather than being phased out over the next two years and DREAMS had been scheduled to finish in August 2019.

We have already seen that DREAMS was a great success and the same could be said for Nilinde. Nilinde means "protect me" and it had effectively worked to that end and with that effect for no less than 11,400 orphans and vulnerable children in neighbouring Kamukunji, Starehe and Kasarani, providing for them a range of essential services. Working with PLAN, a programme of USAID, it focused on increasing access to health and social services for OVC and their families, household economic strengthening to protect and care for OVC and strengthening the child welfare and protection systems at national levels. We can identify these targets in some of the previous programmes carried on by the Centre amongst orphans and vulnerable children. Indeed, each of these targets was pursued with the Small Community Projects and detailed in Chapter 25.

A new ambitious international treatment target with the strange numeric title of "90-90-90" has been launched. It aims to bring AIDS to an end.

By 2020, 90% of all people living with HIV will know their HIV status. By 2020, 90% of all people with diagnosed HIV infection will receive sustained antiretroviral therapy. By 2020, 90% of all people receiving antiretroviral therapy will have viral suppression.

The Centre has resolved to adopt the 90-90-90 approach, enrolling children living with HIV and conducting intensive casework, for which it is has the ideal staff and background. Alongside the medical aspect of 90-90-90, the Centre could draw on all the expertise it had developed in the fight against AIDS and the programmes and tools it had used earlier have continued to be relevant.

It is sad and worrying that these major USAID projects are about to end but it speaks about the sincerity and compassion of the Centre that they have already initiated a sustainability measure, establishing at the Centre, a Girls-Only Wellness Centre to cater for the health needs of adolescent girls and young women.

Child and Maternal Health – something different – something new

According to UNICEF, each year over 10.5 million children die before their fifth birthday and most of them from preventable causes.

In a project, supported by Child Rescue Foundation, the Centre sought to achieve sustainable reduction of child mortality among the poorest households in Kiambiu village of Pumwani. Expectant mothers were targeted and were educated and encouraged to attend ante-natal clinics, followed by domiciliary visits.

Also targeted were children less than five years of age, who were identified as being at risk of dying due to sickness. They would include, particularly, the children of parents too poor to afford the cost of treatment or possessing inadequate knowledge related to the sickness.

Such children were identified by screening for any life-threatening condition. Those requiring it would be referred to health institutions and drugs would be procured for those who were critically ill. Domiciliary visits were made following treatment.

The programme officer worked with community health workers to implement the project. Three thousand children, twice the number targeted for the project, were identified as being at risk and this was down to good planning, proper mobilisation and community involvement. In the same way 200 expectant mothers were found. The Centre networked internally with other departments within its own organisation to secure the necessary medical care, education and awareness which the project required.

It was a requirement that the Centre should find four community volunteers and ten mentor mothers to enhance basic health skills and knowledge. It is pleasing to find that some twenty-nine came forward and worked as volunteers in the project. What is more, the mentor mothers have created general awareness in the households within the area. It all goes to show that working along with the community and involving them, at the outset, at grass roots level in basic community needs, can give them a feeling of achievement and self-worth, spilling over for the well-being of the whole community.

Chapter 27 – Empowerment of Women

Political Inequality – a historical perspective

To deal with sexual inequality in Kenya would be unfair without seeing it in an international context. To do this, however, it is inappropriate to attempt anything more than a potted version of the emancipation of women in England.

Perhaps because of their physical strength men have assumed a superior position to that of women in all societies and throughout the ages. At the time of the Renaissance in England, during the sixteenth century, a few outstanding women began to write reflectively about this situation and demands for the emancipation of women in all areas of life continued for another three hundred years. These demands gained impetus in the nineteenth century and more so in the early twentieth century, resulting in the political emancipation of women in 1928, when they were given in England the right to vote. It took another half-century before Margaret Thatcher became the first woman Prime Minister in England.

Inequality in the workplace

During World War II, which ended in 1945, English women served in the armed forces, did dangerous jobs in munitions factories and worked to produce food on the land. After the war they were not prepared to return to their former role and "do women's work". While we were growing up in England in the fifties, dramatic changes in the roles of men and women were taking place culminating in the "women's liberation movement" or colloquially "women's lib" during the sixties. Since then there have been numerous legal reforms aimed at ending inequality of the sexes. In more recent years a new government provision is paternity leave for men, so that husbands can look after their children whilst mothers return to work. Shelters, which were established for battered wives and their children, now accept men who are threatened by their wives.

These changes have come about more quickly and dramatically in some groups than in others. Social class, education and economic conditions all influence situations. Many ambitious women today suspect that a glass ceiling exists, so that despite "equal opportunity rights", the top jobs are reserved for men.

It is not surprising, therefore, that in Africa where the process of political and economic development has been concertinaed into three or four generations, the place of women in civil society and their political empowerment is only now catching up. Nor is it surprising that St. John's Community Centre, which has concentrated upon women's and girls' education, and their employment, should be in the forefront of the movement to advocate women's political involvement.

Sexual mistreatment

Battered wives in England are encouraged to report their situation but many are too frightened to do so. A hidden number of children are physically and sexually assaulted by a parent. Advertisements on national television encourage these victims to use the telephone and ask for help.

The time of "women's lib" in England was very different from the atmosphere of low self-esteem which prevailed among the women in Pumwani during the sixties. This was largely due to the prevalent disregard shown to the status of women and girls. The wife, whose hand was chopped off by her polygamous husband has already been mentioned. Likewise, several men have come before the court accused of defiling very young girls, due, it seems, to a widely held belief that venereal disease could be cured by having sex with a virgin. In the chapter on casework mention has been made of the social workers' problems in their own family lives. The behaviour of their husbands was accepted as normal.

Pat remembers discussing family planning with a group of Luo women, who were shocked and unbelieving when she suggested that sexual intercourse should be enjoyed by wives as well as husbands. To them it was a chore which occurred whenever their partner required it, often when he was drunk.

Children from the Centre protesting

Pumwani

Some of the young girls who came to the Centre were very glamorously dressed. They were young, and working as juvenile prostitutes did not seem to cause them any undue distress or unhappiness. Some attracted men who could afford to buy them expensive clothes and treats. After they became pregnant, they were often able to leave their children with their mothers but eventually, the cycle of becoming single parent mothers and finding it less possible to earn money to feed their children, caught up with them. The majority who attended classes in the Centre were impoverished women of this kind.

The weekly church meeting, however, attracted a different group. The pastor's wife and others who lived on the CMS compound were dressed neatly and soberly and were at ease with church proceedings. Another small group of dignified, immaculate women came from Majengo. They were members of "Dini ya Burnsi", who had been worshipping at St. John's Church for many years. They owned their own houses in Pumwani, having come from Nandi country and from the coast in the early days when Pumwani was first settled. It appeared that they had retired from their earlier profession and were financially secure with their savings and the rents from letting rooms. On our wedding day, one of them, a Mguiriama named Lydia, brought us a present of a Shs.5 note, a generous sum in those days.

These Christian women had security and a confidence that marked them out from other Pumwani women. If they suffered violence from men, it was not openly acknowledged and certainly not discussed with the Centre workers. However, an educated relation of Eunice had to take court action against her husband for physically abusing her and Pat was told by a senior member of the Revival Brethren that even within this apparently enlightened group such behaviour still occurred.

Gender Budgeting of Devolved Funds

A baseline survey conducted in Pumwani by the Centre in 2011 established that there was very little understanding of the meaning of the word "gender" and that women were undervalued.

Central or local government had introduced the concept of "devolved funds", for which local people had the capacity to bid in order to improve their conditions. It had not, however, occurred to those in authority, or indeed to the population as a whole, that women should have a voice as to how these funds might be used. There was, therefore, no conception of gender-based budgeting being used to improve specifically the situation of women. Women needed to be educated to apply for such funds and to see how those funds might be used for their advancement and benefit. Furthermore, it was necessary to change the attitude of men, many of whom felt threatened by any increased confidence shown by women and were defensive in the face of perceived criticism.

The need for political education in Pumwani

First, however, it was necessary to educate the whole of the Pumwani population, both men and women, on the need to become politically active and involved. There was, as is mentioned elsewhere, an acceptance of disempowerment: the local community were resigned to ineffectiveness in promoting change or improvement in their condition. During the life of the Community Centre its workers have seen central and local governments make decisions which have fundamentally affected the daily lives of Pumwani residents. Apart from a very few activists the population appear to have accepted policies, even when they have been to their disadvantage.

Since 2008 the staff of the Community Centre has run a governance and advocacy programme with the aim of empowering local residents to contribute to local government processes. Through this programme known as "Building Local Democracy and Anti-Corruption" chosen members of the community have been empowered as community mobilisers and resource persons, so that they can spearhead and facilitate civic initiatives which involve the community in the management of public resources at a local level.

Women & Youth - the need of literacy

To achieve this, a gender responsive project was set up to ensure that the needs of women and youth in Pumwani are remembered during resource allocation by local government. It was the aim of the project that observance of their human rights should be increased by the year 2014.

At the beginning of this project women were given written hand-outs as the Centre sought to engage them in the subject of Gender Budgeting of Devolved Funds. It became evident, however, that these women would not become involved because they were illiterate. Even then in 2012, many women had never completed primary school education and many more had never been to school at all. The Centre therefore decided to run an adult literacy class and recruited thirty women, of whom twenty-six graduated after four months. There were two classes, one for the women who were completely illiterate and the other for the school dropouts who were semi-illiterate. The teachers were second year students from Kenyatta University and they used Ministry of Education curricula intensively. The results were dramatic and transformed the lives of the women. They learned to count, to read and to write so that they could sign their names, do simple business calculations and watch their children doing their homework. It would obviously be very desirable for more of the illiterate women living in the Pumwani area to attend such a course.

Following this preliminary education and orientation 3123 women from 43 Self Help Women's Groups received direct education in respect of civic and voting issues before the project finished, building up their knowledge and capacity on issues of governance, leadership, local democracy and the constitution. Similar education and capacity building took place amongst 1800 young people, eleven of whom were trained to contest the National Elections in 2013, three of them successfully.

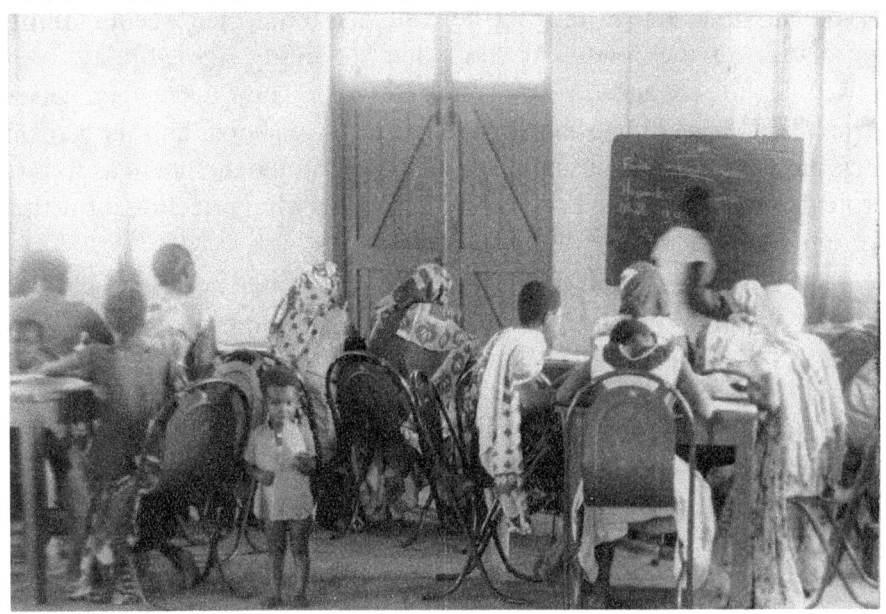

Women learning literacy in the early days

However, the appetite for literacy in the community has not been sustained. It is difficult to think that in only seven years, illiteracy has now disappeared, but literacy programmes have never picked up. Whilst the Centre sees there is still a need for literacy, it is not a priority to the community. The Centre has accordingly stopped all efforts at promoting it, much to the disappointment of the Adult Education Officer for the area.

Area committees

During the gender-responsive project the geographical area covered was divided into three constituencies, in each of which was established a committee, whose aim it was to empower their community and establish links between that community and the officials who administered the appropriate fund. Each committee consisted of fifteen people, nine women and six men, who were given training through community workshops.

The committee members became eager to learn about the relevant devolved funds and to talk to the officials about their accountability for managing the funds. At first, unsurprisingly, the officials were unwilling to engage in such discussions. They were persuaded, however, to participate in empowerment workshops, and as a result they did enter into discussions with the committee members as to how projects were chosen and prioritised and, following selection, how they were monitored.

Monitoring & Audit

In addition, forty women were trained as social monitors, their task being to seek greater transparency and less corruption. It was the purpose of the monitors to sustain the involvement of the community. They were given, and trained to use, scorecards which would enable them to audit the devolved funds. Such an audit was carried out on only one selected project in each constituency as there was no time in the life of the project to do this more than once, although this would have been very desirable.

Ten social monitors were also trained to track the expenditure against the budget, but they did not have the opportunity to do this. To have made it possible, the Community Centre would have had to embark upon advocacy and networking at a national level, and we do not know why this did not take place. If politically it was too difficult or sensitive, to the point that it might endanger the good relations which the Centre enjoyed with relevant Government departments, we can understand its reticence. If, however, it was going to take too long and be unfunded, then we would have thought it would have been worth seeking further funding.

In each constituency seven social committees were trained to find out about appropriate devolved funds and how to apply for them. At the end of the training all these committee members were given application forms and the majority used them.

From the total number of 420 women who were trained, 90 were selected and trained in proposal writing. Each of these women was linked to a government, or local government, official to act as the contact person for members of the community.

Widening horizons

Many years previously, at the beginning of the work of the Community Centre, it was evident that Pumwani was the "world" for many of its residents. So as to expand the experience of the children at that time and widen their horizons, Pat made arrangements to take girls to play netball against teams from other locations. She also took groups of girls to walk through Eastleigh to the City Park in Parklands.

Boys and girls from the youth club were taken further afield to spend time at the Limuru Conference Centre, where they visited the surrounding countryside. They were surprised to find in that beautiful, lush countryside the Bata Shoe Factory and the Uplands Bacon Factory and were fascinated by the industrial processes they saw there. Some years later, women from Maridadi Fabrics started to walk into the commercial centre of Nairobi to market their products.

Part VI - "The Bigger Picture"

Pumwani Youth Club 1961 Netball Team

A visit to City Park exploring the bigger world

Enjoying the facilities of City Park

Underlying the Gender Responsive Budgeting programme was the desire to help women to take a greater leadership role. Attempts were made to increase girls' self-esteem and give them the opportunity to experience life outside their normal pattern. Twenty girls from Forms 1-4 of St. John's High School were taken on a visit to Embakasi Girls' High School. The girls from this school encouraged the girls from Pumwani to aim higher and work harder at their studies reinforcing what the same girls had learnt in their weekly life-skill and governance sessions arranged for them by the Centre. Similar life-skill and leadership sessions were conducted with 160 children from Standards IV - VIII in the Community Centre Primary School.

For very successful publicity, 1000 women's T shirts and 500 shirts for girls, together with 500 bags for each, were produced. They all bore powerful slogans reminiscent of the suffragette movement in England more than 100 years earlier.

The Future

The final activity of this programme was a joint venture, planned with the organisation "Community Action for Rural Development" ("CARD"). This took place at Mbita, a town on the shores of Lake Victoria near to Homa Bay. It is very unlikely that Pumwani women had ever visited that area. CARD organised a forum for monitors from Mbita and those trained in Pumwani to meet with government and quasi-government officials from Homa Bay, including members of government institutions involved in development work. After listening to the proceedings taking place in those forums, the monitors had time for reflection and discussion. They were then able to draw up plans of action for their own areas. Furthermore, the importance of an amicable relationship between the social monitors and government officials became clear to them.

At the end of this project it was agreed that there needed to be continued support for the oversight committees and the monitors if they were to continue to monitor devolved funds. Furthermore, it was expected at that time that there would be a change in the way in which funds would be devolved, making it necessary that the communities be made aware of how they can still benefit.

All funded projects which the Centre has conducted are restricted in their duration. For obvious reasons donors will not fund a project indefinitely. In this case, the funds were made available for a two-year period, during which time the monitors were trained to use only one tool, which had been designed to track just one project. It was not possible to embark upon another project, necessitating the development of a further tool, due to insufficient time. It would, however, be hoped that after using this one tool for a longer period the benefit of increased community involvement would be better understood and appreciated.

Chapter 28 – Non-Formal Education (NFE)

Parking Boys

Parking boys were, and still are, a common sight on the streets of Nairobi. These young lads, with time on their hands and desperate to earn a few shillings, stand on the road by a row of parked cars, ready to wave you into an empty parking space. Parking is at a premium in the City and when on a hot and busy day you are in urgent need of divesting yourself of your vehicle, you will normally want to avail yourself of their services and think it well worth the small sum involved, to park and go about your business. You would have had difficulty perhaps in locating the place yourself due to the heavy traffic or the fact that one's eyes do not see around cars already parked, until it is too late; you have already passed the empty space.

Parking boys, however, can turn out to be a two-edged sword. If you see a whole row of empty spaces, you do not value their services in the same way. If you do not use them, you are fearful that they may vent their feelings on your vehicle. Even if you do use them, you cannot be sure of their loyalty in protecting your vehicle from intruders. They loiter of necessity on the road and one is anxious for their physical safety, concerned that an accident will be caused. There are occasions also when two parking boys will find you the same space.

The public generally would prefer to be without the aggravation of these children and more importantly they should be in school, furthering their skills and education. It was to help them that Father Groll, a Roman Catholic priest, formed the Undugu Society of Kenya. Pat became involved with Undugu at an early stage of its development. We speak mostly of parking boys, but girls were also to be seen on the streets in this role and Pat joined the team of helpers, who assembled in the Chapel on Uhuru Highway to meet with these girls.

Undugu has over the years acquired a good reputation for the service they have provided for parking boys and girls. They could demonstrate that their strategy, including non-formal education, was effective in reaching children out of school and getting them back into the system. The Centre was advised to consult with Undugu.

St. John's Community Centre also admitted street children to its classes, provided they were at least 9 years old. Otherwise these classes were restricted to children who have been growing up in Pumwani. The Centre's efforts aimed specifically at street-children were not, however, well received. The initial street children's programme enrolled 17 of them in the school but within a month all of them had dropped out. How difficult it must be to re-orientate the children's mental attitude, after years of begging, lack of discipline and lawlessness. The Centre has realised that its core competency has developed with greater success in the realm of preventative, rather than curative, activity and this has been seen in the Non-formal education, the Orphans and Vulnerable Children interventions and the Child Development and Advocacy programme.

NFE Schoolchildren washing hands after a lesson on hygiene

The history of the Centre's informal school

St. John's Community Centre has, since its inception, been involved with the non-formal education sector and long before parking boys and girls appeared on the streets, it has endeavoured to rescue children from ignorance, in the realisation that education is the slow but sure way of relieving poverty and that of their families. There is no quick and easy way of equipping destitute children to take their rightful place in society. As we have seen, when Pat arrived in Pumwani, she found in existence classes for the girls taken by Georgina Serpell, with the newly born Christian Industrial Training Centre catering for the boys. In some way or another, that work has continued throughout the life of the Centre, almost without a break.

As we have also seen, Pat shunned the idea of sponsorship, conscious that information publicised about the background and social state of our young girls was an invasion of their privacy. It was important that their dignity and self-respect should be preserved.

Of course, there are different ways in which such information can be released and there is no doubt that over the years many destitute children have found their education furthered through sponsorship programmes. Certainly, in the years following our departure from Kenya, the Centre has obtained sponsorship for children on a regular and organised basis. We have seen that, when Eunice Kamau was appointed Warden of the Centre, she found the Children Incorporated sponsorship was being abused and that some children from the Church congregation were benefiting from scholarships which should have been allocated to children of the Pumwani community with greater need.

The Current Programme

The Non-Formal Education Programme in its present form has been operating since 1992. It offers classes to children who are aged 9 years or more, who are either from the Pumwani community or who have been rehabilitated from the street.

Until 2010, the Programme stopped short of providing a full Primary School course because it did not attempt to complete the final year of primary education, namely Class 8 [12]. As it had always been, it was a first-aid or catch-up service, seeking to lift children out of total ignorance, and providing basic education, including numeracy and literacy skills. It was the hope that they might be enabled to integrate into the normal state schools. If children had ability and wanted to go beyond Class 7, they had to seek registration in private or government schools. Alongside the academic education, children were also given vocational skills. These included knitting, woodwork, metal sheet work, sewing, fine art and cookery. If the pupils did not then register with other schools offering Class 8, they would be provided with vocational training with employers. most frequently in the form of apprenticeships operating within Pumwani.

This, however, changed in 2010 when it introduced Class 8; pupils could remain at the school to complete their primary education. That sounds quite right and logical. This would be the year of examination to determine whether they would be suitable to go on to secondary education. Who wants to change schools at such a critical time, with different friends and a different culture, just for one year? Different teaching staff will not have the same awareness of a child's individual problems and be able to give that extra support which they need. To change schools is an unwanted trauma, which, unless it can be avoided, turns a challenging year into a difficult and perhaps even frightening experience.

However, that extra year would, of itself, have been insufficient. If children were to remain to take the examination for secondary education, they needed to have studied the full curriculum. The school accordingly adopted this in 2011. This change of curriculum, combined with the introduction of Class 8, has meant further choices have had to be made and before considering those, it would be helpful to understand how schools and educational establishments in Kenya are classified.

---

[12] 'Classes' of the NFE correspond to 'Standards' in State schools.

Gordon, himself a former pupil here, now a skilled carpenter inspiring non formal school pupils with his work

Classification of the Non-Formal Education (NFE) Programme

There is the distinction between private and government education, the latter being called "public", unlike the public schools in England, which are anything but! There is, of course, within the public sector the whole range of educational establishments, from primary through to colleges and universities. These are further classified according to their performance, the best being given the status of "national" schools, the others of "provincial" or "district" schools.

The non-formal sector, which by its very nature falls within the private sector, is subdivided into two categories, schools or education. The former delivers a formalised curriculum leading to formal school examinations. The latter, on the other hand, can consist of any organised, systematic and quality educational and training programmes, outside the formal education system, which aim at meeting specific learning needs of the children, young people and adults.

The Centre's programme offers skills training alongside the academic subjects and it is, therefore, a non-formal school according to the government classification. It cannot be registered by the Ministry of Education but, if it chose, it could seek registration as an examination centre.

"Choices"

Having now taken on the task of providing full primary education, the Centre's non-formal programme has now to decide what registration it should seek. Should it seek to register with the Ministry of Education as a private school?

If the school continues to offer the formal curriculum during school hours and skills training after the school hours, then the school can seek registration as a private school. There are few advantages to this type of registration and one distinct disadvantage. The perception of private schools is that they are affluent and well endowed. They are not, therefore, targeted to receive aid from the government or from development partners. On the other hand, the government has been supporting the non-formal schools, which are seen to be needing help, as they support children from vulnerable families. Development partners also focus on the non-formal schools attended by the poor.

It does seem, therefore, that the school should seek registration with one of the other government agencies, such as the Ministry of Culture & Social Services, at the same time registering with the Ministry of Education as an examination centre. It has been recommended that it should also join the Independent Schools Association to receive and give mutual support to other non-formal schools.

The other main choice which requires to be made concerns the continuation of the Skills Courses. It is noteworthy that when pupils were asked their principal aim following the completion of Class 8, 86% wanted to go on to secondary school. One choice which the school could make would be to go with the aspirations of the vast majority of the pupils and pour all the energies and resources of the school into academic studies. Only 7% wanted to continue with skills training.

What would be the effect of such a decision? It would certainly help to improve the standards of academic learning, in that pupils would be able to concentrate their efforts on those studies while the school would be able to allocate all its resources of time and money to the same end. The disadvantages would be at least twofold.

Whilst the children are at the school, their skills training enables them to earn small sums of money from the sale of products made using the skills acquired from the school. They are able to buy food and some school items such as stationery. Damaris in Class 7 has been making mats and she had sold 7 mats for Shs.1500/-, which is not a small amount for a school-going pupil. Joseph, interested in carpentry, had sold 2 chairs for Shs.500/- each, while Antony had sold 4 caps, each realising Shs.150/-.

Even more importantly, the skills classes provide the pupils with a source of livelihood, in the event they do not pass the entry examination for secondary school. Indeed, even if they do, it may not be everybody's choice to obtain a white-collar job and they might prefer to start their own business, especially in periods of unemployment.

Following the assessment, it was unanimous amongst both the pupils and the teachers that skills training should be retained for Classes 3 to 7. Class 8 pupils should be left to focus on preparing for the national examinations. The skills training should, however, be given outside of normal school hours, in the evenings and perhaps also at weekends and during school holidays.

At the time of going to publication, we learn that registration of the Non-Formal School has not yet been achieved, due largely to the bureaucracy which we have noticed. A special registration now seems likely, however, under a new Government system for all children in school called NEMIS[13] and the Education Authorities are reacting positively to the Centre's new application to register.

---

[13] NEMIS - the "National Education Management Information System".

Assessment

Conscious that the school has now upgraded itself to a full primary school, the Centre has, true to form, decided to assess its present and potential impact. In line with the other major projects currently operated by the Centre, its assessment has been carried out in accordance with strategic planning culture. A consultant was employed and focus group discussions were held with all relevant parties. These included pupils from the 6 senior classes, all the teachers, a large representation of parents and guardians, Board members and senior staff of the Community Centre. Meetings were also held with the Director of basic education in the Ministry of Education and the officer in charge of non-formal schools, as well as the officer in charge of basic education at Undugu.

The investigations and research made by the consultant were exhaustive and sufficient to provide a strategic direction for the non-formal school.

Performance

When a group of some 30 parents or guardians met with the independent consultant to discuss the school, they were ostensibly fair and constructive. They were appreciative of what was being achieved but at the same time anxious that standards should be improved.

It is clear that the school excels in the realm of sports. There were too many sporting activities and achievements in this direction had, it seemed, been made at the expense of academic performance. Sporting celebrities have become role models almost everywhere and one can imagine a child, who has been out of school, has in the past used the time to play informally and competitively with other children in their favourite sports and games. Coming into a learning institution at the age of 9 or more, they would find it easier, and therefore more attractive, to focus on activity with which they are more accustomed and in which they are likely to be more successful and competitive.

Furthermore, nine or more years spent living aimlessly, without any timetable to regulate their lives and maybe without any person in authority whom they must obey, they will find the culture of school life very alien and difficult. Lack of discipline has, therefore, been highlighted as one of the principal causes for poor academic performance of the school.

It would be easy to criticise the teaching staff for the lack of discipline and poor performance. It is suggested that the school has been perceived as "a slum school for slum children" based upon a pre-conception that standards will inevitably be lower than those in schools where the children come from better homes. It would be easy to condemn such an attitude, but the realism is that children with devoted parents, who offer help and support in a home which is lending itself to discipline and study, have an enormous advantage over their less fortunate counterparts.

Nevertheless, the Centre accepts there is room for improvement and that excellence is something for which to strive, whatever the challenges that may present. It is accepted that first and foremost, discipline must be instituted, and that teaching staff require training to assist them in achieving this. School rules and regulations require to be written and enforced. Standards need to be inculcated, so that the parents do not remove their children in Class 8 to schools which are obtaining better results. More than half the teaching staff have been there for more than eight years and none for less than four, so the poor performance was not due to inexperience or frequent staff changes. Perhaps the challenges have been so great that they have settled for mediocre results in the expectation that they cannot be improved: or perhaps the demands and difficulties have lulled them into acceptance of the status quo.

There is talk of the need for lesson preparation, and for homework to be set and marked: for greater dynamism in the leadership of the head-teacher. At the same time, the parents and guardians of the children have said that the teachers are good compared with those of other schools. It is not a cause for despair. In England we are so used to hearing of Ofsted[14] reports and the naming and shaming of schools which do not perform well in their "stats" or appear at the bottom of their "league tables".

One interesting criticism has been the physical cleanliness of the premises. The desks need sanding. It has been one suggestion that parents might be asked to contribute their time and energies in this direction, especially if they are one of the majority who are unable to contribute financially to their children's education. Here would be yet another way of involving the community more intensively in the life of the Centre.

The assessment report has identified the problems but not without giving credit for the achievements. The parents have related home visits by social workers, signalling the concern of the school for the children. Indeed, the school has adopted a holistic approach and provides psycho-social support and counselling for the children and parents, forums on life skills for parents and pupils, sponsorship because most parents are poor, spiritual growth for behaviour transformation and seminars on leadership skills for the pupils. It is the view that children living in difficult circumstances require these supportive interventions for character building and education.

Such was the position five years ago. The position today, however, is more encouraging.

Update

Children Incorporated, the organisation which in the past sponsored individual children, has in recent years made donations for capital improvements. The second phase of a construction programme now houses the offices and half of the classrooms in the Non-Formal School. They are spacious, including room for talking walls and they provide an environment which does much to boost the self-esteem of the students.

It is always a bonus when new premises afford the opportunity for increased activities. At weekends and during school holidays the school

---

[14] Ofsted - "Office for Standards in Education, Children's Services and Skills".

is temporarily converted into a "Talent Academy", where hundreds of children are provided with the opportunity of identifying and harnessing any God-given skills of a creative nature.

Thousands of children have over the years benefited from the NFE programme, children who otherwise would be untaught and unemployed. They have accessed quality and functional education, embracing also behaviour change, spiritual nurture and talent development. Today, most of these children have graduated to become responsible, hardworking citizens, engaged in constructive ventures, which make them self-reliant.

In the meantime, during the period of their education at the Centre, their lifestyle was markedly improved. The NFE programme introduced a feeding programme in the year 2015, so that the children ate a healthy lunch three times a week. The challenges produced by hunger had affected their attendance, concentration and participation. A more than significant improvement was noticeable in these areas. Their well-being was also addressed by assisting their parents or guardians. Economic strengthening intervention meant that more than half of them were able to provide the basic needs of their children, especially with essential items such as food, shelter, clothing and healthcare.

The community also has benefited. Retention of the children in school has significantly contributed to reduction in juvenile delinquency and crime. Criminal gangs would exploit children to facilitate their activities. Being in school meant that many of the children would concentrate on their studies, building positive characters and becoming goal orientated, which should be the right and aspiration of every child.

One such child was Ezekiel Kamau. He was raised by a single mother of seven in one of the villages of Pumwani. His mother enrolled him in Class 1 at the NFE Programme and he completed his seven years of schooling. While at NFE, he proved to be a brilliant, God-fearing and disciplined boy and, as such, represented the school in many events including International Exchange Programmes.

Ezekiel pursued his secondary education after passing his primary exams with flying colours. He got an educational sponsorship from the government which was solicited by the new secondary school. Once again, he excelled in his secondary education, proceeded to University, where he graduated with a Degree in Social Statistics.

Today, Ezekiel is back at St. John's Community Centre to offer volunteer services as his way of giving back to the community. He is a mentor and role model to the current students of NFE, the High School and the upcoming youth. His inspiration infects the young generation with enthusiasm and determination to make it.

Ezekiel Kamau mentoring pupils at St. John's High School during a coffee break

Future Challenges

Success should always point the way to further improvement. There is a projected Phase III to the building construction programme, and this would enable the Non-Formal Education Programme to expand the number of classrooms as well as provide ancillary accommodation. A dispensary, mainly for children, a kitchen for the school feeding programme, additional offices and most importantly a multi-purpose hall are projected. Apart from its value as an asset for school activities, the hall would generate recurrent financial resources for the ongoing work of the Centre.

The general perennial problems of Pumwani are intensifying rather than abating and urban poverty is increasing, not only in scale but also in gravity. The high prevalence of HIV/AIDS continues to affect the target group of the NFE programme and lack of awareness of the consequence of risky behaviour remains a problem for children and young people of the Pumwani community, whose poverty renders them more vulnerable.

More specifically but rather differently, girls' education is hampered by tradition, which puts a high premium on the usefulness of their labour on the domestic front. There have been achievements as far as primary education is concerned but for the higher levels of education, the girl-child is grossly affected.

Most especially, the children enrolled in the Non-Formal Education Programme hail from difficult backgrounds. As such, they require a special approach to learning which cannot be obtained from the formal schools and sometimes includes quality counselling. Unfortunately, the Programme faces a shortage of teachers to facilitate quality learning and character formation.

Shortages of money and skilled personnel are unlikely ever to go away. Let's hope that the non-formal education programme, which has survived for sixty years, will continue to flourish and provide a much-needed education for those who would otherwise be deprived of what others simply take for granted.

Part VI - "The Bigger Picture"

Thousands of children have over the years benefited from the NFE programme

"...the children ate a healthy lunch three times a week"

Chapter 29 - "Blessed Are the Peacemakers"

Election fears

In the letters and cards which we received from our friends in Kenya at Christmas 2012, we were not surprised to detect a general concern that the presidential elections scheduled to take place in March should do so peacefully. That, of course, was a concern which was shared by all of us, who over the years have had close connections with Kenya and been involved with the lives and future of its people.

What was more surprising was the degree of concern expressed in those communications and the kind of people by whom they were sent. They came from those who had spent many years in the country and several from those who had been born there, most of them our contemporaries who were now retired and of advanced years. They had been very much a part of the country as it passed through independence, taken Kenya Citizenship and remained to devote their skills and the rest of their working life to this developing country. They had seen all kinds of unrest and problems but had for the most part gone about their normal lives and moved about freely without becoming too phased by these occurrences.

They were, however, deeply concerned about the forthcoming elections. They had seen something of what had occurred after the 2008 election, when large sections of the population believed that the results had been rigged and that they had been cheated. According to some estimates over 1200 people had died in the violence and 400,000 persons displaced from their homes.

Church involvement and initiatives

St. John's Community Centre shared this concern and sought resources to institute a programme of peacebuilding and conflict-management in the slum areas of Nairobi where it operated. Some of those areas, notably Kiambiu and Mathare, had experienced post-electoral violence in 2008 and poverty, so prevalent in those villages, was seen as a cause of the violence. Ethnicity, race, identity, religious and political tensions, bad governance were all identified as causes but within the slums, poverty was perceived to play a significant part. These causes in turn gave rise to attitudes of anger, hatred, suspicion, mistrust and tribal marginalisation and it was the aim to try to deal with these in a methodical way.

The Centre had the advantage that it was an established part of the Nairobi Diocese of the Anglican Church of Kenya. It could lock into an organisation which would readily identify with the need to heal these attitudes and the search for more positive ways of eliminating injustice and dishonesty than the resort to violence and destruction. Indeed, all the dioceses had an established Department of Justice and Peace Commission, which would be the appropriate vehicle through which this project could be rolled out. These Departments were already involved in church activities concerned with justice, human rights and democratisation.

Nairobi North outreach

Five districts were selected in Nairobi North for implementing the project, namely Kamukunji, Kasarani, Starehe, Makadara and Embakasi. These districts together comprised ten slums and within those slums 7,000 church and community members would be chosen to participate. They would reach out directly to 21,000 people, who in turn would each be expected to influence another two or three residents. If things worked out according to plan, over 60,000 people or 16% of the total area population would have been involved.

Key strategies would be employed to build peace and resolve conflicts and systems were introduced to predict conflicts and respond to them. Violence was to be prevented by increased tolerance of, and respect for, neighbours and other communities and finally civic and voter education was to be provided. One of the responses to be employed would be that to "Do no harm", calling for a commitment not to increase tensions within and across communities.

Such was the planning. In the event, four neighbourhood watch groups were formed at community level in each archdeaconry of the Nairobi diocese to co-ordinate the peace building activities and these acted as a link between the community and the local administration. Peace messages reached nearly 35,000 people in church congregations and community dialogue forums.

Monitors & Peace Committees

The Centre trained 68 peace monitors, who were drawn from church community members of each of the five districts, who then established peace committees in their churches. The committees met in coffee bars, holding inter-active sessions on peace building with community members. This dialogue would be inter-faith and representatives from all the churches would be expected to share information and come up with homemade solutions to their conflict and violence issues, developing their own mechanism for maintaining peace.

Training

There would also be the training of Teachers of Trainers (TOTs) to provide civic education to the community through the Church structure. Once trained these trainers would be expected to use church forums for that purpose. Theatre shows were staged during which the community was asked to give their opinions on the development of the play and solutions to the problems. These Interactive Community Participatory Theatre forums were conducted not only in the Churches but also in public community grounds to capture the wider community who do not attend Anglican church services.

The Situation Room

Another interesting feature of the project was the creation of the "Situation Room", a kind of Headquarters which would become of increasing importance as the time for the elections drew near. Peace monitors, working in the community and facilitating peace forums, who identified women, young people or children who needed to rebuild trust in their relationships, whether community, family or personal would bring them to the Situation Room to receive help and advice from counsellors trained by the Community Centre. Peace monitors, provided by each district on a daily rotational basis, were responsible for supervising the Situation Room and it would also be their task to organise peer groups for women, young people and children who could discuss among themselves issues to do with conflict in their families and in the community.

The Situation Room became useful during the electoral period, acting like a community-based resource centre for co-ordinated peace responses in the five districts. Arrangements were made for the peace monitors to have mobile phones: a blog and webpage were set up where the community could post information on peace activities and early warning signs of conflict in their area. The Situation Room also had social media pages like Twitter and Facebook, in order to interact with the community and security personnel on peace issues.

Indeed, the Situation Room served other useful purposes connected with the election.

Conclusions

The election 2013 passed quietly despite the very close vote between the two principal Presidential candidates, the need for recounts and finally a complaint made to the judicial authorities. After the decision of the Supreme Court, peace monitors in Mathare were able to quell unrest in the community. In five of the seven constituencies, accountability forums were held with elected leaders

The importance of this project is the foresight it demonstrates on the part of the Community Centre in involving itself in making provision for the contingency of violence, which would have been so destructive to Kenya and its people. Most especially, it demonstrates yet again the way in which the community in Nairobi North were made to feel responsible for peace building and conflict management within their borders. They were to look for "homemade" solutions and women were to become increasingly involved in decision-making positions within the community structures and in the peace committees.

The importance, realised by the Centre in other contexts and projects many years ago, was to involve the community members at an early stage. Decisions had to be their decisions, reached by their committees, so that the planning, as well as the work itself, was owned by them. Capacity building, though costly and time-consuming, was the way to ensure not only that a project was successfully implemented but would have the best chance of surviving when Centre support had to be reduced or withdrawn and outside financial resources were finally expended.

Part VII – "Conclusion"

Chapter 30 – Outcomes in Pumwani

International & National Challenges

It is striking that the challenges facing the Centre today are almost unchanged since its inception. The sectoral areas in which it is working are strikingly similar. Economic hardship and unemployment remain the basic problems and from them spring educational needs, health problems, crime, vice and low self-esteem.

So, you ask, what has changed and, more importantly, what has been achieved by the Centre in Pumwani in all these years? Before we question the accomplishments of the Centre, it is imperative that we see why the national challenges themselves have gone unchanged in over sixty years.

First and foremost, the scale of the problems has increased beyond all recognition. The national increase in childbirth was phenomenal following independence, Kenya ranking amongst the top six countries world-wide. Whilst the population figures have been offset by the impact of HIV/AIDS, the economic effect of that disease has been disastrous. Men and women have died in their prime and their most productive years have been cut short. We have seen how this has directly affected the Centre in its outreach to the community at large and not least to those orphaned by its fatal effect.

Corruption has also taken its toll. Overseas aid, which might have alleviated the problems of the disadvantaged, has been syphoned off by those in positions of power and authority. This is now endemic across the African continent and, whilst corruption is clearly on the increase in the more developed countries of the world, its effect in nations like Kenya has been more profound. For instance, we saw the scandal of dishonest claims for Parliamentary expenses in England. Whilst this was damaging in terms of example, it had little or no effect upon the general well-being of the populace as a whole. In the German private sector, the built-in secretion of harmful diesel emissions from their cars during tests went widely unnoticed despite its serious ecological effect.

In the same vein, there are the extravagant salaries and benefits paid by global and national businesses to their senior executives. They turn them into poor role models for the less privileged members of their workforces, creating images of greed and selfishness. Whilst in the Western world they produce resentment, they do not impact upon the standard of living which would be enjoyed by the average person. Sadly, in Africa, the polarisation of wealth does prejudice the lot of the ordinary citizen.

These external factors have, therefore, significantly affected the scale of the challenges facing the Centre. In the face of insurmountable odds, the Centre has made a difference. Lives have been changed. Potential solutions have been tested and some have been found. Morale in the community has been raised. Working practices have kept pace with the unprecedented speed of technological advance.

Sectoral Areas of Activity

The programmes of the Centre were directed to four areas of activity which the Centre had selected as those likely to alleviate the most pressing needs of Pumwani. In this final appraisal of the work, we shall confine our comments to the activities which relate to Pumwani, the work in the national programmes having been touched on in the preceding chapters. Those four sectoral areas are Economic Empowerment, Education & Training, Health & HIV/AIDS and Governance & Human Rights.

Economic Empowerment

Economic empowerment, not unexpectedly, heads the list. Working primarily in what is still one of the poorest areas of Nairobi, the Centre aimed at alleviating the needs of at least four thousand poor households by seeing their income increased some twenty per cent over the five-year period up to 2014. The number of households was in fact exceeded but the percentage increase of the income was difficult to measure due to lack of data.

It has to be remembered that, in carrying out this exercise, hand-outs are not the purpose of the Centre but rather the empowerment of these vulnerable communities to address effectively the root causes of poverty and to lobby against injustices which make it difficult for them to attain a sustainable livelihood.

Using an established working model, the Centre encouraged the formation of new self-help groups, with opportunities to increase their savings and to borrow. It was the aim that 80% of the members would consistently access financial support. By the end of the five-year period about 80 Groups had been formed and survived, each with an average of just under 20 members. The capacity of the members in entrepreneurship, business and group management was enhanced and quality of life for participating households improved by increased disposable income.

This was further achieved through product development courses, the community acquiring new skills and establishing new enterprises, which did not necessarily compete with those in neighbouring localities. Making beads, soap and mats assisted self-help group members to diversify their businesses and look for markets beyond the Pumwani area

The Centre also helped the new groups by arranging visits to businesses which have proved successful and aimed at providing mentoring for new businesses to ensure that they did not fall into pitfalls which would otherwise bring about their downfall. Then there are the matters of licensing and registration of businesses, which are complicated; some new entrepreneurs might not even be aware of their existence. The centre seeks to provide that awareness and to advocate in suitable circumstances the relaxation of those requirements with the powers that be.

Finally, success all too often comes from whom you know, rather than what you know, so the Centre sought to improve market access for products and services and to facilitate business linkages with service providers and micro-credit organisations.

Education & Training

From its very inception, education has been seen as the way forward to easing people out of extreme poverty. The girls' classes in the very

Part VII - "Conclusion"

early years of the Centre, followed by women's classes, gave those disadvantaged by their poverty, social position and sex, a chance to break out of the inevitable cycle of prostitution and beer-brewing. We have, however, seen how from these humble beginnings the Centre developed a more sophisticated educational programme, even to the point of building a secondary school, which was handed over to the Parish.

The non-formal education provided by the Centre has, nevertheless, always remained a project of the Centre and has now become one of its most important activities, due very largely to the incidence of HIV/AIDS and the large number of orphans and vulnerable children who are left without the financial resources for their education and up-bringing. They are not, however, the sole beneficiaries of this programme, which caters for the children of very poor families.

Character formation is a central theme within this educational project. Children are taken through life-skill sessions and exposed to other areas such as health and child rights. The Centre solicits sponsorship for the children since their families are too poor to keep them in school

Countless children had obtained access to basic education and vocational skills through the Non-Formal Education School. The pupils themselves and their parents or guardians rated it highly, compared with government schools in the area. The children had been provided with food for lunch and this had had the effect of increasing their powers of retention and hence their performance.

Children continue to be helped following the basic education they receive. On becoming young people, they have been provided with skills training opportunities and others are gainfully employed or self-employed and are earning a living for themselves and their families. Hundreds of young people have been given sufficient education and have acquired sufficient skills from which the majority can derive an income.

From the year 2010, the strategic planning of the Centre forecasted a dramatic increase in the numbers requiring non-formal education and skills training due to the high incidence of AIDS, leaving many orphans and vulnerable children without continuing education. It resolved over the next five years to target nearly 1,000 children and young people, to whom they would offer quality education, skills training and talent development, aware that it would stretch actual and potential financial resources to the limit. The scale of the problem means that numbers are meaningless; for a significant element, however, hope was held out in the form of learning, training and work.

To achieve this, a whole variety of programmes was introduced including facilities like homework clubs or the provision of basic learning materials. As always, the integration of out-of-school children into schools was always the preferred option. In consequence, at least 200 of the out-of-school children were helped back into school and over 1300 children were assisted to access education in one way or another.

Facilities like homework clubs were introduced

Assistance was provided for others in more comprehensive ways. Psycho-social support was also given, resulting in positive behaviour transformation of nearly 1000 young people and children in three of the Pumwani villages. This was provided by peer educators, who were sent on exposure visits, trained in monthly skills sessions and mentored by role models and quarterly forums. Parents and guardians had their part to play, receiving training in parenting and having a role perhaps in children's clubs. Over 4,400 children were reached in this context.

Youth Empowerment

Having looked at education and the Centre's role in it, and especially the Non-Formal education it provided, we have also seen how some of that spilled over to older children as they moved through adolescence into the age when the world of work was beckoning – or, in so many cases, not beckoning and resulting in unemployment. In what ways has the Community Centre reached out to these young people when they have left school, either because their schooling was complete or prematurely when perhaps the money ran out or school was no longer an appropriate place or option for them?

Throughout the long history of the Centre the staff have worked to improve the education, skills and confidence of the young people who lived in Pumwani. The poverty surrounding them, and the depressing attitudes of their families left them feeling helpless and incapable of improving their situation. The Christian Industrial Training Centre, which gave hope of change and skilled employment, graduated from being a club for unoccupied young boys to a sophisticated trade school which selected only the most able applicants from all over Nairobi. Many young people from Pumwani were not suitable and a lot of these turned to crime. To find some excitement and much-needed wealth, they organised themselves into gangs and devised criminal activities. This unemployed youth population is often feared in the community as a threat to peace and security.

For those young people, who are rather too old to go back to school and need assistance to find employment or to make a living, the Centre has worked with Kindernothilfe, a long-standing partner, which has supported some young people working in business groups and others who were individually self-employed. Not everybody, however, is commercially orientated, and they have benefited from vocational and skills training interventions. Many others who already possess other skills or talents have been assisted to nurture them. Sports teams have been assisted with equipment and registration into leagues.

In most of these ways the beneficiaries have been able to derive some income from these activities. It has, however, to be remembered that young people need an outlet for their energy and aspirations and even in those cases where these activities have not led to financial benefit, many have been weaned off a life of crime and lawlessness, quite apart from incentivising them to achieve. The Centre is proud that Pumwani has a pool of talented youth and the existence of PYGRON, the Pumwani Youth Groups Network is evidence of this.

It was in or around 1998, that Eunice Kamau and her team initiated the Environmental programme to which we have alluded earlier. An important part of that programme was the refurbishment of the toilets and Eunice used those facilities as an opportunity of helping the disadvantaged youth who had no chance of education or training. She prevailed upon Nairobi City Council to let the young people of Pumwani manage the toilets and to do so as a business. In consequence, hundreds of young people have since secured a viable source of livelihood, which has seen many of them move from juvenile delinquency to positive living.

How have they done this? They organised themselves into groups, each one assuming responsibility for, and management of, one of the eighteen refurbished toilets. They chose names for the groups, such as "Millenium", "Kitui", "Bidii" meaning "Hard Work", "Dawn to Dusk", "Pumwani United", "Uprising" and so on.

Eunice Kamau (far right) with community leaders who had organised the care of the lavatories and stand pipes

Uprising

Uprising Youth Group was established by 25 unemployed young people whose common goal was to reduce idleness and fight poverty in Mashimoni village, a part of Majengo slums. Mashimoni had for a ong time been known as a haven for hard-core criminals, drug peddling and abuse, prostitution and petty theft, and as a result, had been blacklisted by the administration. Prior to the establishment of the group, many youths had been gunned down by the police and conflicts between the police and youth were a common sight. Most of the founder members of the group are reformed criminals who are now out to challenge a culture of careless living and crime, which had become entrenched in the lifestyle of the youth.

The group, which was formally registered with the department of Social Services in 2005, started off running a video parlour to raise funds. It now has a membership of 30 people, who have diversified into running projects such as a car wash, a fourteen-seater public service vehicle, garbage collection, hot shower and poultry farming. It also owns buildings. Starting with a small kiosk it has gone on to erect a multi-storey building, the ground floor being occupied as shops and go-downs. Laudably, it has a children's resource centre, which is free of charge. When completed, it will have five floors including residential apartments for letting.

"Uprising" is also an example of what one person can achieve given the chance. Winstone Nanjeso is the former Chairman of Uprising Youth Group, a position he held for five years. He joined Uprising Youth Group as a teenager in the year 2000, the year it was formed, and saw the group grow over the years. Uprising's transformation from a little known group of juvenile delinquents to a robust and respected group is a role model for youth in the County.

Winstone attributes the success of his group and its members to good planning, self-sacrifice and determination, at the same time admitting that through the capacity building and economic empowerment programmes of the Centre, his group grew beyond their imagination.

Winstone Nanjeso - Chairman of Uprising (centre of photo wearing white shirt)

Part VII - "Conclusion"

Uprising has gone from a small kiosk to a multi-storey building for housing

"Chipukizi Youth Group"

Like Uprising, Chipukizi was also formed to address the same two problems, namely unemployment and the high crime rates in Pumwani which were escalating out of control. As with Uprising, they intended to do so through environmental management, being deployed to clean the trenches and manage garbage which had piled up in some sections of the community. It was their task also to unclog blockages on the existing community toilet, which was in a deplorable state and had been largely abandoned due to poor waste disposal mechanism. The facility required to be expanded and complementary services provided such as shower rooms. Taught by the Centre to "think outside the box" they persuaded the local Anglican Church to allow them to clear, maintain and use a dumping site along the perimeter wall of the Church and erect temporary rental houses. The newly cemented site, which they undertook to keep clear of rubbish, was available to local residents at a fee as a laundry area and to offer motor-bike cleaning services. They expressed their appreciation of the "livelihoods training" given to them by the Centre which had enabled them to improve their services through their own efforts rather than looking for outside support.

Mustakabal Women Group

A different kind of group originating in a different way was Mustakabal, a group of women who had been friends. They all had domestic financial needs, such as school fees and household emergencies but also stagnating businesses. They had borrowed from each other and their relatives but had no means of repayment and relationships had become strained.

They therefore came together to form a savings system and in 2015 the group was registered and starting with an almost non-existent weekly contribution, the group grew both in terms of income and membership. They had started receiving Livelihood Training provided by the Centre and this taught them to examine their personal gifts, talents and assets. In consequence they started to sell eggs which they purchased wholesale and they produced a profit of US$30 each month but challenges of various kinds made the business untenable. They turned to buying

Part VII - "Conclusion"

Leaders interview Chipukizi Youth Group

Mustakabal Women Group – "enhanced relationships"

household foodstuffs in bulk, which was purchased by the members and the surplus sold to friends and neighbours. This was profitable and made for cohesiveness amongst the members. Savings have increased and due to the Livelihood Training of the Centre they have started to manufacture and sell peanut butter. They say that the training has enabled them to see the need for unity and their social relationship is greatly enhanced.

Group Training

The training of these groups has involved different aspects of viability. Assisting people, who are on the breadline, the Centre has had to address both the personal circumstances of the individual members and the viability of the projects in which they are or might be involved.

It is not easy to tell people who find it difficult to make ends meet, that they need to economise on expenditure, when they are living from hand to mouth on essential items such as food, rental, medication and school fees. It is striking that when Mustakabal Group came together as a group, some started saving as little as US$0.01 per week. It was the culture that all must save, however little and it would become a necessary personal habit fostered by the group dynamic and reinforced by the esprit de corps.

Viability of projects was essential and it was necessary that groups should know when their chosen projects would not, or had not, become profitable. The Centre had the expertise and it was the intention that PYGRON would assume the task of overseeing the groups and dealing with gaps occurring in such issues as viability.

However, everything comes at a cost. The costs of PYGRON itself has had to be borne by the groups some of whom see their subscription to PYGRON as either an unnecessary, or a burdensome, expense depending upon the success or otherwise of the group.

The Centre's continuing involvement, in partnership with Tearfund, has therefore been essential and the future of their role in oversight and co-ordination is an issue to be resolved. Perhaps the value of the Centre's input through its Livelihood Training programme is best summed up by Chipukizi: "We are very grateful to St. John's Community Centre for giving our group an opportunity to gain more knowledge on how we can sustain ourselves through the livelihoods training. As a group, we were really impacted by the principle 'to think outside the box'. For a long time, we had put ourselves inside an imaginary box – the training helped us to realise that we were limiting ourselves."

Pumwani Youth Group

Pumwani Youth Group was formed in 2002 as the only football team in the area of Majengo to represent the area in sporting activities. By then most of the team players were idle with no source of income and had opted for a life of crime and drug abuse, finishing up in life-imprisonment and even death.

In 2016 the group was re-organised and registered with fifty male members, who each contributed at least US$14 per month after tournaments or casual labour. The purpose was to bring together the members and their accumulated savings and to make them available to members to support their basic household needs. Then, after some years a local leader helped them acquire a small piece of land, upon which they built car washing services. The group encountered many difficulties both with regard to their car wash business and also their personal financial contributions and relationships.

They were helped, like Chipukizi, by the Livelihood Training, following which they accepted that the space could produce a bigger income, despite its challenges and they resolved to deal with those challenges. They cleared up their land space and with the aid of a US$200 capital contribution from the Centre they cemented the floor of the car wash, expanding the area to include a public toilet and motor-bike services, employing labour to assist in meeting increased demand for those services.

Pumwani Youth Group Car Wash

Sponsorship

Readers will recall that in the very early years, sponsorship was resisted by the Centre, so as not in any way to compromise the children's self-respect. Pat thought this was particularly important for the girls whose background was confidential. This was later changed as we saw when Children Incorporated became a partner but again this was stopped, because the children being sponsored were not the poorest who really required sponsorship. The scheme was being abused. Clearly this policy has now been reversed, and the authors wonder whether this became necessary due to the enormity of the problems and needs following the HIV/AIDS epidemic, in terms of the numbers affected and the need to obtain education for the orphans and vulnerable children affected.

Now, once again, sponsorship of a very different kind, has been offered since 2010, with the help of one of the Centre's friends in Norway. Drammen School in that country was touched by the plight of the children in the Nairobi slums, who could not afford secondary education by reason only of poverty. Drammen School organises an annual event when all the interested students work for a day and donate their earnings to the Centre for secondary school sponsorship. At the time of writing 180 needy, but bright, children have been supported. Furthermore, there is a bonus. Every year a team of teachers and students from Drammen School visits the Centre for a week and every second year a team of seven visits Drammen School, also for a week. Through the Drammen School Sponsorship Programme hundreds of children have been supported to complete their secondary education and over 20 of them have even pursued University education. Scores of others have been enrolled for vocational training with many of them graduating and engaging in self-employment. Building relationships like that and establishing friendships lead to a better understanding of what it means to be bearing each other's burdens.

We thought in an earlier chapter of the needs of parking boys and the case of Peter Mweke is a boy who was actually found on the streets. Peter Mweke does not know when he was born. His name, Mweke (Swahili for "alone") was given to him by the person who found him abandoned in the streets of Nairobi. He was raised by an old woman who later died, leaving the young boy with no guardians to look after him. It comes as no surprise that, afterwards, he joined street boys and started engaging in crime and drugs. He was arrested and being a minor, was sent to reform school, where he decided to turn his life around. After being released from government reform school, he started attending the Non-Formal Education school at the Centre where he was sponsored by a Ms Astrid. During this time, Peter also developed skills in singing and rapping and became a successful gospel artist and a comedian. It is a great story when somebody who has had the most impossible start in life finds a way of extricating himself from a downward spiral which looked inevitable. It is even greater news when that person wants to use his experience to help others.

The boy who was given the name "Alone" is anything but alone in the motivational sessions he has with street children. As a TV entertainer, they will respect his advice and hopefully use him as a role model. It is also encouraging, especially for the Centre staff, when people who

Chapter 30 – Outcomes in Pumwani

Peter Mweke in motivational discussions with street children

have benefited from the Centre's activities want to give back their time and support as volunteers and contribute in a practical way as part of a community which the Centre seeks to promote. The Centre is considering the formation of an Alumni Association to bring together its many beneficiaries who can give back as Peter has done, especially as mentors and role models. Currently there are six beneficiaries working at the Centre in different capacities, three of them being employed as Programme Officers.

Health - HIV/AIDS – Child Mortality

HIV/AIDS is one of the most serious epidemics ever to face Kenya. Statistics indicated in 2008 that Kenya ranked sixth globally in HIV infection. In some parts of the country, especially in urban areas, one in every six people was infected with HIV/AIDS but in some vulnerable population groups it was as high as 35%. In response to the spread of the virus the Government declared AIDS to be a national disaster and set up the National Aids Control Council to spearhead the fight against the disease and co-ordinate the HIV/AIDS programme in the country.

We have seen in an earlier chapter how the Centre became heavily involved in HIV/AIDS in five different areas throughout Kenya and in the following chapters how the DREAMS and Nilinde projects worked successfully in Nairobi amongst a huge number of people. With $7 million in funding for HIV/AIDS prevention, care, support and treatment over the past 15 years, St. John's Community Centre has a strong track record in managing multi-faceted health programmes for orphans and vulnerable children and young people. It has done it through programmes that mobilise communities, build capacity and create linkages among community-based organisations, local NGOs, Faith-Based organisations, self-help groups and the Government. Since 1993, the Centre has combated HIV/AIDS, the most important public health and development challenge of our time. Suffice it in this section to look more generally at health problems in Pumwani itself.

One quite new and different project, supported by Child Rescue Foundation, was to achieve sustainable reduction of child mortality among the poorest households in Kiambiu village of Pumwani. Expectant mothers and children less than five years old were targeted because the parents have inadequate knowledge and are too poor to afford the costs of treatment if it is required.

The children under five were screened to identify risky conditions. Referrals were made to health institutions, drugs were procured for those in critical conditions and after treatment cases were followed up. As a matter of routine, expectant mothers were encouraged to attend anti-natal clinics and were followed up in their households.

Due to good planning, proper mobilisation and community involvement, some 3,000 children under five were identified and dealt with, just twice the number targeted at the inception of the project. It was also due to successful networking with other programmes within the Centre. Most significant, however, was the degree to which members of the community were mobilised to deal themselves with the targets. It was planned to build up a capacity of 1760 households with knowledge of nutrition, preventative health practices and the importance of immunisation. In the result 1850 households were mobilised, because the households which were mobilised ended up mobilising others.

Even more striking, was the willingness of members of the community to volunteer. It was envisaged that four community volunteers and ten mentor mothers would be trained to enhance basic health skills. No less than 29 were willing to work as volunteers in the project and even more encouragingly, women who were beneficiaries of the project formed a group, quaintly called the "mentor mothers group", who are educating other women on good preventative health practices and child care, an effective way of passing on key health messages to the mothers and the community at large.

When the project started in 2007 the child mortality rate in Kiambiu village was 5.7% but within four years it had reduced to just 1.4%. When the project ended, the enablement of the community, and the training of 20 community health workers, ensured that the community continued to receive health services.

Governance & Human Rights

It would be easy for the Centre, in the face of all the human deprivation revealed in the last three sectoral areas, to concentrate all its efforts into alleviating the physical suffering and need which they exhibit. The temptation would be for the Centre to throw all its efforts into Economic Empowerment, Education & Training and HIV/Health issues because the needs of the people in those areas are all too obvious and urgent. To redress them would bring immediate relief and clearly demonstrate the practicality and effectiveness of the Centre's activities.

To do that, however, would be to ignore the self-esteem of the people of Pumwani. The lack of this, as we have seen, has been a root cause of their acceptance of the status quo. It was an attitude of laissez faire that led to the persistence of serious physical problems because people did not believe that change is possible. The Centre has, therefore, also operated programmes related to human rights; the chapter dealing with devolved funds and the empowerment of the people, particularly the women, to claim and follow these is a case in point. Similarly, the tackling of abuse of human rights, especially on behalf of orphans and vulnerable children following the loss of their parents due to HIV/AIDS, has been vital. The exploitation of such children by opportunistic neighbours or villagers is an outrage and the action of the Centre in activating, and in some cases establishing, Local Area Advisory Councils and insisting they exercise their responsibility to safeguard such children, has been timely.

The Centre has also formed change-agents, training monitors and paralegals to support and empower self-help groups with various programmes it has fostered.

Gender mainstreaming is a cross-cutting theme of the Centre going across all its programmes. Amongst the population of Pumwani, where women have played a major role in the life and activities of the community, it is important that their position is respected, their views taken account of, their rights safeguarded, their persons and possessions, such as they are, protected.

In all the networking done by the Centre, it has, of course, established contacts not only with the Churches and voluntary sector, but also with the public sector, making regular contact with the various Government Ministries, such as Health and Education, which are relevant to the areas of work in which the Centre is involved. The same would be true in the local government field and the need to co-operate and network with the Nairobi City Council. The Centre's values and the clear stand which it makes on matters such as empowerment, sexual equality and transparency, will have its quiet, but steady, impact upon policy-makers and legislators.

Chapter 31 – The Future Role of the Centre

The Centre workforce

A brief glance at an organogram of the Centre staff would demonstrate not only how the size of the operation has grown, but the extent to which professional expertise and loyalty has developed within it. Peter Njuguna, who was the head of the educational work when Eunice Kamau left the Centre, was appointed Director and he is supported by a Deputy Director and two senior officers, one responsible for Finance & Administration and the other for the Centre's programmes. In turn, a Chief Accountant and three other Accountants, a Principal in the Training Institute and High School, an Administrator and a Chaplain, all provide essential skills for the overall running of the organisation. Team Leaders of the individual programmes supervise the Programme Officers, teachers and other staff, who are working at the grass roots with those who are served by the Centres activities.

Peter Njuguna – Director of St. John's Community Centre

Strategic Management

A strategic plan was first introduced in 1993 and thereafter a strategic management culture has been developed. Following adoption of the plan by the Board of Management, it is then cascaded down through the different levels of staff for implementation, which in turn is monitored and evaluated at all stages. Organisation experience within the Centre has shown that positive benefits have been derived from this culture such as team synergy. Furthermore, donors and other stakeholders who have been dealing with the Centre are able to focus on the direction being taken by it. All parties can maximise their resources on areas of priority and the different programmes are better co-ordinated.

In the last plan it was noted that there was room for better co-ordination and in view of the number of cross-cutting themes, this is important. There have now been five strategic plans and the key focus remains, unsurprisingly, in Preventive Health, Education and Training and Economic Empowerment.

There is, however, a new development of special importance, in the closer working relationship of the Centre and the Diocese of Nairobi in the wider mission of the Church to the community at large. It goes under the name of "Church Community Mobilization Transformational Development" (CCMTD) - something of a mouthful but, if when it is unpicked, it does prove to be "transformational", then it will indeed be an exciting "development" and mark an entirely new chapter in the life of the Centre.

Participatory involvement & Institutional Achievement

Shortly before the end of one strategic plan, a strategic planning workshop was held with twenty-two participants, comprising several board members, senior management and programme staff. Time was taken to re-assess the needs of target groups of the Centre programmes as well as those of the general Pumwani community. This period was used to discover from people's experiences lessons learnt in programme implementation and the conditions then prevailing amongst the people of

Pumwani. Building on these experiences, the planning team was better able to define new objectives for the ensuing plan.

At the same time, an evaluation was made of the outcomes of the current plan. Resources had been effectively mobilised to ensure that 75% of the planned targets had been met. That, we believe, was a good result, bearing in mind all the imponderable assumptions necessarily made at the beginning of a five-year plan, such as the state of the national economy and the estimates of donations and grants. It is laudable that the strategic planning of the Centre took into account external criteria, such as the risks attendant in a developing country and possible circumstances likely to affect the growth rate. Particularly impressive is the care taken to examine how the Centre's activities matched up to the Millennium Development Goals set by the United Nations Millennium Summit 2000, and how far they were aligned to the national aspirations set by the Kenya Vision 2030.

They were able to identify areas of Centre activity totally in keeping with the three so-called pillars of the vision: Economic, Social and Political. This demonstration of compatibility with, and support of, international and national goals would undoubtedly impress the overseas donors who do and give so much to resource the Centre's work. How encouraging, also, for the staff, as they see their work at the grass roots promoting the hopes and aspirations of their country. How important, too, that the national and regional programmes of the Centre fit with the national targets adopted by the government.

Even more importantly during that period, through proper accountability for resources and transparency in all their dealings, the Centre maintained a cordial and supportive relationship with the development partners who have been financing its work. This was made possible by the enhancement of staff capacity to monitor and evaluate the outcomes of their activities, so that reports had been made to the partners keeping them in touch.

One of those achievements was the completion of a new wing of offices and classrooms. This had been professionally built and was completed on time, a move applauded by the partner who had provided the funds.

Over the years the Centre had also kept abreast of the fast-changing developments in the world of IT. Internal communication has improved through access to email by all the staff. This must have been particularly important where there are cross-cutting programmes serving the same target groups and beneficiaries.

Empowerment of local groups

Readers will recall the paradigm shift to which we have referred earlier. All those years ago, the Centre had decided to discontinue hand-outs and to empower the people of Pumwani themselves to deal with the problems which they face.

Even in the 1960's, before the paradigm shift itself really occurred, Anne Barnett had insisted that the provision of cooked food should be

Mealtimes at the centre in the past

discontinued because women were not providing in a traditional way for the feeding of their families. In the same way, Eunice Kamau was insistent that the community had to get their act together to maintain the lavatories and take ownership of them, before she would release funds sent by the Tudor Trust in England to repair and renovate the toilet blocks.

This modus operandi has been progressively developed over the years. The Centre had operated micro-credit facilities for clients who needed them but found that it is much more effective to work through Self-Help Groups rather than to be involved with the day-to-day administration of those activities itself. This is especially so, where the Centre is also working in a supportive role. The reader will recall how successfully the Small Community Projects had managed revolving funds to help the guardians of Orphans and Vulnerable Children provide for the children's economic needs.

Micro-credit has proved to be useful for small businesses, providing saving and borrowing facilities. In a recent strategic plan, the Centre has set itself a target of facilitating the formation of fifty new self-help groups, training them in the concept of micro-credit and finding finance through other sources.

Young People & Crime

Youth-perpetrated crime in the slums is still a major concern for Nairobi City residents and development organisations like St. John's Community Centre share that concern as much for the perpetrators as for the victims. Sadly, many of the people who get drawn into criminal activity are the very young people with whom the Centre has been working, endeavouring to woo them from crime and the destitution and hopelessness, which precipitate it. The Centre is, however, confident that youth crime is now less prevalent and that the interventions, which it has introduced into its youth programmes, have significantly contributed to that reduction. Gone are the days when gunshots would rend the air in Pumwani, almost on a daily basis, as the police gave chase to criminals, most of whom had been the Centre's students. Gone too are the days when unsuspecting visitors to the Centre would be mugged as they entered or left the Centre premises.

Indeed, crime used to be so commonplace that almost every member of the Centre staff could recall at least one occasion when they had been the victim of a mugging. So blatant was this activity that a staff member would not be safe, even within the Centre premises. The most dangerous area was the street immediately outside the Centre gates, a position in which thieves would even board and seize cargo from moving vehicles as they slowed to negotiate the sharp bend in the road.

The saddest moments occurred when members of staff were called from their offices to view the corpses of young people, who had been gunned down by the police after criminal involvement. It was particularly distressing to find young people, who had passed through their hands, finishing their lives in that way. Furthermore, it was demoralising, because the Centre felt that they had in some way failed those young lives.

The Projects Manager of the Centre, Ms. Sally Gatei recalls the concern of her father, who had run a discotheque business in the area. He had felt so strongly that she should not work in an area of such high criminal activity that he tore up the appointment letter which she received from the Centre before she started work there. Sally's mother, Emily Njeri Arunga was perhaps not so concerned, having worked in Pumwani as the Secretary at St. John's Church from 1985 until 1998, when she was appointed to Matumaini House as Matron of the old women and the girls, a position she held until her retirement in 2005.

Sally thanks God for the way in which muggings and robberies, especially in Munyema Street, the notorious route outside the Centre gates, have drastically reduced. She is convinced this is due to the dynamic Youth Programme interventions initiated by the Centre, which have already been mentioned in connection with the Youth Groups. The Lifeskills Training, Vocational Sponsorship, Careers Awareness Trainings and Talent Development programmes have all been effective.

Part VII - "Conclusion"

Sally Gatei – Projects Manager

We have written about the lucrative income-generating projects such as car wash, public toilets, bathrooms and shops: many of these have been created alongside the paths where the muggings were previously rampant. These facilities in themselves now offer the much-needed security because the owners and workers identify persons known to them as criminals. Sally quotes the old adage about "setting a thief to catch a thief."

Uprising Youth Group, which started off with reformed criminals, are now making great efforts to mentor the upcoming generation, openly sharing their nasty experiences in the crime-world and advising them not to follow suit. Uprising has been in the forefront of initiating a children's resource centre to improve the academic performance of children in their area and even securing educational sponsorships for some of the children. They are ready to mentor and offer the next generation a life away from crime and a taste of success through entrepreneurial hard work.

*Community cleaning Munyema Street,
the "notorious route outside the Centre gates"*

The Centre has also introduced Talent Development initiatives and has seen dozens of young people unleash their God-given talents to pursue their dreams. Like Peter Mweke, some are making it big in such areas as theatre, music and comedy, whilst others have displayed innate talent in carpentry, sculpture and even sport. The Centre is proud that one of their very own mentored groups emerged as the winners of a recent talent search competition and scooped the half-a-million-shillings award.

Youth Group in Dancing and Performing Arts

The Performing Arts

Some of the best actors and comedians who graced the television screens and radio shows in Kenya in the eighties and early nineties came from Pumwani slums. They were household names almost anywhere in the country. Unfortunately, unlike their Western counterparts, they did not benefit greatly from their amazing talents. It is said that they obtained raw deals because their negotiating skills were not strong and being poor their modest remuneration was better than none at all.

Bearing in mind that these actors had never had any training, it is remarkable that they successfully entertained Kenyans for years and the slums which had a reputation for crime and prostitution suddenly acquired a new kudos and dignity from their stage celebrities. Unfortunately, that generation of fine actors has come to an end without being succeeded by the next.

The Centre is trying to revive this lost art by revamping the performing arts clubs for children and youth. This is already paying off. In 2016, using a host of locally talented artists mixed with professional actors, the Centre produced a powerful movie on advocacy entitled "Maria"[15], which went on to win a number of regional and national awards. Produced with the support of the United Nations Democracy Fund, the Centre held screenings in social halls around the slums and less affluent parts of Nairobi.

Clearly the Centre has, over the years, come to understand the importance of allowing its students to dream. Amidst the poverty of the area and location and the need to focus on economic issues, especially in the tuition, the Centre staff realise the importance of realising the people's God-given talents, as they put it. In the same way, the Youth Groups were taught to "think outside the box". Lifting people out of poverty seems more successful when they are being encouraged to use their own initiative, start their own businesses, pursue their own dreams and ideas. Lifting people out of crime works when they want a different kind of life and reach their own conclusion that life will offer more adventure, more hope, more satisfaction in living their lawful dreams and letting other people do the same.

The Centre also finds it most gratifying that the young people, when engaging with their programmes also enrich their spiritual lives. Many of them start attending Church on a consistent basis and join the youth programmes in their churches. A significant proportion of the youth who are active in St. John's Church Pumwani are beneficiaries of the Centre's programmes including the acting Church Secretary.

We have seen how important the environmental conditions of Pumwani have been and the part played by young people in their improvement. Just as important as the work itself, was the part played by the Centre and the effect it had on young people, lifting them out of the poverty surrounding them and the depressing attitudes of their families. The opportunities

---

[15] Some information is taken from the Kenyan Daily Nation article *'Maria': A picture of dirty politics* dated 10th February 2017.

offered to the young people to earn even a modest sum in the environmental work had demonstrated to them that crime was not the only option and that the search for work, however menial and however difficult to secure, was the only safe and long-term solution to alleviate their need of an income. The formation of the youth groups, as we have seen, provide now the clear evidence which other young people needed to witness.

The International Arena

In Part VI we spoke of the Bigger Picture and we see that a small project to alleviate suffering in one small region of Nairobi city has grown into an organisation with national programmes and international contacts.

In developing programmes across Kenya, St. John's Community Centre has attracted the attention of donors and partners from abroad. Its long association with the German charity Kindernothilfe led to funding from USAID for the HIV/AIDS projects and working closely with Kindernothilfe and the New Partners' Initiative enabled the Centre to build its own capacity, introducing new standards, policies and operational systems across the whole of its work.

From an earlier date, in its darkest days, the Centre found friends in the people and churches of Norway. It was given a new lease of life by a baseline survey of its activities carried out with their help and financial support given on the back of it. The other Scandinavian countries have also been generous friends and supporters. Recall the miraculous visit of the Danish foreign minister, who found a warm welcome at the Centre when his planned, high-powered, Government interviews fell through at the last moment. That happy visit was well rewarded and the relationship with Danida was cemented. Then there was SIDA, the Swedish International Development Cooperation Agency, which gave the essential grant for the building of the new Maridadi Fabrics factory: and, do not let us forget neighbouring Finland, who sent us Immi, our talented designer.

Fredkorpset, a programme of the Norwegian Foreign Ministry, operates a project through St. John's Community Centre facilitating the exchange of personnel for a one-year period between the Centre and similar institutions in two other African countries. Young professionals are given the opportunity to work and share their knowledge and practice in the fields of health, information technology, community development and accounts. The Centre has been involved in this programme for ten years and has during that period sent ten members of staff to these other countries. In turn it has hosted fifteen personnel from the Churches Health Association of Zambia and the Churches Health Association of Malawi. It is noteworthy that St. John's Community Centre is the co-ordinating partner and as such is responsible for the administrative and financial responsibilities of the programme.

Church Community Mobilization Transformational Development (CCMTD)

In Chapter 2 we referred to the emphasis which the Kenyan church inherited from the conservative evangelical missionaries, whose evangelistic zeal brought the Christian gospel to the country in the 19th Century. This theology later gave rise to stress and misunderstanding when the missionaries, who came with the same zeal and sense of vocation to the Community Centre in the 1950s and 1960s, displayed also a concern for wider issues affecting the people whom they had come to serve than those which the members of the established church would have then thought it necessary to address. We have referred to the suspicion with which Helen and Charles Tett thought they were viewed by the Revival Brethren. They each worked amongst those who needed help in all sorts of ways, regardless of their religious persuasion. It was equally difficult for members of St. John's Church to understand why Muslim women, dressed in their black bui-buis, sat waiting outside Pat's casework office. In chapter 22 we noticed how Eunice Kamau experienced animosity from one of the clergy who had no understanding of her conception of Christian ministry and did not seek to share with her the evangelistic work of the Christian church. Thankfully, the work of CCMTD is changing these earlier attitudes.

Statistics produced by Habitat estimate the current population of Nairobi to be over 3.3 million, of whom 60% live in informal settlements or slums, such as Pumwani. In the year 2000 the World Bank said that 70-75% of slum dwellers are poor, living on an income of less than $1.25

per day. This economic poverty has created a social and political poverty. The staff of St. John's Community Centre have attempted to improve the lives of Pumwani residents not only spiritually but also economically and socially, showing compassion and concern according to the Centre's scriptural motto - "bearing each other's burdens." This activity is now recognised as a legitimate activity of the Anglican Church of Kenya so that outreach is understood to include not just spiritual transformation but also economic and social transformation.

This new concept in political and development thought is beginning to take root in church thinking. Since 2014, St. John's Community Centre has been capacity building and mentoring 14 local churches in CCMTD.

The Bishop of the Diocese of Nairobi, the Rt Rev'd Joel Waweru and senior clergy, went to Ethiopia in the latter part of 2018 to see and understand how the Kefe Heywott Church engages with and implements CCMTD. The Director of St. John's Community Centre, Peter Njuguna, went with them on this exposure visit, the Bishop having approved a sustainable strategy that will see the project take root in the Diocese with the Centre playing a facilitative role.

CCMTD workshop of clergy from implementing parishes and a team from the Centre with the Diocesan Director of Mission mapping the way forward

Chapter 31 – The Future Role of the Centre

What of the future?

The penultimate Strategic Plan Evaluation concluded its recommendations for the future in the following terms:

> "In spite of the excellent performance of the centre, its visibility has remained low and success stories and history has largely not been documented. It therefore projects an image of a small church project which can be a challenge in fundraising and networking.... There is need to implement activities to enhance visibility of the organisation, consider rebranding by perhaps a new name and a national or regional geographical focus. Most of the staff are of the view that the organisation needs to target other geographical areas apart from Pumwani"

"What of the future?"

Re-branding and a national and regional focus might well be appropriate but the people of Pumwani will, hopefully, always remain a priority for this very special organisation and, likewise, the people of Pumwani will continue to think of it as belonging to them in a special kind of way. Because here, amongst the mud and wattle dwellings, there has grown up not just a community, but also a relationship, built upon the clear vision of bearing each other's burdens.

Staff, community members and the local government area chief at a stakeholders forum

Epilogue

We began with opaque glass and its effect upon the Church's view of the outside world. St. Paul used a similar metaphor to describe the view we have in this life of Christ and His Kingdom. In his first letter to the Corinthian Church he spoke about seeing "through a glass darkly". One way, in which Jesus invited us to find Him, was in the faces of the hungry, the thirsty, the alien, the naked, the sick and the prisoner. He invited us, further, to provide appropriate assistance to those who suffer in these ways, and that, in so doing, we would catch a glimpse of His Kingdom and experience what it means.

St. John's Community Centre, and those who have worked for it and with it, have responded to these invitations. We have joyfully shared in the Centre's mission of bearing each other's burdens and have derived enormous satisfaction in the process, glimpsing albeit "darkly", the meaning of the Kingdom of God, of which selfless service is an ingredient.

Opaqueness has, in consequence, given way to transparency and plain glass to a prism. Through the work and witness of St. John's Community Centre, light has been refracted to illuminate and bring colour to the lives of those who inhabit the dark and dingy recesses of Pumwani homes. It shines forth also as a beacon of social development, empowerment and change throughout the land of Kenya and beyond.

This book has been many years in the writing and its publication just sixty years after Pat boarded the "*Rhodesia Castle*" is timely, if it serves to demonstrate the growth and development of the Centre in the supervening years.

The 'Rhodesia Castle' on which Pat sailed to Kenya in 1959

Index

A

abstinence • 259, 261
accounting • 230
Adhiambo, Christine • 249
Adult Education • 96
Advocates • 133
African Evangelistic Enterprise • 206, 207, 210
Africanisation • 132, 135, 142
African Revival Brethren • 255
Afro-Arts • 145
Age Concern England • 196
Aggrey, Raheli • 122, 133
AIDS • *See* HIV/AIDS
All Saints' Cathedral Nairobi • 15, 50, 59, 91, 94, 127, 150, 186
Amani School of Dressmaking • 171, 186, 216
American University in Nairobi • 226
American volunteers • 113
American Women's Association • 141, 143
Amin, Idi (General) • 127
Anglican Church of Kenya (ACK) • 336
Aphia Plus • 262
Appleby, Lee (Miss) • 17
Apprenticeships • 245
Archbishop of Canada • 170
Area Advisory Councils • 250, 251, 322
Arunga, Emily Njeri • 329
Ashton, Clive • 151, 159, 161, 162
Ashton, Ken • iii, 183
Astrid, Ms • 318
Auchinlech, Claude (Field Marshall Sir) • 23
Awori, A.A.W. (Mr) • 158

B

Ball (Captain) • 64
Barnardos • 135
Barnett, Anne • 47, 70, 76, 87, 94, 101, 157, 158, 168, 185, 327
 Rev'd • 65
Barolina • 263
Barton Hill • 3
baskets • 102, 103
bearing each other's burdens • xviii, 88, 115, 244, 338, 339
Beecher, Leonard (Most Rev'd) • 18, 68
 Archbishop Leonard Beecher • 61, 66
 Gladys • 19
Beer-brewing • 32
beer hall • 106, 171
being faithful • 261
Bewes, Cecil (Canon) • 27
Bickersteth, John (Rt. Rev'd) • 62
Bidii • 309
Bishop of Winchester • 151
Bowen, Roger (Very Rev'd) • 127
Bread for the World • 70, 185
Bristol • 3
British Council of Churches • 75
British Government • 134
Buku, Joel • 211
Burns, George • 13
 Archdeacon George Burns • 13
 Archdeacon George Burns OBE • 15
 Bwana Burns • 13
 Canon Burns • 36
 Sibella Bazett • 13
Burns, Joyce • iii
Burns Memorial Hall • 6, 18, 165, 184, 208, 212, 218

C

Caretaker Committee • 186, 188, 189, 191, 196
Carlebach, Julius (Rev'd) • 90
Caroline, Sister • 155, 187
Carr Stanyer Sims • 209
cash flow • 177
CCMTD • 325, 335, 336
Channels of Hope • 257
Chao, Leah • 160
Chege, James • 195, 197
Chika, Gladys • 94, 98, 99
Child Development and Advocacy • 282
Child Head of Household • 241
child mortality • 320
child protection committees • 250, 251
Children Incorporated USA • 189, 190, 194, 198, 206, 209, 283, 290, 317
Child Rescue Foundation • 268, 320
Child Welfare Society • 90, 126
Chipenda, Eva • 159, 160
Chipukizi Youth Group • 313, 316
Choose Life • 259
Christian Council of Kenya (CCK) • 22, 24, 41, 52, 75
Christian Hostels Fellowship • 179
Christian Industrial Training Centre (CITC) • 24, 56, 59, 70, 109, 171, 215, 283, 308
Christian Partnership on AIDS in Kenya • 257
Church Army • 13, 187
Church Army Community Centre • 122, 133
Church Bookshop • 184
Church Commissioners for Kenya • 139, 183, 196, 198, 208, 210
Church Community Mobilization Transformational Development • *See* CCMTD
Church Mission Society (CMS) • iii, 10, 134, 135, 148, 152, 207
Church of the Province of Kenya (CPK) • 60, 186
City Park • 277
Coast Youth Dramatic Society • 22
Coffee Bar Forums • 260
Collins, Alan • 133
Community Action for Rural Development (CARD) • 280
Community Centre Board • 208
community development • 229
Community Development Worker • 86
Community Empowerment • 85
Community Health Workers • 251, 252, 264
Contact Club • 118
CORAT AFRICA • 84, 149, 162
Coronation Street • 249
  Corrie goes to Kenya • 249
corruption • 303
Court, Elsbeth • 166
Craig, Daniel (James Bond) • 249
crime • 331, 332, 333
criminal gangs • 291
criminals • 310, 330

D

Dakin, Stanley (Rev'd) • 98
Danida • 219, 226
Danish Embassy • 226
Danish Minister for International Development • 226
Dawn to Dusk • 309
Department of Justice and Peace Commission • 296
Diocese • 59, 183, 188, 189, 190, 195, 196, 206, 208, 212, 216, 218, 227, 261, 296, 325, 336
District Children Officer • 251
Dr. Aggrey Primary School • 19, 24, 49, 89
Drammen School • 317, 318

Index

dream • 333
DREAMS • 262, 265, 266, 267, 320
drug peddling • 310
drugs
  bhang • 6, 30
  miraa • 30
Drury, Dorothy • 104, 111
dukas • 11
Dulverton Trust • 101, 102, 111

E

East African Industries • 216
East African Literature Bureau • 22
Eastleigh flats • 138, 198, 201, 209, 227
Economic Empowerment • 304, 322, 325
economic hardship • 303
economy
  prostitution and beer-brewing • 32
Ecumenical Church Loan Fund (ECLOF) • 170, 196, 210
education • 305, *See* Talent Academy
  Adult Education • 44, 96
  book-keeping classes • 97
  dropout • 215, 219
  Empowerment Through Education • 89
  First-aid Education • 91
  Girls' Training Scheme • 90
  High School • 24, 186, 192, 199, 200, 206, 207, 208, 209, 210, 211, 212, 238, 279, 292
  Informal school • 41
  Non-Formal Education • 95
  nursery school • *See* Nursery School
  Primary School Classes • 42
  Secretarial College • 216, 227, 228
  Sewing classes • 102
  Sewing Project • 158
  Special Group for Teenage Girls • 44
  typing classes • 97
  Women's Classes • 91

Education & Training • 304, 305, 322, 325
Election fears • 295
Elliot, Ross and Pauline • 57
Embakasi • 296
Embakasi Girls' High School • 279
employment
  Empowerment Through Employment • 100
  Home Industries project • 101
  Sewing classes • 102
empowerment • 323
environmental conditions • 215, 220
Ericsson, Janie • 111, 158
Ethiopian refugees • 127
Eyre, Mary (Miss) • 22, 50

F

Fahari ya Kenya exhibition • 112
Faithfulness in Marriage • 260
Faloon, W.M. (Rev'd) • 16
feeding programme • 291
Finance & General Purposes Committee • i, 138, 153, 155, 158, 178, 183
Fisher, Tom and Mary • 58
Foxbury • 10
Fredkorpset • 334

G

Gacanja, Elijah (Canon) • 15
Gachira, Mr. • 192, 193
Gachui, John Mwangi (Justice) • 186
garbage • 313
Gatei, Sally • iii, 329
Gender Budgeting of Devolved Funds • 273, 274
Gender Responsive Budgeting programme • 279
Gertrude's Gardens • 119
Gikonyo, Martha • 111, 141, 153, 161, 162, 165, 186, 196

Giltrap, Stanley • 55
Girls' Training Scheme • 90
glass ceiling • 266, 271
Governance • 304, 322
Griffin, Geoff • 137
Groll, (Father) • 281
Group Training • 315
gunned down • 310

H

Hake, Andrew (Rev'd) • 56
Harries, Raymond (Very Rev'd) • 79
Health • 304, 322, 325
Help the Aged Kenya • 206
Hess, Richard • 148, 164, 168, 170
Hillman, Jesse • 54
HIV/AIDS • 209, 219, 241, 242, 249, 252, 255, 256, 257, 258, 262, 263, 264, 265, 267, 268, 293, 303, 304, 306, 317, 320, 322, 334, See Nilinde, See DREAMS, See Aphia Plus, See Hope, See Faithfulness in Marriage, See Choose Life, See abstinence, See Channels of Hope, See Christian Partnership on AIDS in Kenya, See Springs of Life, See stigma, See village pharmacies, See Community Health Workers, See child protection committees, See self-help groups, See Revolving Fund scheme, See Apprenticeships, See Small Community Projects, See President's Emergency Plan For AIDS Relief (PEPFAR)
90-90-90 • 267
Holla, Mr. • 189, 194
Home Industries • 111, 143, 162
  Home Industries Committee • 111, 113, 142, 145, 150, 153, 154, 158, 162, 168
  Home Industries project • 101, 141, 165, 215
  Home Industries shop • 114
Hooper, Cyril • 55
Hope • 262, 264
Horani-Hoffert, Dr. • 126
Houston, Hazel • 91
Howe, Norman • 169
Human Rights • 304, 322

I

Idle, Tony and Myra • 57, 58
Imani House • 186
Independence
  Uhuru • 36, 94, 131
Integrated Youth Development Programme • 233
Israel • 111

J

Jackson, Elizabeth • 125
Jackson, Tudor • 133
Jennings, Hilda • 13
Joint Refugee Service of Kenya • 127

K

Kabiru, Rev'd • 199
Kalebi, Esther • 159, 160
Kamau, Eunice (Mrs) • iii, 186, 189, 205, 209, 210, 212, 218, 219, 222, 223, 226, 227, 228, 229, 230, 231, 236, 238, 283, 309, 324, 328, 335
Kamau, Ezekiel • 291
Kamau, Sarah • 114
Kamukunji • 265, 267, 296
Kang'ori, Paul • 211
Karani, Jacob • 245

Kariuki, Obadiah (Bishop) • 23
Eugenia • 23
Kasarani • 267, 296
Katembu, Mr. • 186, 187, 188, 189, 190, 191, 193
Kathii, Henry • 176, 181, 207
Kefe Heywott Church • 336
Kellehear, Allan • 85
Kenya Association for Professional Counsellors • 259
Kenya Council of Legal Education • 133
Kenya Girl Guides Association • 265
Kenya Institute of Administration • 217
Kenya-Israel School of Social Work • 87, 111, 126, 127
Kenya National Council for Social Services • 134, 196
Kenya National Youth Service • 137
Kenyanisation • 132
Kenyan Minister of Health • 226
Kenya Planters Co-operative Union • 5
Kenya Posts & Telecommunications • 198, 209, 210
Kenya School of Law • 133
Kenyatta College • 217
Kenyatta Hospital • 219
Kenyatta, Margaret (Miss) • 94
Kenyatta, Ngina (Mama) • 102
Kenyatta University • 211, 216, 275
Kenya Voluntary Works Camp Association • 108
Kiambiu • 268, 295, 321
Kibera slum • 226
Kikuyu • 24, 28, 41
Kindernothilfe • 242, 309, 334
Kiplagat, Bethuel • 80, 99, 138, 152, 154, 155, 159
Kiplagat, Honorine • 214
Kitui • 309
Kiyegga, Tom • 147

Koinange, Mary Mbui (Mrs) • 197, 199, 201, 207
Kuria, Bessie • 114
Kuria, Manasses (Archbishop) • 207, 209, 211
Kymana, Sammy • 233

L

Lacey, Janet • 75
Langford-Smith, Neville (Bishop) & Vera (Mrs) • 116
Lari • 25
Chief Luka • 25
lavatories • 219, 221, 223, 227, 232
Lee Abbey Fellowship • 179
life skills • 290
Lifeskills Training • 329
Likalama, Mrs. • 197
Livelihood Training • 232, 233, 236, 316
Local Area Advisory Councils • 322
London Federation of Boys Clubs • 23
Lowther, David • 116

M

Macgoye, D.G.W (Mr) Wellington • 184
Macgoye, Marjorie Oludhe • iii, 183, 184, 185 (nee King) • 183
Machakos • 126
Machakos College of Social Studies • 126
Macharia, Elizabeth • 196
Majengo • 8, 28, 35
Makadara • 125, 296
Makerere University • 125
Malatya, Elizabeth (Mrs.) • 206
Mambo, George (Rev'd) • 197, 198
Maridadi Fabrics • 84, 99, 120, 139, 143, 145, 153, 154, 155, 158, 159, 161, 163, 165, 166, 176, 177, 180, 181, 186, 187, 188, 191, 196, 206, 210, 215, 217, 231, 277

Marshall, Ella (Mrs) • 103, 158
Mashimoni • 310
Mathare • 262, 295, 298
Matumaini House • 70, 71, 119, 155, 185, 187, 199, 206, 207, 208, 209, 216, 329
   Matumaini House Committee • 187
Mau Mau • 3, 24, 28, 41, 60, 116, 183
   Hola Commission • 27
   Hola massacre • 27
   Hola Report • 27
Mbugua, Leonard (Canon) • 179, 185, 187, 188, 191, 200
   (Archdeacon) • 201
McDougal, Barbara • 24, 41
Micro-credit • 246, 328
Millenium • 309
Mill Hill Fathers • 206, 209, 217
Mincing Lane Market • 5
Ministry of Culture & Social Services • 286
Ministry of Education • 112, 253, 286
Ministry of Social Services • 125
Missionary Aviation Fellowship • 103
Mithamo, Reuben • 135
Mliwa, Shadrack (Canon) • 18
Moi, President Daniel Arap • 226
Moller, Miss • 17
Motor Mart Trust • 122
Mount Kenya Safari Club • 144
Mpita, Lucas • 197
MS Kenya • 226
Muchira, Johnson (Mr) • 197, 206, 211
Mugo, Ephantus • 38, 40, 63, 95, 96, 99, 134, 135, 136, 154, 162, 163, 165, 168, 178, 179, 181, 206
  Mary • 135
Mukhwanya, Jackton • 97, 151, 162, 163, 168
Mukugu • 262
Mulatya, Elizabeth • 186
Munyema Street • 329
Mustakabal Women Group • 313, 315

Mutual Responsibility and Interdependence • 61, 62, 67
Mvumi • 116
Mwadime, Jefferson • 154
Mwangangi, Jane (Canon) • 214
Mwangi, Michael • 169
Mwangi, Rev'd • 207
Mwangola, Dishon (Rev'd) • 6, 53, 65
   Ethelreda • 6, 116
Mweke, Peter • 318, 331
Mzungu, David (Rev'd) • 21, 22

N

Nairobi Baptist Church • 47, 91
Nairobi City Council • 125, 171, 185, 210, 219, 220, 222, 223, 232, 323
Nairobi diocese • 296
Nanjeso, Winstone • 311
National Aids Control Council • 320
National Council of the Churches of Kenya (NCCK) • 75, 198
Nderitu, Samuel (Rev'd) • 198, 200, 201, 205, 206, 207, 209, 211, 238
Ndungu, John (Rev'd) • 197, 199, 200
neighbourhood watch groups • 296
NEMIS • 287
netball • 277
New Partners' Initiative • 243, 256, 257, 334
Nilinde • 262, 267, 320
Njoka, Peter (Rt. Rev'd) • 212, 257
Njonjo, Charles • 125
Njuguna, Peter • 216, 228, 236, 238, 324, 336
Non-Formal Education (NFE) • 95, 281, 282, 283, 285, 291, 293, 306, 308
Non-Formal Education school • 287, 306, 318
Northcott, Roger • 221
Norway • 126, 128, 317
Norwegian Church Aid • 205, 206, 207, 210, 215, 216

Nunn, Michael • iii, 183
Nursery School • 178, 180, 187, 192, 197, 199, 206, 207, 210

O

Obote, Milton • 127
Obunga, Emma (Mrs) • 123
Olang, Festo (Most Rev'd) Archbishop • 68
Old People's Home • 119, 185
Oloo, Wilfred • 125, 127
Onyango, Margaret (Mrs) • 196, 198, 200
Opiyo, Millicent • 196
Orphans and Vulnerable Children • 255, 262, 267, 282, 306, 307, 320, 328
Orphans and Vulnerable Children's Project • 256, 264
Ouma, Valary • 245
overseas aid • 70, 303
Owour, Emma • 120

P

paradigm shift • 84, 216, 218, 228
parking boys • 137, 281, 283, 318
participatory education theatre • 249
Pattinson, Ken • 155, 170, 175, 180
   Margaret • iii, 155, 183
peace committees • 297, 298
peace monitors • 297, 298
peer educators • 308
Pethybridge, Maude (Sister) • 16, 21, 50
   Bibi Bahoia • 18
   Pethy • 17, 23
Pittway (Mrs) • 17
PLAN • 267
Plummer, Mary (Miss) • 17
Policy Committee • 76
Politeyan, Mary • 101, 105, 111, 113
Pooley, Margaret • 45, 76, 90, 95, 100

poverty • 230, 305, 308, 333, 336
   urban poverty • 293
   Walking with the Poor • 232
poverty - a mind-set • 231
President's Emergency Plan For AIDS Relief (PEPFAR) • 243
Princess Anne • 137
Princess Margaret • 23
product development courses • 305
prostitution • 32, 310, 332
   juvenile prostitutes • 44
   red-light district • 35
psycho-social support • 308
Pumwani • 36, 175, 219, 220, 226, 338
   California • 38, 206
Pumwani Maternity Hospital • 118
Pumwani United • 309
Pumwani Youth Group • 316
Pumwani Youth Groups Network (PYGRON) • 309, 315
Purchase, Stella • 88, 115, 120, 128

Q

Queen Elizabeth Hospital • 13
Quinter • 214

R

Racecourse Road • 24, 49, 89
Ramtu, Timothy • 186, 187, 188, 195
Revival Brethren • 22, 23, 44, 49, 52, 115, 117, 121, 122, 335
Revolving Fund scheme • 246, 247
Rhodesia Castle • 3, 339
Richardson, James and Pat • 61, 98, 118
   Jim • i, 52, 54, 154, 158, 162, 165, 180, 183
   Pat • i, 26, 39, 44, 52, 58, 87, 90, 100, 115, 125, 126, 127, 220, 221, 236, 281
Rickman, Mary • 19
Ridley, Mary • 125

Ridout, John and Shirley • iii, 153
role models • 320
Rudge, (Rev'd Dr.) • 163

S

Sams, Michael • 163
Sasaka, Rev'd • 185, 189, 191, 192, 193, 195, 207
Secretarial College • *See* education: Secretarial College
Selassie, Haile (Emperor) • 127
self-help groups • 248, 305, 320, 328
Self Help Women's Groups • 275
Sentamu, John (Most Rev'd) • 62
Serpell, Georgina • 8, 21, 24, 42, 44, 56, 89, 283
Serwanga, Daniel (Rev'd) • 206, 207
Sewing classes • 102
Sewing Project • 158
Shadrack, Mary • 8
Shauri Moyo • 52, 167
Shaylor, Margaret • 151
Shewera, Alexander • 47, 49, 76, 90
Shiundu, Mark • 47, 49, 187
sibiriti • 106
SIDA • 170
Sidhom, Swailem (Rev'd) • 37, 76, 88
Situation Room • 297
Skills for Southern Sudan • 228, 237, 238
skills training • 286, 307
Slade, Humphrey • 126
Small Community Projects • 243, 244, 246, 247, 250, 251, 253, 254, 267, 328
Snell, Stuart (Rev'd) • 162, 163
Sorsbie, Malin (Sir) • 126
Southern Baptists • 52
sponsorship • 283, 317, 331
Springs of Life • 256, 262, 264
  Committee • 260
Stade, Mrs • 141

St. Andrew's Church • 260
Starehe • 265, 267, 296
Starehe Boys Centre • 137
stigma • 255, 256, 257, 261
St. John's Church Pumwani • xvii, 36, 55, 67, 184, 210, 227, 234
St. John's Community Centre • i, xviii, 3, 24, 41, 54, 59, 66, 67, 189, 191, 208, 228, 265, 271, 282, 336
St. John's High School • *See* education: High School
St. John's Parish • 205, 207, 208, 209, 210, 218
St. John's Parochial Church Council • 183, 185, 195, 211, 212
St. Mark's Church • 214
Stovold, Ken (Archdeacon) • 153
St. Paul's Anglican Church • 205
St Paul's Theological College • 37
strategic management culture • 325
strategic plan • 88, 325
St. Stephen's Church • 122, 123, 186
Studio Arts 68 • 103, 114, 144

T

Talent Academy • 291
Talent Development • 331
Tattersall-Wright, Ralph • 150
Taylor, John (Right Rev'd) • 3, 53
Tearfund • 233, 257, 315
  Integrated Youth Development Programme • 233
Tett, Charles and Helen • 5, 41, 50, 56, 335
  Charles • 24, 28, 55, 215
  Helen • 23, 44, 91
think outside the box • 313, 316, 333
Thomas Barnardo House • 119, 125, 135, 136, 159
Thomas, Jim • 56
Tivola, Immi • 145

Torchbearers • 56
Triad • 169, 170
Tudor Trust • 221, 222, 230, 328
Twining, Lady • 126

U

Udall, Dorothy • 102, 103, 109, 111, 145, 157, 158
Undugu Society of Kenya • 281
unemployment • 303
UNHCR • 127
UNICEF • 268
Uprising Youth Group • 310, 330
USAID • 267, 268, 334
U.S. President's Emergency Plan for AIDS Relief (PEPFAR) • 265

V

village pharmacies • 252
volunteer • 321

W

Wachagga • 116
WaGathoni, Kuria (Mr.) • 220
Waithaga • 116
Wambua, Mr. • 91
Wambui • 107
Wambui, Martha (Miss) • 24, 42, 49, 92, 115
Wanjiku, Mary • 196
Ward, Don • 150
Waruhia, Ruth • 158
Waswa, Daniel • 22, 23
  Mrs. Daniel Waswa • 22
water • 30, 31, 35, 219, 221, 227
Water Aid • 237
Waweru, Joel (Rt Rev'd) • 336
Waweru, Mr. D. • 189, 193
Wilding, Pam • 58
Wiseman, Edith • 19
Wolfendale, Professor • 102, 114, 136, 161
Wood Avenue • 139, 187
work permits • 132, 142
World Bank Conference • 146
World Council of Churches
  Biblical Studies and Research Committee • 79
World Vision • 137, 257

Y

Young Mothers' Group • 232, 233
youth crime • 328
Youth Groups • 232, 329, 333, 334
Youth Programme • 329

www.ingramcontent.com/pod-product-compliance
Lightning Source LLC
Chambersburg PA
CBHW071555080526
44588CB00010B/918